Breaking the WTO

Breaking the WTO

How Emerging Powers Disrupted the Neoliberal Project

Kristen Hopewell

Stanford University Press
Stanford, California

Stanford University Press

Stanford, California

Printed in the United States of America on acid-free, archival-quality paper

Library of Congress Cataloging-in-Publication Data

Names: Hopewell, Kristen, author.

Title: Breaking the WTO : how emerging powers disrupted the neoliberal project / Kristen Hopewell.

Other titles: Emerging frontiers in the global economy.

Description: Stanford, California : Stanford University Press, 2016. | Series: Emerging frontiers in the global economy | Includes bibliographical references and index.

Identifiers: LCCN 2016011055 (print) | LCCN 2016011401 (ebook) | ISBN 9780804798662 (cloth : alk. paper) | ISBN 9781503600591 (pbk : alk. paper) | ISBN 9781503600027 (ebook)

Subjects: LCSH: World Trade Organization. | International economic relations. | Neoliberalism. | Brazil—Foreign economic relations. | China—Foreign economic relations. | India—Foreign economic relations.

Classification: LCC HF1385.H67 2016 (print) | LCC HF1385 (ebook) | DDC 382/.92—dc23

LC record available at http://lccn.loc.gov/2016011055

Typeset in 10.5/15 Brill.

Cover design: Angela Moody.

To my family

Contents

Preface

IN the fall of 1999, fifty thousand protestors took to the streets of Seattle in opposition to a meeting of the World Trade Organization (WTO) and its effort to launch a new round of multilateral trade negotiations. The WTO had come into force only four years before—as a successor to the General Agreement on Tariffs and Trade (GATT) that had governed international trade since the end of World War II—but it had already generated an intense reaction from civil society groups. The creation of the WTO involved a significant expansion in supranational authority and the scope of trade rules. The WTO was at the heart of the neoliberal revolution sweeping the globe, and its officials saw themselves as writing a new constitution for the global economy. Civil society actors were gravely concerned about the implications of WTO trade rules for a wide range of issues including human rights, poverty, inequality, development, the environment, education, labor, and health. Moreover, this immensely powerful institution was seen as exclusionary and undemocratic in its decision-making and void of transparency or accountability. Organized by a broad network of social movements, nongovernmental organizations (NGOs) and trade unions, the Seattle protests united a diverse collection of actors seeking, as many of their banners read, to "Stop the WTO." Environmentalists clad in turtle costumes marched alongside Teamsters, black-clad anarchists alongside the Raging Grannies. The protests closed the downtown core of the city for four days and disrupted the meetings of negotiators. The "Battle of Seattle," as it came to be known, was a coming out party of sorts for the antiglobalization movement (also known as the global justice movement) and set off a wave of other mass protests at meetings of multilateral economic organizations—including the International Monetary Fund (IMF), the World Bank, the World Economic Forum, and the G20—at different sites around the world.

In the lead-up to the Seattle Ministerial, I was working in the Canadian embassy in Washington, DC, contributing to the formulation and development of Canada's position in the upcoming negotiations. My job was essentially intelligence gathering—to act as a fly on the wall in Washington, collecting data on and analyzing the development of the US negotiating position and reporting back to Ottawa, so that Canada's negotiating team could prepare its own position accordingly. In this, I was one of hundreds, or possibly even thousands, of people around the world preparing their governments for the new "Millennium Round" of negotiations to be launched at Seattle. This was to be a monumental undertaking, as the first trade round since the creation of the WTO in 1995.

Events in Seattle, however, turned out to be far more interesting than anyone anticipated. Entirely unprecedented and largely unexpected, the Seattle protests came as a shock to the trade community surrounding the WTO. Until then, the GATT/WTO had been virtually unknown to general public, a sleepy and arcane world of policy-making and diplomatic negotiations left to trade lawyers, economists, and bureaucrats. The Battle in Seattle had an explosive effect in thrusting the WTO into the media spotlight and rocking the very foundations of the institution. The Seattle protests also generated significant academic interest in global civil society and its potential to act as a transformative force in global economic governance. In 1999 and the early 2000s, this was one of most dynamic and exciting aspects of global politics—the emergence of a vibrant and colorful antiglobalization movement contesting the construction of neoliberal globalization through institutions like the WTO.

Almost a decade later, I arrived in Geneva in the late-2000s with plans to study the interaction between global civil society and the WTO during the Doha Round, which had been launched two years after the failed Seattle meetings. Several things, however, quickly became apparent. First, as I have written about elsewhere (Hopewell 2009; Hopewell 2015b), many civil society actors had become far less critical of the WTO and its neoliberal agenda. In contrast to the oppositional, anti-WTO stance that characterized the civil society protests at Seattle, over time many prominent civil society actors had adopted advocacy positions—such as on agricultural and fisheries subsidies—that fit within, rather than challenged, the dominant neoliberal trade paradigm. As a result, civil society contestation surrounding the WTO had diminished substantially. In fact, when the WTO held a key Ministerial Meeting in 2008, it went virtually without protest from global civil society.

Second, the most interesting and important conflict was no longer taking place between the WTO and civil society, but among states *within* the WTO, with the battle lines drawn in ways that were totally unanticipated a decade before. Observing and analyzing the development of the American negotiating position in Washington in advance of the Seattle Ministerial, it was clear that the US was preoccupied with a limited number of actors—chiefly, the EU, Japan, and, to a lesser degree, Canada. Other states barely registered on the radar screen: China was not even a member of the WTO yet, while Brazil and India were seen as struggling developing countries preoccupied with getting their domestic economies in order after decades of economic crisis and upheaval. There was certainly no concept of "the BRICs"—the Goldman Sachs report that would coin the term and give birth to the concept had yet to be written—and, if anything, in the wake of the 1997 Asian financial crisis, developing economies appeared vulnerable and insecure. In sharp contrast, in the late 1990s, the US economy was booming and, with the fall of the Soviet Union earlier in the decade, its global power had reached new heights. Just ten years later, however, as this book will show, the world looked radically different. When I began my field research in the late 2000s, the environment at the WTO was virtually unrecognizable from what it had been a decade before: the US and the other Western powers had lost their hold on the institution; Brazil, India, and China had emerged as central players; and a new fault line had become deeply entrenched between the developed and developing worlds.

Third, at the time of Seattle, neoliberal globalization was widely seen as akin to a steamroller, progressing inevitably through powerful institutions like the WTO. Yet, if we flash forward to the present, the Doha Round is now effectively dead and the WTO is consequently in crisis. The future of the institution is in doubt as debates swirl about whether it has become irrelevant. How do we explain such a remarkable change in such a short period of time?

That question lies at the heart of this book. As I show, what has disrupted the Doha Round and thus effectively "stopped" the forward march of the WTO is not contestation from global civil society but shifting power among states. The neoliberal project has in fact broken down at WTO. Contrary to expectations, however, this is not because of a counterhegemonic movement in opposition to neoliberalism. Rather, it has been caused by changes in the distribution of power among states and the rise of new powers—Brazil, India, and China—which are not contesting but seeking to work within the paradigm of global neoliberalism. By embracing the rules and principles of the multilateral trading system, rising powers brought its contradictions to the fore and precipitated a crisis at the WTO. The case of the WTO suggests that, surprisingly, one of the most serious threats to neoliberal globalization—as it has been pursued to date within the multilateral institutions—has come not from a direct ideological or political challenge, but the emergence of new powers from the developing world that have broadly accepted the neoliberal orthodoxy.

Preparation of this book has benefited from the generous assistance of a large number of individuals and institutions around the world. I would first like to thank the many WTO negotiators, trade policy-makers, and other actors who agreed to be interviewed for the study. Their firsthand knowledge of global trade politics is represented in the many quotations and references throughout the book, and their insightful comments were vital for analyzing specific events and informing my understanding of contemporary struggles over international trade regulation. The research for this book received support from several institutions, including a Fulbright Fellowship, the US National Science Foundation, the Chinese Academy of Social Sciences, and the Social Sciences and Humanities Research Council of Canada. I would also like to thank Tianbiao Zhu at Peking University, Joost Pauwelyn at the Graduate Institute of International and Development Studies, and Sigrid Quack then at the Max Planck Institute for the Study of Societies for generously hosting me at various stages during the research and writing of the book.

This endeavor began at the University of Michigan, where I was fortunate to work with and be challenged by a wonderful group of faculty members. I owe a tremendous debt of gratitude to Jeffery Paige, who spent hours discussing many of the themes and arguments that ultimately came to form this book, with an incredible knack for asking precisely the right questions to spur new and deeper analysis. Greta Krippner was extraordinarily generous of her time and intellectual energy, and her detailed and incisive feedback profoundly shaped the development of this book. Margaret Somers, Susan Waltz, and Mark Mizruchi offered highly valuable input at key points in the project and were all deeply involved in pushing my thinking forward.

My sincere thanks go out to the colleagues and friends who have read drafts and commented on various parts of the project, listened to and critiqued my arguments, and provided useful inputs and advice along the way. They include Barbara Anderson, Sarah Babb, Jennifer Bair, Tim Bartley, Carolyn Biltoft, Betsy Carter, Gregory Chin, Nitsan Chorev, Jennifer Clapp, Sandra Comstock, Joseph

Conti, Ole Elgström, Peter Evans, Marc Froese, Surupa Gupta, Terrance Halliday, Gary Herrigel, Roselyn Hsueh, Maria Johnson, Tiffany Joseph, Anna Lanoszka, Zakiya Luna, Andreas Nölke, Nicola Phillips, Amy Quark, James Scott, Andrew Shrank, Beverly Silver, David Smith, Michael Smith, Matthew David Stephen, Lynn Verduzco-Baker, Fred Wherry, and Rorden Wilkinson. Matias Margulis has been critically engaged in this project from the start, patiently reading and commenting on enumerable drafts and acting as the chief sounding board for many of the ideas developed here.

I am grateful to the University of British Columbia, where I spent two and a half years as an assistant professor, for the resources, time, and encouragement to further develop the project. I completed work on this book in the School of Social and Political Sciences at the University of Edinburgh, where I have been fortunate to find a highly engaging intellectual environment and a group of wonderful colleagues. I would particularly like to thank Christina Boswell, Iain Hardie, Eve Hepburn, Julie Kaarbo, John Peterson, and Charlotte Rommer-skirchen for their valuable advice and feedback. I owe special thanks to Margo Fleming, James Holt, and John Feneron at Stanford University Press, and J. P. Singh, editor of the *Emerging Frontiers in the Global Economy* series, for their enthusiastic support of the project and their incredible responsiveness and efficiency. I would also like to thank two reviewers for their very helpful comments and suggestions.

Finally, thank you to my family for their unfailing support and encouragement.

Abbreviations

ACP	African, Caribbean, and Pacific
AD	antidumping
AMS	aggregate measure of support
ATC	Agreement on Textiles and Clothing
AoA	Agreement on Agriculture
BPO	business process outsourcing
BRICs	Brazil, Russia, India, China
DG	Director-General
EEC	European Economic Community
FDI	foreign direct investment
FTA	free trade agreement
G7	Group of 7
G8	Group of 8 Leaders' Summit
G20	Group of 20 Leaders' Summit
G20-T	Group of 20 (WTO coalition)
G33	Group of 33 (WTO coalition)
G77	Group of 77
GATS	General Agreement on Trade in Services
GATT	General Agreement on Tariffs and Trade
GDP	gross domestic product
GSP	Generalized System of Preferences
IATP	Institute for Agriculture and Trade Policy
ICC	International Criminal Court
ICONE	Institute for International Trade Negotiations
IMF	International Monetary Fund
ITO	International Trade Organization
IP	intellectual property

ISI	import-substitution industrialization
LDCs	least-developed countries
MFA	Multi-Fiber Agreement
MFN	most-favored nation
NAM	Nonaligned Movement
NAMA	nonagricultural market access
NGO	nongovernmental organization
NICs	newly industrialized countries
NIEO	New International Economic Order
OECD	Organization for Economic Cooperation and Development
OTDS	overall trade distorting support
PPP	purchasing power parity
Quad	US, EU, Canada, Japan
SAP	structural adjustment program
SDT	special and differential treatment
SSG	special (agricultural) safeguard
SPs	special products
SSM	special safeguard mechanism
TPP	Trans-Pacific Partnership
TRIMs	Agreement on Trade-Related Investment Measures
TRIPs	Agreement on Trade-Related Intellectual Property
UNCTAD	UN Commission on Trade and Development
WTO	World Trade Organization

Breaking the WTO

Chapter 1

Introduction

F OR over half a century, the global economy and its governing institutions have been dominated by the United States and allied advanced-industrialized states. From its hegemonic position in the international system, the US has played a vital role in managing the making of global capitalism as we know it today—from the golden age of postwar reconstruction and embedded liberalism to the contemporary era of neoliberal globalization. Yet the global political economy is currently in the midst of profound change. There has been a significant shift in global economic activity from the advanced countries of the Global North to the developing countries of the Global South, with China, India, and Brazil, in particular, emerging as major players in the world economy. The share of global GDP produced by developed countries has dropped dramatically—from 80 percent in 1960 to 44 percent today—while the share of developing countries has risen from 20 to 56 percent, such that developing countries now account for more than half of global economic output. Just three developing countries alone—China, India, and Brazil—now make up 25 percent of the global economy, whereas the entire Group of 7 (G7) advanced economies (US, UK, France, Germany, Italy, Japan, and Canada) accounts for only slightly more, at 33 percent.[1] China provides the most striking illustration of this change: three decades of sustained economic growth at rates averaging 10 percent a year have made it the world's largest manufacturing exporter and second largest economy.[2] India's growth rates have been nearly as impressive, with it becoming one of the world's leading exporters of information technology (IT) and IT-enabled services. Brazil has emerged as an agroindustrial powerhouse, threatening to unseat the US and EU as the world's largest agricultural exporter. These large emerging economies are now major consumer markets, with their own globally competitive multinational corporations, and an important source of outward investment, loans, and aid. As Martin Wolf (2009) declared in the

Financial Times, "[F]or the first time since the industrial revolution, economic power is no longer concentrated in Western hands." Instead, we are seeing the emergence of multiple centers of global economic power. Along with their increasing importance in the global economy, the emerging powers are demanding a greater role in its management, including at the World Trade Organization (WTO), International Monetary Fund (IMF), World Bank, and Group of 20 Leaders' Summit.

The rise of new powers and the corresponding decline in the hegemony of the US—and of the Global North more broadly—are reshaping the world economy and the institutions charged with its governance. This transformation has been identified as one of the most important in modern history (Ikenberry 2008; Warwick Commission 2008) and generated significant debate about the agendas of the emerging powers and the implications of their rise. This book focuses on how changes in the distribution of power among states are affecting the governance of neoliberal globalization. By neoliberal globalization, I refer to growing global economic integration occurring through the increased movement of goods, services, and capital across borders, propelled by free market ideology and policies, championing open and competitive markets, freed from the fetters of the state. In the prevailing popular discourse, economic globalization is depicted as a spontaneous and agentless economic process, propelled by the ingenuity of markets and the magic of the invisible hand (Friedman 2004; Wolf 2004). Extensive scholarship, however, has shown that globalization is neither a natural nor an inevitable force but a *project*, driven by specific agents, political struggles, and institutional changes (Chorev 2008; Gill 2002; McMichael 2004). It is thus as much a political as an economic process. Moreover, contrary to its own mythology, neoliberal globalization entails not the removal of economic regulation but the construction of new rules, regulations, and institutions to facilitate the spread and deepening of global markets (Block and Evans 1994; Braithwaite 2008; Fligstein 2005; Levi-Faur 2005; Peck and Tickell 2002). In other words, it is an *institution-building project*—and one that remains ongoing.

The US has been the primary driver of neoliberal economic restructuring globally (Babb 2009; Cox 2008; Evans 2008; Fligstein 2005; Harvey 2005; Helleiner 2001; Mann 2001). As the world's largest and most advanced economy, the US actively propelled the liberalization and opening of global markets, as a means to gain access to foreign markets, investment opportunities, and cheaper inputs. Multilateral economic institutions, such as the WTO, IMF, and World

Bank, have played a central role in this endeavor, creating and enforcing new rules to govern the global economy, while inducing states to adopt neoliberal economic policies and open their national economies to foreign trade and capital. For their part, developing countries have historically been marginalized and excluded from decision-making in the multilateral economic institutions, while the "Washington Consensus" policy prescriptions they propagated produced economic and social dislocation across much of the Global South and provoked intense protest in many countries (Babb 2005; Shadlen 2005; Wade 2003).

In short, neoliberal globalization to date has been a US-led project, pursued in large part through the multilateral economic institutions and often resisted by the Global South. A key question, therefore, is what impact the rise of new powers from the developing world is having on the neoliberal project. This book sheds light on the nature and implications of contemporary power shifts by analyzing the case of the WTO, a core institution in global economic governance, responsible for setting and enforcing the rules of the global trading system. Changes in the global distribution of power, I argue, have ruptured the WTO's ability to fulfill its intended purpose in driving forward the process of neoliberal restructuring on a global scale, as signaled by the collapse of the Doha Round of trade negotiations. The rise of new powers has thus precipitated a crisis in one of the central governing institutions of global neoliberalism. Paradoxically, however, the rising powers should not be seen as carriers of a counterhegemonic movement in opposition to neoliberalism. They are certainly counterhegemonic in the sense that they are challenging US hegemony, but not the institutional structures and logic of global neoliberalism. Yet, even if the emerging powers do not represent an antisystemic movement—they are decidedly *not* seeking to bring about fundamental changes in the contemporary workings of global capitalism or to bring down the governance system that supports it—their rise has nonetheless had powerful, though unintended, antisystemic effects. Ironically, what has disrupted the continued expansion of the neoliberal project at the WTO is not an oppositional countermovement but just the reverse—the wider embrace of the neoliberal trade agenda by emerging powers from the developing world. The emergence of new powers, I contend, has led to the disintegration of multilateralism and a moment of disjuncture in the project of neoliberal globalization, by heightening and bringing to the fore inherent contradictions contained within the liberal international economic order constructed under American hegemony.

Debates about Contemporary Power Shifts

Given the rapidly changing and still unfolding nature of contemporary power shifts, much of the existing literature on this subject has been of a highly speculative nature, attempting to predict the consequences of shifting power. With limited clear data yet available, such accounts have been heavily shaped by prevailing theoretical divisions in the study of international political economy. Different theoretical camps have produced at least three sets of competing analyses and predictions.

The realist tradition of international relations provides a pessimistic view of the prospects for global governance and multilateral cooperation in the context of shifting power. Hegemonic stability theory contends that an open, liberal economic order requires a single hegemonic or dominant power (Gilpin 1981; Kindleberger 1973; Krasner 1976). An international system without a leader is seen as unstable and potentially dangerous (Bremmer and Roubini 2011; Haass 2008). In a context of shifting power, realists foresee conflict, with many viewing emerging powers as holding fundamentally different interests and agendas than those of the dominant powers and, therefore, as system-challengers rather than system-supporters (Gilpin 1981; Kagan 2010; Kupchan 2014). As Stewart Patrick (2010) of the US Council on Foreign Relations states, for example:

The United States should be under no illusions about the ease of socializing rising nations. Emerging powers may be clamoring for greater global influence, but they often oppose the political and economic ground rules of the inherited Western liberal order, seek to transform existing multilateral arrangements, and shy away from assuming significant global responsibilities. The emerging non-Western powers do not share the United States' view on global governance. The ideal scenario for Washington would be for the rising powers to embrace Western principles, norms, and rules. . . . But the emerging nations are intent on altering existing rules, not adopting them hook, line, and sinker. . . . They believe that they are entitled to reshape international arrangements to suit themselves.

It is assumed that the emerging powers will reject the rules, norms, and principles of the liberal economic order created by the Western powers (Bremmer and Roubini 2011; Castañeda 2010; Kupchan 2014; Patrick 2010). Realists thus expect the decline of US hegemony and the emergence of new powers to weaken multilateral cooperation and threaten the international economic arrangements that support globalization. Realism foresees a possible breakdown of the liberal international economic order, triggering rising nationalism and mercantilism, and ultimately "deglobalization" (Layne 2009; Patrick 2010).

In contrast, liberal institutionalism is considerably more optimistic about the prospects for multilateral cooperation and the maintenance of the liberal economic order in the absence of a hegemon (Keohane 1984). Liberalism envisions a smooth integration of new powers into the Western-made liberal world order. It suggests that emerging powers will be supporters of the existing order, based on the belief that in the current situation of global economic interdependence, all states have an interest in participating in and maintaining the system (Cox 2012; Ikenberry 2011; Nye 2015; Snyder 2011; Xiao 2013). The old and new powers will therefore find ways to jointly manage the international economic architecture and collective action will prevail to preserve an open, liberal international economic system. Liberal institutionalism thus sees multipolarity as congruent with cooperative and successful multilateralism (Bailin 2005; Snidal 1985). Ikenberry (2009), for example, foresees a "post-hegemonic liberal internationalism," arguing that reform of the global governance institutions to increase the weight of rising powers would lock in their support for an international order based on the Western model (see also Drezner 2007; Zakaria 2008). Many thus argue that the incorporation of new powers would strengthen the multilateral system by making it more inclusive, representative, and legitimate (Vestergaard and Wade 2015; Warwick Commission 2008; Zoellick 2010).

Critical approaches informed by world systems, dependency, and neo-Marxist theory yield yet another view of the potential impact of contemporary power shifts. Critical scholars contend that developing countries are systematically disadvantaged within the global political economy and that its rules and governing institutions have worked to maintain relations of domination and exploitation between the advanced-industrialized core and underdeveloped periphery (Bailin 2005; Chang 2002; Gallagher 2008; Jawara and Kwa 2003; McMichael 2004). Given the particularly harsh effects of neoliberalism in the Global South, many have looked to the developing world as the potential source of an emancipatory movement of resistance to neoliberal globalization (Roberts 2010; Silver and Arrighi 2003). Among critical scholars, there has been a great deal of speculation and debate about whether the rise of new powers from the developing world could rupture the current trajectory of neoliberal globalization and help usher in an alternative form of globalization and a more equitable and progressive global economic order (Arrighi 2007; Evans 2008;

Gills 2010; Gray and Murphy 2015; Pieterse 2011; Pinto, Macdonald, and Marshall 2011; Thakur 2014). Arrighi and Zhang (2011: 45–46), for example, raise the prospect that the emerging developing country powers could "lead to the formation of a new and more effective Bandung—that is, a new version of the Third World alliance of the 1950s and 1960s better suited to counter the economic and political subordination of Southern to Northern states in an age of unprecedented global economic integration."

Certainly, for most of the period since World War II, the Global South has been a fierce source of criticism and opposition to the US-led global economic order. In the 1950s–70s, Third Worldist movements such as the Nonaligned Movement (NAM) and the Group of 77 (G77) called for a radical overhaul of the rules and principles of the global economic system and the establishment of a New International Economic Order (NIEO) (Krasner 1985; Mortimer 1984; Prashad 2012). The new powers emerging today were central figures in and around these movements, and the international trading system was one of their primary targets. Brazil, India, and China "all historically espoused conceptions of international order that challenged those of the liberal developed West" (Hurrell 2006: 3), from the socialist revolutionism of China to the Third Worldism of India and Brazil. Even after the demise of the NIEO, these countries adopted generally defensive positions in relation to the norms of economic liberalization being advanced by the West (Hurrell 2006: 11). Within the international trading system, for example, Brazil and India led fierce resistance from the developing world to the neoliberal agenda pursued by the US and other Northern states in the 1980s and 90s.[3]

There are thus major debates among scholars, policy-makers, and foreign policy analysts and observers about the objectives and intentions of the emerging powers—whether they will challenge or support the rules, norms, and principles of the existing international economic order—as well as whether their rise is likely to generate conflict or enhanced cooperation in the international system and what its implications are for the management of economic globalization. The case of the WTO provides an important point of empirical intervention into these debates. As I will show, contrary to the expectations of liberal institutionalism, the rise of new powers has created a crisis of multilateralism that profoundly threatens the way global trade governance has functioned for the last half-century. However, this is not for the reasons predicted by either realists or critical theorists: the emerging powers have imperiled the existing institutional order not because they sought to bring about its collapse but precisely the opposite—because they bought into the system and sought to lay claim to its benefits.

The Case of the WTO

The WTO provides a critical case to understand current transformations in global economic governance. With its system of rules and trade disciplines underpinning international economic relations, the WTO has been compared to a constitution for the global economy (Ruggiero, former director-general of the WTO, cited in McMichael 2004: 166). It is a core pillar in the management of economic globalization and the construction of global neoliberalism, since its rules define the "line between legitimate and illegitimate state intervention in the market" (Mortensen 2006: 172).

As one of the only international institutions whose rules are legally binding on states and backed by a powerful enforcement mechanism, the WTO is one of the strongest and most important institutions of global governance. Consequently, the WTO has been a key site of struggle over global power relations. The WTO was one of the first global economic governance institutions in which the new developing country powers successfully disrupted traditional decision-making structures and became core players. Over the course of the book, I provide empirical evidence to demonstrate that a significant shift in power has indeed taken place at the WTO.[4] This is important because there remains debate among scholars about whether power shifts in global economic governance are real or merely symbolic. Skeptics contend that reports of declining American hegemony have been exaggerated, the US and other traditional powers retain their primacy in the international order, and the emerging powers have yet to exercise significant voice and influence or become a source of initiative and agenda-setting in global economic governance (Babones 2015; Beeson and Bell 2009; Cox 2012; Norloff 2012; Nye 2015; Pinto, Macdonald, and Marshall 2011; Subacchi 2008; Wade 2011). As I will show, however, at the WTO, the rise of new powers has dramatically circumscribed the power of the US and other Northern states and brought an end to their dominance; Brazil, India, and China have not only joined the elite inner circle of power within the WTO but they have also had a profound impact on both negotiations and dispute settlement.

The WTO is also an important case because power shifts occurred there far earlier, in 2003, than in other institutions such as the G8/G20, IMF, and World

Bank, which did not begin until 2008. In contrast to the IMF and World Bank—whose weighted voting systems serve to lock in historical power disparities, are stickier and more resistant to change, and therefore are less reflective of the changing balance of power—the more informal and consensus-based system of decision-making at the WTO made that institution more fluid and responsive to shifting power (Narlikar 2013). In addition, the power shift that occurred at the WTO in many ways laid the groundwork for subsequent changes in other institutions. The emergence of new developing country powers at the WTO was groundbreaking and had far-reaching reverberations, giving recognition to these states as important actors in global economic governance and further delegitimizing their subordination or exclusion in other institutions, such as the G8 and the IMF.[5]

In order to understand current transformations in the multilateral trading system, I conducted fifteen months of field research at the WTO in Geneva, as well as in Beijing, New Delhi, Sao Paulo, Brasilia, and Washington. The research involved 157 interviews with trade negotiators, senior government officials, and representatives of industry and nongovernmental organizations; more than three hundred hours of ethnographic observation; and extensive documentary research (see Appendix).

The Rise of New Powers at the WTO

This book analyzes the role that Brazil, India, and China have played at the WTO and assesses their impact on the multilateral trading system.[6] The central thesis of the book is that power shifts have disrupted the institutional project of neoliberalism—the construction and expansion of rules and institutions to further the advance of globalization and neoliberal market restructuring—at the WTO. However, this is not because the new developing country powers have rejected neoliberalism as the ordering principle of the global economy, as we might expect. Rather, I argue that the emerging powers have embraced the WTO's discourse of free trade and liberalization and its tools for opening markets and sought to use them to their own advantage. The surprise is thus that a wider acceptance of the neoliberal global economic order—the norms, principles, and institutional arrangements governing the global economy—by the emerging powers has led to the breakdown of one of its core institutions.

This is a story rich in paradox.

Although Brazil, India, and China employ rhetoric that is strongly reminiscent of the era of Third Worldism in the 1950s–70s and its calls for a radical overhaul of the international economic order, I show that the agendas they are actually pursuing at the WTO fit solidly within—rather than challenge—the neoliberal trade paradigm. The new powers are not calling the neoliberal global economic order into question; on the contrary, they have accepted its constitutive institutional arrangements and are seeking to advance their interests within them (rather than trying to go outside or overthrow them, as they did in the past). Although the new powers have challenged the traditional workings of the WTO, their opposition has been to the dominance of the US and other advanced-industrialized countries, not the fundamental norms and principles of the institution or the protrade ideology that animates it. In other words, theirs is a power challenge, not an ideological one. Their objection is not to global neoliberalism, per se, but the unbalanced way in which it has been pursued through multilateral institutions under US hegemony.

In the extensive debate about whether the new powers are likely to be "system challenging" ("revisionist") or "status quo" preserving, there has been a tendency to conflate challenging the dominance of the US and other Western powers with challenging the system itself (see, for example, the quotation from Stewart Patrick of the US Council on Foreign Relations, above). Consequently, a country that refuses to concede to US demands is often labeled as playing "nasty" (Narlikar 2010), or failing to act as a responsible international citizen. The case of the WTO, however, illuminates the important distinction between challenging the dominance of the traditional powers and rejecting the existing system of global economic governance. It also shows, though, that even by adopting positions in keeping with the norms of the liberal economic order, the rising powers have still thrown it into jeopardy, however inadvertently.

How are we to understand the enduring power of the neoliberal trade paradigm in a context of shifting power, particularly when the rising powers are originating from the developing world? If developing countries have been victimized by the global governance institutions and the regime of global neoliberalism, why are the emerging powers from the Global South not challenging the neoliberal paradigm, as many would predict? The answer, I argue, stems from what we might call *the structural paradox of global power.* Only those countries that are successful within the neoliberal paradigm become powerful enough to challenge the system, but having benefited from the liberal trading order, these countries have little incentive to jettison it. As their booming exports attest—Brazil in agriculture, India in services, and China in manufactured goods—these countries have been among the primary beneficiaries from liberalization of the global economy. The neoliberal turn and the free trade policies adopted by many countries have opened markets for their exports, fueling their rapid growth and rising economic might. While many developing countries have been profoundly disadvantaged by global neoliberalism, certain countries have been able to profit from the export opportunities created by the wrenching open of markets under neoliberalism. The countries now rising to power—Brazil, India, and China—are those that have made significant gains within the existing system. As a result, far from challenging neoliberalism at the global level, they have become some of its strongest champions, frequently extolling the virtues of free trade and impressing upon other countries—developed and developing—the need to further open their markets. If anything, the position of the new powers is that liberalization has not gone far enough—in their areas of export interest, that is.

An important caveat is in order. In claiming that the emerging powers have become advocates of neoliberalism, I am referring specifically to their behavior and policy objectives at the global level. There is considerable debate among scholars over how the domestic economic and development policies of the emerging economies should be understood, whether they are neoliberal or represent a rejection of neoliberalism and the development of alternative economic models (such as a "Beijing Consensus," "neodevelopmentalism," or "social neoliberalism"; see, for example, Ban and Blyth 2013). The intention here, however, differs and is more narrow: setting aside the issue of how to characterize the internal policies of the rising powers, I concentrate instead on their behavior and objectives in the international rather than the domestic realm. Despite considerable variation in their domestic political economies and policies, I show that the new powers are pursuing strikingly similar goals in global economic governance: all are actively seeking to profit from and continue the liberalization and expansion of global markets. Regardless of their domestic policies, the new powers have embraced global neoliberalism at the international level.

This interpretation of the behavior of the new powers at the WTO runs counter to the dominant one advanced by many Western WTO observers and international relations scholars. There has been vocal criticism of the new powers—especially from those connected with the US trade and foreign policy establishment (Bergsten 2008; Schwab 2011)—eager to point the finger of blame at China, India, and Brazil and hold them responsible for the breakdown of the Doha Round. The emerging powers have been variously characterized as illiberal, recalcitrant spoilers and vetoers, irresponsible stakeholders shirking their international responsibilities, and more (Castañeda 2010; Hampson and Heinbecker 2011; Patrick 2010). What I will argue, however, is that this is based on a fundamental misrecognition of the behavior of the traditional powers at the WTO and the actual workings of the institution.

It is my contention that the new powers have taken up and become strong proponents of the ideology of self-regulating markets at the global level, but they have done so exactly as the traditional powers always have—*selectively*. The US and other Northern states have frequently been accused of hypocrisy for demanding market liberalization from developing countries while simultaneously evading and limiting the application of the same principles in their own markets. The goal of the new powers, just like the old, is to open foreign markets to facilitate the growth of their exports. In the neoliberal global economy, exports are vital to a country's economic stability and prospects for growth. In areas where their exports have the potential to flourish, the new powers have become vocal advocates of free trade and the opening of global markets. At the same time, the new powers, just like the old, also seek to varying degrees to protect uncompetitive and sensitive areas of their domestic economies. Thus, in arguing that the new powers have become advocates of global neoliberalism, I am referring to their efforts to secure free and open markets at the global level, while nonetheless seeking to maintain protectionist policies in parts of their own markets. Their commitment to neoliberalism is thus as contradictory and hypocritical as that of the traditional powers. The new powers are embracing neoliberalism to the extent that it serves their purposes, just as the US and other Northern powers always have.

This represents a marked change in the multilateral trading system. Historically, developing countries have been in a defensive position at the GATT/WTO—seeking to resist pressures to liberalize their markets from the US and other rich countries. In an organization that views its mandate as expanding trade liberalization, this is a highly vulnerable position to be in. Now, however, driven by the rise of its highly competitive, export-oriented agribusiness sector, Brazil has emerged as one of the most aggressive proponents of agricultural trade liberalization. In a remarkable about-face, India has gone from being the primary opponent of freer trade in services in the last round of trade negotiations to one of its leading advocates in the Doha Round. And China, having undertaken more liberalization at the WTO than any other state and with keen interests in the continued liberalization of global markets for manufactured goods, is deeply invested in maintaining and expanding the (relatively) open, rules-based multilateral trading system.

Over the course of the Doha Round, the emerging powers turned the tables and went on the offensive vis-à-vis the US and EU, making their policies a central focus and target of the round and radically altering the dynamic at the WTO. As I will chronicle, the key turning point occurred when Brazil and India, backed by China, led the developing world in an attack on US and EU agricultural subsidies, one of the most substantial and conspicuous examples of protectionism and distortion in world trade.[7] This became a critical juncture that overturned the traditional power structure at the WTO and catapulted Brazil and India into the inner circle of power, later to be joined by China. In effect, the new powers turned the WTO system against its originators, demanding market liberalizing reforms from the US and its industrialized allies. Beyond the Doha negotiations, the new powers have become aggressive users of the WTO dispute settlement system to challenge and discipline developed country trade policies. This represents a dramatic change: for all eight previous trade rounds, the US was the primary *demandeur*, pushing other countries to open and liberalize their markets. But now in the Doha Round, for the first time, the new developing country powers seized the offensive and made the policies of the US and other advanced-industrialized states a central target at the WTO.

Yet the result has been a clash between the old and new powers, with each side demanding additional liberalization from the other but refusing to yield itself. The situation at the WTO is now one in which the traditional powers—the US and EU—are faced off against the rising powers—Brazil, India, and China. The two sides are locked in a fight over the outcome of the Doha Round that centers on where its costs and benefits should fall. This is not an ideological or paradigmatic conflict but a distributional struggle taking place within the neoliberal normative and institutional framework of the WTO. The two sides in this struggle are relatively evenly matched, such that neither has been able to overpower the other and impose its preferences, and the result has been repeated breakdown and stalemate in the Doha negotiations. With the traditional and emerging powers unable to reach agreement, the Doha Round has effectively collapsed.[8] It now appears that it will likely be impossible to conclude the Doha Round; and, even if states do one day manage to salvage some kind of conclusion to the round, it will be a greatly diminished version of what was originally intended.

The emergence of competing powers has thus severely disrupted the workings of the WTO. Under conditions of more equitable power relations among states, multilateralism—the ability of states to agree on the construction of global laws, rules, and institutions—has disintegrated.[9] States have been unable to cooperate in pursuit of the WTO's agenda of expanding the institutional architecture governing trade. With the collapse of the Doha Round, the WTO is an institution in crisis. The WTO was created to push forward trade and market liberalization and neoliberal restructuring on a global scale, through successive rounds of interstate negotiations. Yet the first trade round to be conducted under its auspices has been a dramatic failure.[10] The emergence of competing powers capable of countering the traditional dominance of the US—and pushing back with their own agenda of liberalization—has brought the advance of the WTO's neoliberal project to a halt. This is not to say that the WTO has collapsed, and it does not necessarily imply "deglobalization" or a retreat to autarchy. The WTO continues to exist as an institution and its existing rules and dispute settlement mechanism remain in force. However, its project of driving forward the continued progress of liberalization—which is central to its raison d'etre—has broken down.

The collapse of the Doha Round signifies a crisis of multilateralism and of the international institutional architecture that has played a central role in the advance of neoliberal globalization to date. The puzzle, then, is why a broader acceptance of global neoliberalism—specifically, its embrace by rising powers from the developing world—produced a crisis in one of its governing institutions. How are we to explain the apparent ideological triumph of neoliberalism—in the sense that it has come to transcend its original backers and been taken up by other actors that were once its fervent opponents—occurring alongside the breakdown of its institutional project at the WTO?

The Contradictions of the (Neo)Liberal Economic Order

The solution to this puzzle, I contend, lies in contradictions at the heart of the governing institutions constructed under US hegemony. The existing international order is premised on the ideology of liberalism. Politically, this has taken the form of a system of multilateral institutions based on the notion of equally sovereign states freely coming together and agreeing to cooperate to govern the global economy and polity. Economically, this meant an expansion of global capitalism purportedly fueled by increasingly free and open global markets, theoretically intended to maximize global economic welfare by providing competitive markets and the most efficient allocation of resources. These twin pillars of political and economic liberalism have provided the foundation of the international economic order. Yet the discourse of liberalism served to mask or obscure, to varying degrees of success, inequality and relations of power within the global economic order.

The deadlock in the Doha Round lays bare how much the successful multilateralism of the past was predicated on highly unequal power relations. Previous agreement among states required the ability of the more powerful to force the less powerful to consent; now, in contrast, under conditions of more equal power, states have proven unable to cooperate and reach agreement. Power asymmetries thus provided the hidden foundation for multilateralism. The goal of the new powers is not to counter liberalization—far from it, they have undertaken extensive liberalization unilaterally and are keen advocates of liberalization for others—but they resist the external imposition of policies just as much as the US does. And now, for the first time at the WTO, they are demonstrating the power to do so effectively. Brazil, India, and China are asserting their own sovereignty vis-à-vis the US—demanding that their sovereignty be recognized and treated as equal to that of the US—while simultaneously demanding that the US be held accountable to the same rules, norms, and principles that it has propounded and pressed on other states.

For more than fifty years, the US has enjoyed the privileges of hegemony, acting and being treated as the exceptional state in the international system. While the US created a system of laws, norms and institutions to govern the globe, it always to some extent positioned itself as outside of that system, refusing to relinquish its sovereignty or be fully bound by the rules in the same way it demanded of other states. The US has long claimed the right to intervene in the affairs of other states, through its dominant position in multilateral institutions like the IMF and WTO and justified by the discourse of neoliberal economics (Cox 1992). Now, however, the rising developing country powers are behaving in the same way and demanding an equal right to intervene in the internal trade and economic policies of the US and other states of the Global North and pressure them to open their markets. The new powers have sought to curtail the privileges of the US and insist that it be treated as a state like any other and therefore truly bound by the international economic architecture it constructed and equally subject to its norms, laws, and principles. Yet, in the process, they have destabilized that very system of global economic governance.

Contemporary power shifts, I argue, have shattered the mythology of the liberal American-led world order. They have laid bare the extent to which the principles of multilateralism and free trade, which supposedly animated the WTO and other global economic governance institutions, were in fact what Richard Steinberg (2002) calls "procedural fictions" and Stephen Krasner (1999) refers to as "organized hypocrisy." To characterize these principles as myths is not to suggest that they were simply blatant falsehoods, but instead that they were partial truths that concealed as much as they revealed about the actual workings of the WTO. In practice, both the multilateralism of the WTO and its pursuit of free trade have been highly unbalanced and heavily shaped by power disparities among states. The emergence of new powers has underscored the discrepancy between the WTO's liberal rhetoric and its reality of power politics. Moreover, in an ironic twist, the twin myths of multilateralism and free trade that underpinned the system of global economic governance constructed under US hegemony—and for decades helped to legitimate that order and enhance the exercise of American power—ultimately proved its unraveling. In demanding that the multilateral trading system live up to its liberal rhetoric, the emerging powers have thrown that system into jeopardy.

Each successive hegemon to date—the Dutch, the British, and the American—has used its political and economic dominance to construct a new and distinct world order, characterized by distinctive institutional forms at the global level (Arrighi and Silver 1999; Ruggie 1982). Periods of hegemonic transition therefore present "as moments of change both in the leading agency of world-scale processes of capital accumulation and in the political-economic structures in which these processes are embedded" (Arrighi and Silver 1999: 22). I argue that the case of the WTO suggests that we are indeed in the midst of a fundamental change in the political-economic structures in which global capitalism is embedded. The system of global economic governance established following World War II was a distinct and defining feature of the era of US hegemony. However, the failure of the multilateral trading system to produce a successful new round represents a break in the institutional architecture that has governed the global economy for the last half-century and enabled and fueled the process of neoliberal globalization. With states unable to reach agreement, the multilateral trading system is no longer able to function as it was designed to by the US and other Western powers in the years following World War II.

Arrighi and Silver (1999: 33) posit that escalating competition and conflict in a period of hegemonic transition is likely to destabilize existing political-economic structures and produce rising systemic disorganization. I make the case that this is precisely what we are seeing in the realm of trade. The collapse of the Doha Round suggests that the means by which neoliberal globalization has been advanced to date—through multilateral institutions and propelled by US power—has been disrupted and may now be blocked. Yet global capitalism is fluid and adaptable and has continually evolved in response to periodic crises. With the Doha negotiations at a stalemate and the WTO therefore unable to fulfill its function of pushing forward the progress of trade liberalization, there has instead been a proliferation of alternative arrangements, such as bilateral and regional trade and investment agreements. I argue that in contrast to the centralization that characterized international trade regulation under American hegemony, we are now seeing increasing fragmentation in the governance architecture of international trade and global capitalism more broadly. Analysis of the WTO thus suggests that the current historical moment represents an important turning point in the evolution of neoliberal globalization.

Neoliberalism Turned on Its Head

The case of the WTO illustrates how, paradoxically, neoliberalism—which arose as a projection of US power—unleashed unintended structural, discursive, and institutional consequences that ultimately had the effect of undermining American dominance. First, neoliberalism was advanced globally by the US in an effort to maintain its economic supremacy and benefit from its competitive advantage in high value-added areas of production. Yet, by opening global markets for their exports, global neoliberalism played a significant role in fueling the economic rise of Brazil, India, and China and their emergence as major new competitors to the US and other traditionally dominant states.

Second, in a testament to the hegemony—and mobility—of neoliberalism, neoliberal discourse became a tool used by the rising powers to delegitimize the position of the traditional powers. A significant part of the reason these countries have been able to gain power and be so effective in challenging US hegemony at the WTO is that they are advancing an agenda which resonates with its dominant free trade ideology and principles. This enhanced their ideational, or normative, power and added considerable force to their position. By appealing to the neoliberal ethos of the institution and its proliberalization agenda, the emerging powers could claim the moral high-ground, which served to enhance their status and influence. Conversely, if they had intentionally sought to overthrow the liberalization mandate of the WTO or pursued a radical agenda of restructuring the international trading system (along the lines of the NIEO, for example), the rising powers likely would not have been as successful in gaining power within the institution and contesting the dominance of the traditional powers. This points to how, in the current era, power in global economic governance is constrained and enabled by the ideology of neoliberalism.

Finally, an institution that emerged as an instrument of US (and more broadly Western) power—the WTO—ultimately provided the tools that enabled subordinate actors to challenge their domination. With the WTO, the US and other Western states created a Frankenstein's monster; the system they constructed eventually spun beyond their control and came to be used against them. The new developing country powers usurped the master's tools, mobilizing the discourse of neoliberalism and making use of its rules and institutions at the global level in pursuit of their own ends. Neoliberalism thus both gave rise to and empowered challengers to American hegemony.

Relations within and between
the New Developing Country Powers

An important theme running through the book is the heterogeneity both *within* and *between* the new developing country powers. Scholarship on international politics has frequently been criticized for treating states as unitary actors pursuing an objectively pre-given "national interest," without attention to how those interests are determined. This "black box" model of the state considers the origins of a state's policies and objectives at the international level as largely outside the frame of analysis. In contrast, my objective in analyzing the new powers is to open up that black box and look at the domestic forces and actors shaping their negotiating positions at the WTO. This requires disaggregating these countries and analyzing the internal dynamics within them. Each is composed of multiple actors with diverse interests and agendas, and their negotiating positions at the WTO are the product of ongoing domestic political struggles. The stances that these countries take at the WTO—or in global economic governance more broadly—are the product of contests between competing social forces within them. The interplay of domestic social, political, and economic forces in each of the new powers is therefore critical to understanding how the structure of global power is currently being transformed.

The dynamics evident at the WTO also draw our attention to the diversity among the new developing country powers. In the emerging scholarship on the rising powers, there have generally been two tendencies. One is to lump these countries together—for example, as "the BRICs"—which tends to homogenize them and erase important differences in their behavior. The opposing tendency has been to treat each country separately and analyze it independently. As a result, there has been little explicit comparison of the role of new powers in global economic governance or analysis of the interaction among them. While sharing some similarities, Brazil, India, and China differ in many ways (including the nature of their economies, political systems, and social structures; the identities, interests, and power of domestic social groups and political actors; and their economic and development policies and priorities). These three countries have widely divergent trade interests and objectives, and they face different opportunities and constraints in multilateral trade negotiations. In consequence, as I will show, there have been significant differences in the behavior of the rising powers at the WTO. At the same time, however, I will also demonstrate that, despite diverse and even potentially conflicting interests, Brazil, India, and China have a strong collective identity and alliance rooted in their oppositional position in relation to the traditional powers. The interaction among the new powers is essential to understanding contemporary power shifts and the emerging dynamics in global economic governance.

This leads to a second important theme within the book: the relationship among the new powers and their relationship to the rest of the developing world. I argue that the rise of Brazil, India, and China cannot be understood in isolation. Their growing importance at the WTO corresponded with a rising tide of developing country activism and unrest within that institution. In the years following the Uruguay Round of trade negotiations that created the WTO in 1995, there was growing dissatisfaction among developing countries about their exclusion from decision-making and the profoundly unbalanced results of the round. It is no coincidence that the rise of new powers from the Global South was intertwined with a broader revolt on the part of developing countries. Brazil and India were key figures in fostering and channeling this uprising, and it played a major role in fueling their rise to power. Although China was more a follower than a leader of this movement, it nonetheless benefited in more subtle ways from its solidarity and alliances with other developing countries. As I will show, developing world leadership and alliances have played a central role in changing power dynamics at the WTO. Yet the rise of the new powers has had complex and ambiguous effects for the rest of the developing world.

Overview of the Book

The chapters in this book chronicle the emergence and impact of new developing country powers at the WTO. It is my contention that the case of the WTO illuminates important transformations taking place in the US-led project of neoliberal globalization and its governing institutions.

Chapter 2 explores in greater detail the economic, institutional, and ideational foundations of the global economic order. Liberalism has provided its ethos; yet, as I will show, liberalism has always simultaneously contained possibilities of oppression and emancipation, of reinforcing and challenging power, and been imbued with the contradiction between a rhetoric of universalism and practices of exclusion. This tension has been equally present within the liberalism underlying the American hegemonic order. While multilateralism and free markets served as its core pillars, both were in practice highly asymmetrical. The US created and used multilateral institutions as a means to exercise its authority over the international system and promote its own national political, economic, and security interests abroad. In the economic realm, the US hegemon deployed the discourse and policies of free markets—propagated through multilateral institutions—to compel other countries to open their markets to its goods and capital, while nonetheless maintaining substantial protections in its own. This exercise of American power, however, contained the seeds of its own undoing: the expansion of global markets gave rise to new economic competitors and involved the creation of institutions and discourses that could eventually be used against the hegemon.

Chapter 3 examines the WTO as a central institution in the American-led project of neoliberal globalization. This chapter therefore sets the broader context for understanding the magnitude and significance of the contemporary power shift that has occurred at the WTO. It provides an overview of the history and evolution of the multilateral trading system, from the origins of the GATT in the immediate postwar years to the creation of the WTO in the Uruguay Round. Driven by the US and other advanced-industrialized states, the establishment of the WTO as a successor to the GATT represented a significant transformation in the governance of international trade, by dramatically expanding the scope of the institution and its authority over states. The WTO was created to be a key carrier of the neoliberal globalization project, and subsequent rounds of trade negotiations were intended to further its agenda of neoliberal economic restructuring. While providing historical context, the chapter concentrates on highlighting the tensions within the liberal principles of multilateralism and free trade that lie at the center of the GATT/WTO. It shows how the superior economic and political resources of the US and to a lesser extent other Northern states have enabled them to dominate the institution and design and structure the rules of international trade to serve their economic and strategic interests. It also looks at the historically disadvantaged position of developing countries within the multilateral trading system and the particularly onerous costs exacted from them in the previous Uruguay Round.

Chapter 4 examines why and how a significant shift in power has occurred at the WTO. In doing so, it challenges the conventional wisdom that the emergence of new powers in global economic governance is merely a function of their growing economic might. Instead, I argue that while China's rise has been more closely tied to its economic weight, Brazil and India used their activist and entrepreneurial leadership of developing country coalitions to propel themselves to power. In contrast to the widespread view that China is the primary threat to American hegemony, I show that, in fact, Brazil and India led the charge in challenging the US and became major players at the WTO several years before China. Despite their relatively small economies and limited roles in world trade, Brazil and India assumed a more aggressive and activist position in WTO negotiations than China and played a greater role in shaping the agenda of the Doha Round. Later, China did come to exercise significant influence as the negotiations neared a potential conclusion, but in a reactive veto capacity, unlike the proactive agenda-setting of Brazil and India. Furthermore, even China, though eschewing a leadership role akin to that of Brazil and India, has still sought the protections afforded by developing world alliances.

The next chapters turn to examining the objectives of the new powers in global trade governance. Each chapter concentrates on one of the three countries, in order to highlight a distinct aspect of the agendas being pursued by the emerging powers at the WTO. Chapter 5 focuses on the Brazilian case, which provides perhaps the most striking illustration of why the ascension of developing countries into the core power structure has not resulted in a direct challenge to the neoliberal agenda of the WTO. I show that Brazil's stance at the WTO has been driven by the rise of its sophisticated and highly competitive agroexport sector, which has emerged as an influential force in Brazilian trade policy and at the WTO. Working in close partnership, the Brazilian state and its agribusiness sector have actively made use of both the WTO's dispute settlement mechanism and the Doha negotiations to further their commercial interests. Far from rejecting the discourse and tools of global neoliberalism, Brazil has become arguably the most active and aggressive proponent of trade liberalization in the current Doha Round. I further show that Brazil has advanced the interests of its agribusiness sector by portraying them as a universal interest of the Global South and strategically mobilizing a discourse of development and social justice and the politics of the North-South divide. The influence of Brazil and its agribusiness sector is critical to explaining why agriculture has been such a central part of the round. It has also significantly shaped the direction that developing country "activism" has taken in the current round, with an intense focus on liberalizing agriculture markets through the removal of subsidies, rather than advocating policies that would mark a more radical departure from the WTO's traditional neoliberal trade paradigm.

Chapter 6 shifts the focus to China in order to highlight the constraints on the emerging powers. As the world's largest exporter, China—like Brazil—has a major interest in reducing trade barriers, further opening markets to its exports, and strengthening the rules of the multilateral trading system. Yet, I demonstrate that China has been less aggressive in pursuing its offensive trade interests in the Doha Round. China's more cautious stance, I contend, is a reflection of the delicate dance of the new powers, whose economic rise is heavily dependent on exports. For China, the massive expansion of its industrial capacity and export of manufactured goods are perceived by states around the world as a threat; aggressively seeking to expand its market access through the Doha Round would risk provoking a backlash that could ultimately jeopardize its exports and economic growth. Finally, I show that a further constraint, operating not just on China but on all the emerging powers, stems from the need to maintain their developing world alliances. Thus, although they have indeed gained power and exercise considerable influence at the WTO, the new powers are not unconstrained in their ability to pursue their offensive trade interests within the institution.

Chapter 7 turns to India's agenda at the WTO, in order to show how the emerging powers must balance a complex mix of offensive and defensive trade interests. Of the three emerging powers, India is the most frequent target of condemnation by Western negotiators and observers, who typically portray it as an illiberal and irresponsible player in global trade politics, intent on derailing the WTO's liberalization agenda. In this chapter, I challenge this characterization, arguing that it is a reflection of efforts by the US and other Western powers to make India a scapegoat rather than an accurate portrayal of its trade policy. I show that, like China and Brazil, India's process of domestic economic reform and liberalization, coupled with the development of a world-leading services export industry that has substantial interests in liberalizing foreign markets, has fundamentally altered its orientation toward the multilateral trading system. Far from an opponent of global trade liberalization, India has major offensive trade interests that it has sought to advance through the Doha Round. At the same time, however, India also has significant defensive interests, particularly in agriculture, because of its large and heavily impoverished peasant population. India's negotiating position at the WTO has therefore combined efforts to promote liberalization in its areas of export interest and secure protections in sensitive areas where it is vulnerable to liberalization. Although the traditional powers decry India's behavior and objectives as an affront to the liberal trading order, this is no different from how the US and other advanced-industrialized states have operated in relation to the GATT/WTO, with extensive accommodations for the sensitivities of those states consistently built into the fabric of the multilateral trading system.

The concluding chapter returns to the central questions raised in this introduction regarding the impact of contemporary power shifts on the multilateral trading system and, more broadly, American hegemony and the governance of neoliberal globalization. I argue that the new powers have imperilled the neoliberal project at the WTO; yet, paradoxically, this was an unintended consequence not of rejecting its goals and principles but embracing them. Through a process of strategic maneuvering, rising challengers usurped the dominant norms, discourses, and institutional tools of the WTO, which had once been instruments of US hegemony, and used them to destabilize the existing hierarchy. Yet the emerging powers' challenge to American dominance has had profound and unpredictable consequences: when the weapons of the powerful became appropriated by formerly subordinate states, the system itself broke down. A situation of more equitable power relations among states has caused the Doha Round to collapse and thus cut short the American-led neoliberal project at the WTO. The current crisis at the WTO is a crisis of the liberalism underpinning the international economic order created under US hegemony, unleashed by power shifts that exacerbated the contradictions contained within its foundational myths of multilateralism and free trade

Chapter 2

Liberalism and the Contradictions
of American Hegemony

CONTEMPORARY power shifts have had a profoundly disruptive and destabi-lizing effect on the ability of the WTO to function and fulfill its intended role in the institutional project of neoliberal globalization. To better understand why this is the case, I contend that we need to situate the WTO within the larger context of the liberal international economic order. The central question is why the rise of new powers from the developing world—Brazil, India, and China—has had such a subversive effect on the workings of the WTO, when, as I will show, those states have largely bought into the existing norms and principles of that institution. The reason, I argue, is that these power shifts have exacerbated systemic contradictions in the American-led liberal world order.

This chapter begins with a discussion of the international economic order constructed under US hegemony. It goes on to focus on the liberal underpin-nings of this system, exploring enduring tensions within liberalism between equality and domination, and universalism and exclusion. It then examines how these tensions have been manifest in the contemporary system of global economic governance. The discussion centers on two core tenets at the heart of the WTO: multilateralism and free markets. I argue that neither was ever in-tended to be fully realized but served instead as foundational myths to mask and enhance the projection of power by the US and other dominant states. Finally, however, I show that the American hegemonic order also contained forces that would give rise to and empower its challengers. The chapter closes with a summary of the argument developed so far.

The American-led World Order

The existing international economic order was forged during the era of American hegemony and heavily shaped by US power (Gilpin 1987; Ruggie 1996). In the aftermath of World War II, as the former Great Powers of Europe lay crippled by the devastation produced by two consecutive and massive wars, the US emerged with an unprecedented concentration of power. The US accounted for one-third of global GDP, with an economy three times the size of the USSR's and five times that of Britain, commanding half of the world's industrial output and three-quarters of its gold reserves (Anderson 2013: 22; Wilkinson 2011). Its overwhelming economic and political power enabled the US to impose upon the world an order of its own choosing (Arrighi and Silver 1999; Walt 2011). Consolidating its power in the wake of the war, the US stabilized the international system and went about constructing a new and historically distinct global order that reflected its predominance. Dispensing with the traditional form of imperialism based on territorial expansion and direct colonial rule, which was both highly risky and expensive, the US constructed an "informal empire" based on its position at the epicenter of global capitalism and institutionalized through an extensive system of global governance (Babones 2015; Go 2008; Panich and Gindin 2012; Steinmetz 2005; Wood 2005).[1]

From its hegemonic position, the US fashioned an increasingly open and integrated global economy, based on the doctrine of free markets and trade. While seeking to advance the interests of its own investors, exporters, and multinational corporations, the American hegemon became the guardian and promoter of global capitalism, taking responsibility for creating the conditions necessary for international markets to operate (Panich and Gindin 2012). The US assumed a pivotal role in ensuring the stability and functioning of global capitalism, by providing military security, a large and relatively open market, foreign investment and aid, liquidity for the global economy, and a reserve currency, and by acting as global crisis manager (Gilpin 1975; Ikenberry 2011; Keohane 1980; Kindleberger 1973; Krasner 1976; Lake 2009).

Simultaneously, the US—backed by Britain as a junior partner—engaged in an extraordinary and unprecedented building of multilateral institutions, which included the United Nations (UN) and the Bretton Woods institutions— the General Agreement on Tariffs and Trade (GATT, later to become the WTO), International Monetary Fund (IMF) and World Bank. The US put in place an integrated system of rules, laws, and norms centered on such international organizations in order to create stable and open conditions for the functioning of global markets. These institutions served as the pillars of the new US hegemonic order (Gilpin 1987; Keohane 1984; Ruggie 1996).

In constructing the contemporary global economic architecture, the US made multilateralism a foundational principle (Ruggie 1993). American post-war planners viewed the interruption of trade in the 1930s, resulting from the Great Depression and the autarchic policies imposed by states, as exacerbating the Depression and contributing directly to the outbreak of World War II; they were eager to see a rebuilding of the economies of Europe and Japan and a resumption of trade. The devastation wrought by war in Europe, in particular, stifled demand for US goods, and American capitalism was considered at risk without access to foreign markets (Anderson 2013). American policy-makers were also motivated by antipathy toward trade-restricting and trade-diverting policies, whether in the form of Nazi and communist models of bilateral and state-controlled trading systems, or the imperial preference systems of the co-lonial powers. The latter closed much of the colonized world to America's com-mercial reach: the preferential systems of the colonial powers both guaranteed markets for their products and provided them with exclusive access to vital raw materials, which had the effect of restricting American commercial presence in and ability to extract raw materials from these markets (Wilkinson 2006).

The US sought a worldwide liberalization of trade orchestrated through in-ternational institutions, confident that from its position of industrial and finan-cial dominance, it was in a position to supply the world with goods and capital. The triumvirate of the IMF, World Bank, and GATT/WTO, in particular, oper-ated in concert to promote the overarching goal of enabling free trade. While the World Bank financed postwar reconstruction, and later Third World devel-opment, and the IMF stabilized the international financial system, the GATT/WTO provided a framework for negotiations among states to lower trade bar-riers. Although the economic order created at Bretton Woods in 1944 and the specific functions of these institutions have evolved over time, the principle of free trade has remained constant at the core of this system.

The American-led institution-building project involved extending the logic and imperatives of its own domestic economy—by internationalizing its own political ideas, policies, and practices—and drawing others into its orbit (Kup-chan 2014; Wood 2005). Initially, motivated by the desire to ensure the security of the capitalist system and respond to the ideological and political challenge posed by the Soviet Union, the US sought to extend a modified version of the New Deal globally. Its principles of greater government responsibility for eco-nomic and social protection were manifest in the postwar reconstruction of Europe and Japan, development aid to the Third World, and the embedded liberalism that characterized global economic governance until the 1970s. During this period, the US oversaw a generalized expansion of world trade with few precedents in history (Arrighi 1994).

Yet, with the global economic crisis of the 1970s—combining economic stagnation, unemployment, heightened inflation, and indebtedness—the postwar social contract between labor and capital broke down and the Fordist-Keynesian model was abandoned. This hegemonic crisis did not bring an end to American dominance but instead led to "the material and ideological refurbishing of US hegemony" in the 1980s (Gill 2003). As Chorev and Babb (2009) chronicle, the US successfully "reinvented its hegemony by transitioning from the post-war 'embedded liberal' world order to the Reagan-Thatcher model of neoliberalism and global capitalism" (see also Harvey 2005; Morton 2003). As before, the US went about internationalizing its agenda through the global governance institutions. Previously, for much of the period of its hegemony, the US had needed to balance a complex combination of economic and geopolitical/strategic objectives in constructing *Pax Americana*: its desire to expand opportunities for its exports and multinational corporations was tempered, to some extent, during the Cold War by the need to contain the threat of communism and the Soviet Union. In the 1990s, however, the fall of the Soviet Union left the US the world's sole, undisputed superpower, ushering in what Henry Veltmeyer (2012: 64) has termed the "golden age of US imperialism" in regard to the advance of American capital and Washington's influence over the neoliberal policy regimes adopted by governments around the world.

The Ideological and Institutional Foundations of American Hegemony

American hegemony and the existing global economic architecture are deeply intertwined. Hegemony, in the Gramscian sense, is distinct from pure domination because it relies not solely on coercion but on a degree of consent (Cox 1983). Hegemonic powers are distinguished by their capacity to present themselves, and be perceived, as the bearer of a general interest. As Arrighi and Silver (1999: 26) describe, hegemony is "the *additional* power that accrues to a dominant group by virtue of its capacity to lead society in a direction that not only serves the dominant group's interests, but is also perceived by subordinate groups as serving a more general interest." It is this ability of a dominant actor to universalize its interests—by constructing the appearance that they are shared or universal interests—that represents the crucial difference between hegemony and mere domination.

Liberalism has thus played a central role in the hegemony of the US. The existing global order is aptly characterized as an "American liberal hegemonic order" or "a hierarchical order with liberal characteristics" (Ikenberry 2014). It is a "liberal" order in the sense that it is based on articulated principles of economic and political liberalism—free markets and trade, democracy, human rights, and political freedom—and a rules-based system of sovereign states (Lake 2009). These roots in liberal ideas and institutions have lent powerful ideological legitimacy and support to the world order constructed under American hegemony. Yet liberalism contains a number of important contradictions, which, as I will later show, were carried over into the American hegemonic order and its legitimating mythology—with critical implications for the workings of the WTO and, ultimately, its disruption by changes in the distribution of power among states.

The Contradictions of Liberalism

Three contradictory aspects of liberalism are particularly important to highlight here. First, from its birth in the seventeenth century, liberalism has always been Janus-faced, combining impulses of both universalism and exclusion. It has claimed to be about universal emancipation and the revolutionary concepts of the sovereignty and rights of the people, equality, liberty, justice, and the rule of law. Yet, the extension of liberal rights within Europe was not only limited in its scope (recognizing only certain people as liberal, rights-bearing subjects) but also intricately bound up with colonialism, slavery, the taxonomy of race, and a plethora of other mechanisms that served to exclude many from access to purportedly universal rights (McIver 1932; Wallerstein 1995; Wood 2005). Moreover, liberalism was directly implicated in these exclusions, with the very principles of liberal thought used to justify and legitimate the age of European imperialism (Pitts 2005).

Second, the formal, legal equality upon which liberal institutions are predicated often serves to mask substantive inequality. The pretense of equality implied in the liberal universalism of "general rules applying equally to all persons" (Wallerstein 2006: 38) can work to obscure (and thereby reinforce and strengthen) vast real inequality. Liberal political-economic systems, whether democratic nation-states or international organizations like the WTO, are founded on the pretense of legally free and equal individuals (or states), which provides a powerful source of legitimation—even when, in practice, many may be excluded from the system's benefits (Wood 2005). In the words of Pierre Bourdieu (2000: 71), the "mystificatory hypocrisy of abstract universalism" is such that "whether in relations between nations or within nations, abstract universalism generally serves to justify the established order, the prevailing distribution of powers and privileges."

Finally, in many ways, liberalism represents a Pandora's Box, with forces that once unleashed can be difficult to contain. Although liberal ideas and discourse may operate as tools of the powerful, they simultaneously create potential levers of resistance for subordinate actors to challenge their subordination. For, as Bourdieu (2000: 127) describes, "[A]s soon as the principles claiming universal validity (those of democracy, for example) are stated and officially professed," this opens the possibility that those principles may be used "as symbolic weapons in struggles of interests or as instruments of critique." Even when liberal values are only hypocritically embraced by the powerful, it nonetheless creates a point of tension and vulnerability, and potential leverage for the dominated.

As I will show, these contradictions of liberalism—between universalism and exclusion, between formal equality and substantive inequality, and between serving as an instrument of exploitation and domination, while simultaneously creating possibilities for contestation and resistance—have factored powerfully in the American-led and Western-centered system of global economic governance, including its myths of multilateralism and free markets.

The Liberal Mythology of the WTO

In speaking of the WTO's "mythology," I am referring to stories told to explain its nature, history and purpose, which purport to give a true account and are generally accepted as valid. The WTO's foundational principles of multilateralism and free trade are myths in the sense that while they have some basis in truth, they also work to obscure and distort reality. It is, indeed, this combination—of being partially but not strictly true—that makes these myths effective. Such stories serve a purpose: the image they construct carries ideational, or symbolic, power. By wrapping the WTO in the virtues of liberalism, its foundational myths serve as an important source of legitimation. Like many myths, those enshrouding the WTO also operate as a sort of morality tale—in this case, carrying quasi-moral messages about the inherent virtue of multilateralism and free trade. Like any myth, these needed some basis in fact in order to work: as Perry Anderson (2013: 33) states: "To be effective, an ideology must reflect as well as distort, or conceal, reality." But what these foundational myths worked to conceal—to varying degrees of effectiveness—was the disparity between the rhetoric and reality of American-led global capitalism and its associated system of global governance. I will examine each of these core myths, and the contradictions embodied within them, in turn.

The Myth of Multilateralism

The principle of multilateralism—sovereign states coming together to collectively govern the global economy and polity—is a defining feature of the distinct global political-economic structures constructed under American hegemony. The Westphalian state system that provides the basis for multilateral cooperation only expanded globally under US hegemony, as mass decolonization following World War II resulted in the world being divided into a system of sovereign states. The US supported decolonization out of a desire to avoid a restoration of prewar spheres of influence and control of raw materials, as well as to open doors for American capital in the periphery (Anderson 2013; Apeldoorn and Graaff 2012). Rather than replacing the European colonizers by imposing its own direct colonial rule, the US sought to integrate the newly sovereign states into global capitalism and its emerging system of global governance with the promise of self-determination and national development. This enabled the US to construct and maintain its global dominance with only a minimal and selective use of force compared with the former colonial powers. For the most part, the US was able to rely on the economic imperatives of the market, backed by the coercive power of its governing institutions, to do much of the work (Wood 2005). The US was thus able to portray itself as an "anti-imperialist" advocate of decolonization, at the same time that it went about projecting its power globally with unprecedented scale, scope, and effectiveness (Panich and Gindin 2012). The form of dominance that emerged under American hegemony was no longer a relationship between imperial masters and colonial subjects but a complex interaction between theoretically sovereign states bound together by the logic of global capitalism, administered and coordinated by the multilateral governance institutions (Go 2008; Steinmetz 2005; Wood 2005).

The extraordinary proliferation of global governance that has occurred since 1945 produced unprecedented restrictions on the freedom of sovereign states, in both their relations with other states as well as their own internal affairs (Arrighi 1994). The tentacles of the multilateral economic institutions, for instance, are now able to reach into states and compel them to adopt certain policies and principles in running their economies. The authority of such institutions to intervene in the affairs of sovereign states is justified on the principle of multilateralism—that supranational organizations are themselves the creation of states, who freely agreed to relinquish a degree of their sovereignty in order to reap the benefits of international cooperation. The reality, however, is much messier than this.

Sovereignty as a Privilege of Power

The multilateral institutions that constitute a key component of the American-led world order are predicated on the notion of equal sovereignty of states. Indeed, the norms of sovereignty and nonintervention in the affairs of sovereign states are enshrined in international law and the UN Charter. But state sovereignty has never been equal. As Stephen Krasner (1999) argues, although the central organizing principle of the international system, the norm of Westphalian sovereignty—that a state has autonomy to govern its own territory free from external authority or control—is routinely violated and best characterized as "organized hypocrisy." In practice, powerful states abide by the rule of sovereignty only when it is in their interests to do so. Thus, although all states are theoretically sovereign, powerful states regularly intervene in the internal affairs of weaker states. The question of "Who has the right to intervene?" as Immanuel Wallerstein (2006: 27) puts it, goes to "the heart of the political and moral structure" of the international system, where "intervention is in practice a right appropriated by the strong."

With its preponderance of power in the international system, the US has claimed certain rights and privileges denied to other states. While the US created an extensive structure of international laws and institutions to govern the globe, it has nonetheless been highly unwilling to accept external constraints on its own behavior (Ignatieff 2005). The US has consistently refused to subject itself to, or be bound by, the very system of global governance it created to bind other states and reserved for itself the right to alter or break the rules (Mastanduno 2014). Examples of such "American exceptionalism" abound and are evident across a broad spectrum of governance arenas, including the human rights system, environmental treaties, the nuclear nonproliferation regime, the

UN system, the law of war, the Geneva Conventions, the Torture Convention, the International Criminal Court (ICC), and international financial governance (Anderson 2003; Ignatieff 2005; Krasner 1999; Mitoma 2013; Ruggie 2005; Wade 2011; Wood 2005).

The multilateral system has been animated by the fiction of legally free and equally sovereign states entering into agreement with one another. But just as not all individuals enjoy the full rights of citizenship at the national level (Wood 2005), not all states enjoy the full rights of membership in global governance institutions like the WTO, and not all states have been equally constrained by their rules. Instead, as Panich and Gindin (2012: 9) argue, "[T]he attempt to reconcile national self-determination and the formal equality of states with the inherently asymmetric inter-state relations in a capitalist world economy" has operated to obscure the realities of the American hegemonic order. As Robert Wade (2011) describes, with a formal veto in the IMF and World Bank and its informal dominance in institutions like the GATT/WTO and the G8, the US has often—though not always successfully—treated the multilateral economic institutions as arms of its own foreign policy. The US invested in multilateralism specifically because, in the words of then-Senator Barack Obama (2007), "[I]nstead of constraining our power, these institutions magnified it." Despite the lofty principles upon which the multilateral system rests, in practice, it has strongly reflected underlying power asymmetries among states and especially the overarching power of the US.

The Myth of Free Markets

If multilateralism is the political manifestation of liberalism in the international system, then free markets and trade are its manifestation in the economic realm. Both manifestations have been densely intertwined, as the multilateral economic institutions have played a key role in driving the agenda of global (neo)liberalism. Economic liberalism has aimed to enforce the principle of the free flow of goods and services and the factors of production (material inputs, capital, and labor) within the global economy. But economic liberalism, whether the embedded liberalism of the postwar era or its more recent neoliberal version, has also been intended to buttress the competitive edge of the hegemonic power, while delegitimizing the efforts of other states to take actions that would undermine its economic supremacy.

Neoliberalism: For Whom and What Purpose?

Like liberalism more broadly, the discourse of neoliberal economics makes claims of universality and neutrality, which veil how it is implicated in the machinations of power. Neoliberalism presents itself as a scientific, technocratic discourse that has ascertained the universal and natural "laws of the market." It asserts that free trade and free markets are in the service of "the common good," enhancing general prosperity by creating efficient markets and the conditions for economic growth, whereas state intervention and protectionism are fueled by narrow, particularistic interests and undermine the general welfare. Yet, as Nancy Fraser (1992: 131) writes, "[W]hen social arrangements operate to the systemic profit of some groups of people and to the systemic detriment of others," claims to represent the common good "should be regarded with suspicion." Neoliberalism claims to be both natural and neutral when, in fact, it is neither.

Neoliberalism is rife with further contradictions (Brenner, Peck, and Theodore 2010; Harvey 2005). At an ideological level, neoliberalism advocates the "freeing" of markets from all forms of state interference; yet, the actual establishment and ongoing maintenance of free markets demands deliberate and extensive state action (Centeno and Cohen 2012). As Karl Polanyi (1944) observed, the notion of the self-regulating market is a myth: markets are not natural or self-creating, but constructed through rules, institutions, and regulations. Indeed, state intervention is "a constitutive element of capitalism" essential to enabling the functioning of markets (Levi-Faur 2005: 14). Consequently, despite its apparent antipathy toward the state, the contemporary age of neoliberalism has involved a widespread *expansion* of regulation (Baker 2010; Braithwaite and Drahos 2000; Peck and Tickell 2002; Vogel 1996).

Neoliberalism has thus never been as antistate as it claimed; rather, neoliberalism's "fake adulation of the market" (Wallerstein 1995) has been deployed strategically by actors to meet specific ends. As it emerged in the advanced-capitalist countries of the Global North, "neoliberalism was essentially a *political* response to the democratic gains that had been previously achieved by working classes and which had become, from capital's perspective, barriers to accumulation" (Panich and Gindin 2012: 15). And the implementation of neoliberal policies (such as tax changes, financial deregulation, and tight monetary policy) succeeded in producing a major redistribution of income and wealth to the richest strata (Blyth 2002).

Despite the claims of neoliberalism, however, market forces have never been universally or evenly imposed. Neoliberal restructuring projects are contextually embedded, molded by the institutional and political context in which they are situated, including asymmetries of power and political struggles (Brenner and Theodore 2002). As Brenner and Theodore (2002: 361) observe, "Neoliberal programs of capitalist restructuring are rarely, if ever, imposed in pure form." Instead, actually existing neoliberalisms are always "hybrid or composite structures" (Peck and Tickell 2002: 383). Since the application of neoliberalism is structured by power, it has inevitably been highly uneven. At the national level, as Stephen Gill (1995: 407) explains, the neoliberal turn has worked to "subject the majority of the population to the power of market forces whilst preserving social protection for the strong." As a result, neoliberal policies of "fiscal austerity" and a retrenchment of the state in the provision of welfare, education, healthcare, and other social services have occurred alongside massive state intervention in the financial sector and the commitment of trillions of dollars of public funds to bail out insolvent banks and rescue high finance during the global financial crisis. The powerful have sought to implement the rubrics of neoliberalism when they serve their interests, and blithely ignored them when they do not. The goal has never been truly free markets (which are an impossibility), but to selectively use the rhetoric of neoliberalism as a political tool to enable powerful actors to capture economic advantages.

American Hegemony and the Global Spread of Neoliberalism

The spread of neoliberalism at the global level has been similarly inseparable from power. The neoliberal project, to date, has rested heavily on American hegemony: if multilateral economic institutions like the WTO, IMF, and World Bank have supplied the architecture of neoliberal globalization, the US has served as its chief architect. As Christopher Layne (2009: 169) writes, the US "fostered an open, globalized international economic system based on the 'Washington consensus' and multilateral institutions . . . . Globalization has been made possible by America's military and economic dominance." Yet, this project was never neutral; the Washington Consensus "was first and foremost a strategy aimed at re-establishing US power" after its relative decline in the 1970s (Arrighi and Zhang 2011: 27).

Neoliberal programs of restructuring were extended globally through the efforts of the US and other advanced-industrialized states via the global governance institutions. Initially, in the postwar era, the functions of these institutions centered on ensuring global economic stability and preventing a recurrence of the outbreak of protectionism and "beggar-thy-neighbor" trade and currency policies that caused the global economy to break down in the 1930s and contributed to the Great Depression and the outbreak of World War II. With the rise of neoliberalism, the role of such institutions—and their scope and authority—was dramatically redefined and expanded, as they were "transformed into agents of a transnational neoliberalism and mobilized to institutionalize th[e] extension of market forces and commodification in the Third World" (Brenner and Theodore 2002: 350). In the midst of the international debt crisis that afflicted the Global South in the early 1980s, developing countries were forced to turn en masse to the IMF and World Bank for loans, which were made conditional on their adoption of "structural adjustment programs" (SAPs) involving market liberalizing reforms (such as privatization, deregulation, protections for private property rights, and trade and capital liberalization) and fiscal austerity policies (Chorev and Babb 2009). The GATT/WTO simultaneously locked in many of these reforms and imposed further market opening on developing countries. Thus, although formally neutral and the product of voluntary cooperation among states, the multilateral economic institutions have played a highly coercive role in imposing neoliberal policy prescriptions on developing countries (Chorev 2012; Woods 2006).

For many developing countries, the effects of the Washington Consensus were devastating—resulting in one and sometimes two "lost decades" with little, if any, per capita income growth, combined with rising inequality, growing deprivation with a disproportionate burden on the poor, deindustrialization, and the proliferation of precarious forms of employment (Bayliss, Fine, and van Waeyenberge 2011; Saad-Filho 2013; UNCTAD 1997; UNCTAD 2012). The economic performance of developing countries as a whole dropped sharply, with a fall in median per capital income growth from 2.5 percent in 1960–79 to 0 percent in 1980–98 (Easterly 2001).

Ha-Joon Chang (2002) argues that the neoliberal reforms mandated by the multilateral economic institutions represented an effort to "kick away the ladder" for developing countries by prohibiting many of the same strategies that high-income countries like the US had used to develop and grow rich themselves. Far from throwing open their markets to free trade and allowing the market to determine their fate, the US and other now prosperous states relied on the use of high tariffs and production subsidies to foster the growth of their industries and selectively sequence their integration into the global economy. They were also aggressive in adopting technology from more advanced countries, as well as in controlling the inflow of foreign investment and directing it toward the goals of national development. Yet the US and other advanced states have sought to deny other countries access to the very policy tools that were so essential to their own growth and prosperity. The dictates of the Washington Consensus constrained the future development prospects of many poor countries by severely limiting development "policy space" (the room states have to maneuver in seeking to foster national economic development).

There was, however, a wide gulf between the policies that the US sought to impose on others and those it was willing to undertake itself (Silver and Arrighi 2003). As John Braithwaite (2008: 8) states, the Washington Consensus "was what Washington believed was good for other countries to do because it would benefit American business operating in those countries." Yet, in the words of Joseph Stiglitz (2004: 23), "[T]he medicine we dispensed abroad was, in important respects, not really the same stuff we drank at home." In spreading neoliberalism globally, the US position has been imbued with considerable hypocrisy and, given the extent of its power, the result is that neoliberal policies and free trade principles have been only selectively and inconsistently applied in global governance. At the GATT/WTO, for example, the US has historically been the primary aggressor seeking trade liberalization from other countries, although it nonetheless refused to open significant portions of its own market to foreign goods, capital, and labor. While this departs from the "pure" logic of neoliberalism—according to which any country should be willing to unilaterally open its market—the practice of neoliberalism has never been applied in pure form. What the US sought was not true free trade but the careful control of trading conditions, in the service of its own interests; as Ellen Meiksins Wood (2005: 134–35) describes, "If the openness of the global economy were a two-way street, whatever else that might achieve, it would not serve the purpose for which the system was designed." The dominance of the US enabled it to ensure that such asymmetries were built into the very structure of international trade agreements.

As Silver and Arrighi chronicle (2003: 338), "[T]he United States has been both the main propagator of the utopian belief in a self-regulating world market and the main beneficiary of the actual spread of that belief." However, they continue:

even at the height of its liberal crusade the United States did not adhere unilaterally to the precepts of the liberal creed.... While incessantly preaching to others the advantages of behaving by those precepts, the United States has generally chosen either not to adopt them at all ... or to adopt them through carefully negotiated agreements with other states, as in the liberalization of foreign trade.

Despite its fervent rhetoric propounding the virtues of free markets and trade, the US has never been willing to unilaterally open its market. Instead, it has preferred to selectively open parts of its market in exchange for securing even greater gains in other markets, through international trade negotiations shaped by its overwhelming political and economic might (Chorev 2008). As the world's largest market, the US used the prospect of its own liberalization as a weapon to force other governments to liberalize their markets (Arrighi 1994: 72). Its economic power, combined with the military protection it provided to its allies in the context of the Cold War, gave the US considerable leverage to induce other states to enter into trade negotiations and to secure favorable terms within those agreements. Thus, as will be detailed further in the next chapter, there has been a significant disjuncture between American rhetoric and practice regarding opening markets and instances of US protectionism abound.

How American Hegemony Sowed
the Seeds of Its Own Undoing

The international economic order was constructed chiefly to serve the political and economic interests of the United States. Its foundational myths of multilateralism and free trade provided, to borrow a metaphor from Mlada Bukovansky (2010: 69), a velvet glove for "the iron fist of power asymmetry." Yet, I argue that the American hegemon never had complete control of the effects its actions produced. The steps the US took to advance its economic and geopolitical goals had unintended consequences, which eventually came to undermine its preponderance of power and capacity to dominate global economic governance. Ultimately, the system created by the US spun beyond its control. Paradoxically, core elements of the American hegemonic order—structural, institutional, and discursive—that were central to the exercise of US power have now contributed to challenges against it.

First, through the expansion of global capitalism, the US sought to profit from its economic advantages and expand their reach. But in opening global markets to trade and capital flows, however unbalanced and incomplete, the US gave rise to its own economic competitors (Arrighi and Silver 1999). Following World War II, the US assumed a significant portion of the costs of reconstruction in Western Europe and Japan, supplying aid, investment, technological assistance, and favorable trading relations, in order both to expand markets for its multinational corporations, goods, and capital and to counter the looming rivalry posed by the Soviet Union. In large part as a result of American support, the European and Japanese economies were able to make a remarkable recovery from the utter devastation of the war, and the 1950s and 1960s became a period of rapid and sustained expansion of world production and trade. Likewise, in an effort to stave off the communist threat, the US provided extensive economic and military aid, including preferential access to its large market, to pivotal countries in the Third World such as South Korea and Taiwan, setting off their transformation into "Asian Tigers" engaged in the low-cost production of manufactured goods. Yet the flow of US capital abroad fueled growing economic competition from recipient countries, undermining its dominance. By the mid-1970s, as its competitiveness declined, the US trade balance shifted from positive to negative. In the ensuing decades, the US promoted neoliberal policies around the world in an effort to buttress its waning economic dominance; however, the expansion and opening of global markets had the unintended effect of fueling the emergence of new competitors like Brazil, India, and China. Contrary to the rhetoric of its proponents, neoliberalism did not bring universal benefits—and, in fact, hurt the economic growth of many developing countries—but it did benefit a relatively small group of countries that were uniquely positioned to capitalize on the new trade opportunities created by global market liberalization. While the US was able to successfully incorporate earlier competitors, such as Europe, Japan, and the Asian Tigers, into its system of global economic governance, that has proven far more challenging with the new emerging powers.

Second, I show that the global governance institutions that provided a channel for the exercise of US power also contained features that could be turned against it. From the perspective of the US, international institutions like the WTO provided "a legitimate, stable, and inexpensive form of domination" (Conti 2011: xiv). But the decision to govern the globe through international institutions came at a price: it required the US to accept certain restraints on its power. For international institutions to function effectively as instruments of American hegemony, the fact that they were doing so needed, at least to some extent, to be disguised. Under the guise of multilateralism, the international organizations the US created could serve as a powerful mechanism to legitimate its own preferences and values. The catch was that: "Legitimation requires that the organizations be given autonomy. If they are seen as merely handmaidens of the hegemon, they will be ineffective" (Krasner 1985: 10). In order for these institutions to be seen as legitimate, the US had to cede them some real authority and independence and to create at least the appearance of neutrality and genuine multilateralism. For the most part, despite their formal autonomy, the US retained great influence over the international organizations it created. In instances in which the US lost control of international organizations, such as when the balance in the UN General Assembly came to tilt toward the Global South in the wake of decolonization, it tended to abandon them and, by doing so, undermine their power and relevance.

The US could not exercise its hegemony through international institutions without making concessions and compromises to secure the support and backing of other states (Lake 2009; Mastanduno 2014). American hegemony has thus been described as a "penetrated" hegemony, which institutionalized mechanisms for hegemonic rule through compromise with allied competitors (Ikenberry 2011). Other states were induced to buy into and submit themselves to the set of rules and institutions the US created with the promise that these would circumscribe how American power was exercised and provide mechanisms for them to exercise reciprocal political influence. For its part, the US accepted restraints on its power in exchange for institutional arrangements favorable to its larger economic and political interests, trading off "short term gains for longer-term gains" (Ikenberry 2001: 5). As Amy Quark (2013: 13) argues, "Institutions are always the product of political struggle and compromise." Institutions reflect the power relations prevailing at their creation, with institutionalization "a means of stabilizing and perpetuating a particular order" (Cox 1996). Yet, once in place, institutions can have unanticipated results, including reshaping power relations among participants: "[I]nternational institutions may deviate from the original intentions of the dominant states that designed them, and even create spaces for challenging the balance of power that they originally reflected" (Chorev and Babb 2009). I will show in the case of the GATT/WTO, for example, that even at the height of its power, the US needed to make compromises in the design of the institution and its decision-making structure in order to ensure the participation of other states. As a result, the WTO was vested with power that could be turned against its originators and contained specific institutional features—which came about either as an assertion of American power or as a compromise to secure the cooperation of other states—that became tools that rising powers could use to challenge US dominance.

Third, while the liberal discourses of multilateralism and free markets helped to build consent for and legitimate the global economic order, I show that they also created a "hypocrisy trap" (Weaver 2010) with the potential to ensnare the hegemon. This fundamental hypocrisy—the gap between the discourse and practices of the US, and between the rhetoric and reality of the liberal international order it constructed—created vulnerability. The liberal norms propagated by the US became a measuring stick that the American hegemon and the system itself could be measured against and found lacking.

As Joseph Conti (2011) has argued, while the creation of the WTO was a manifestation of US hegemony, it had the effect of producing a new "field of power beyond the control of any single country" (xiv). This is not only institutional but also ideational, as the WTO is "a field of contest and struggle, where many of the critical battles are fought over ideas, identities and symbolic capital" (Conti 2011: 163; see also Eagleton-Pierce 2012). The WTO created ideological resources, or symbolic tools, that could be used by weaker states to bring powerful normative and reputational pressures to bear on the dominant. As I will show, in contesting the dominance of the US and other Western powers, the emerging powers have been engaged, in part, in a symbolic struggle. It is a struggle in which they have, crucially, seized upon and used the very norms that the US played a major role in creating. The rising powers have gained considerable force through invoking the norms and principles of the WTO: by mobilizing the dominant neoliberal discourse of free markets and trade, combined with demands for development, they have been able to claim the moral highground, while simultaneously undermining the traditional authority of the US.

Conclusion

This chapter has set the stage for understanding the nature and impact of contemporary power shifts at the WTO by exploring the American liberal hegemonic order of which that institution is a part. I have developed two core arguments pertaining to the liberal foundations of the contemporary global economic order, which will be further expanded in the remainder of the book. First, the system of global governance constructed under American hegemony—with liberal ideological and institutional underpinnings—provided a highly efficient and effective means for the assertion of US power. But in spreading neoliberal economic policies, the US gave rise to its own competitors, and liberal institutions and discourses provided levers that enhanced the growing power of Brazil, India, and China and supplied them with tools to challenge American (and more broadly Western) hegemony. Because of the contradictory nature of liberalism—its ability to both reinforce and undermine power—what began as hypocritical tools of domination became sources of empowerment.

Second, the liberalism of the global economic order served to mask its underlying power structure and resulting inequalities. The multilateral economic institutions and their neoliberal agenda were veiled in a false guise of universality and neutrality that concealed their relationship to American power. Of course, the supporting mythology of American hegemony has never been totalizing, and its dominance has never been uncontested or without resistance. But these myths functioned to provide powerful ideological support for the US-led global economic order. For decades, the façade remained in place and the system held together. Now, however, as I will argue in the remainder of the book, the emergence of new powers, by showing the lie to these myths, has undermined the foundation of the liberal international economic order embodied in institutions like the WTO.

Liberalism—including its contemporary manifestation in global governance in the principles of multilateralism and free markets—has always contained tensions between advancing universal and particular interests. The WTO and other institutions of global governance staked their legitimacy on claims to universalism but were founded on creating and preserving new forms of inequality and exclusion. In reality, neither access to the rights of sovereignty vis-à-vis the multilateral institutions nor the imposition of free markets was ever truly intended to be universal. At the WTO, I will show, the rising powers have pressed for the liberal international economic order to become more universal and inclusive, in both its recognition of the sovereign equality of states and application of free market economic policies. As a result, however, by pushing for the liberal principles of the system to be more universally realized, the emerging powers caused the system to unravel. The following chapters turn toward a more detailed analysis of the WTO, exploring how the dynamics identified here have played out more specifically within that institution.

Chapter 3

Power, Multilateralism, and Neoliberalism at the WTO

THIS chapter illustrates how the contradictions of the US-led global economic order have been manifest in the governance of international trade. I show that the liberal rhetoric surrounding the GATT/WTO—extolling the universal benefits of the institution and the gains from trade to be reaped by all members—masks the real inequality built into the history and function of the multilateral trading system and obscures its role in maintaining and reinforcing the relative distribution of wealth and power in the global political economy. Despite its professed principles of multilateralism and free trade, the GATT/WTO was designed to reflect and serve the economic interests and commercial practices of its dominant architect, the US, and other advanced-industrialized states.

This chapter sets the stage for the analysis to follow in the remainder of the book by providing a discussion of historical power relations within the multilateral trading system, an understanding of which is important for appreciating the magnitude and significance of contemporary power shifts. It begins by chronicling the history of the multilateral trading system, the workings of the WTO and its predecessor the GATT, and how both institutions have been shaped by the dominance of the US and other rich countries. The chapter then examines the trade policy of the principal architect and leader of this system, the US. It makes the case that the US is far from the liberal, open economy often claimed: on the contrary, while professing the liberal virtues of self-regulating markets and free trade, the US has made extensive use of protectionist measures in its own economy. And, what is more, American dominance has meant that the inconsistencies and tensions contained in US trade policy have been inscribed in the global institutions and rules established for the regulation of international trade.

This is arguably nowhere more evident than in the creation of the WTO as a result of the Uruguay Round of trade negotiations, which marked the start of the neoliberal era in the realm of the international trading system. The WTO was intended to be a key pillar of the neoliberal globalization project, pushing forward the progressive removal of state-imposed barriers to trade and capital flows, forcing changes to domestic regulations to make them more friendly to foreign capital, and privileging the expansion of self-regulating markets over social and environmental protection. Yet this remains an ongoing and unfinished project. Moreover, the process of moving toward freer markets has been far from fair or even, shaped as it is by political struggles and significant power disparities both among and within states. The US and allied advanced-industrialized states have successfully tilted the rules of the global trading system in their favor. At the same time, however, I also identify certain institutional features in the design of the WTO that—regardless of their original intent—have come to play an important role in the process and impact of contemporary power shifts.

Finally, the latter portion of the chapter focuses in more detail on the traditional status of developing countries in the multilateral trading system, with a particular emphasis on the Uruguay Round. With the Uruguay Round, I argue, the inequalities of the international trade regime reached new heights: the US, backed by other advanced countries, demanded a pound of flesh from developing countries and used its coercive powers to secure it. The chapter concludes by charting key developments in North-South relations at the WTO since its creation, from the growing developing country unrest and activism that emerged in response to the disappointing results of the Uruguay Round to the origins of, and initial contestation surrounding, the current Doha Round of trade negotiations.

History of the Multilateral Trading System

Since the end of World War II, the international trading system has been governed first by the General Agreement on Tariffs and Trade (GATT) and later its successor the WTO. The GATT, an international treaty originally signed in 1947, was the outcome of a failed attempt to create an International Trade Organization (ITO). The mandate to begin negotiations on an ITO stemmed from the Bretton Woods Conference in 1944, which brought together world leaders to craft a plan for postwar economic recovery and construct the architecture of the international economic system. Bretton Woods gave birth to the IMF and the World Bank, and the original intention was to create a third institution— the ITO—to govern trade. The GATT was to be a part of the ITO and negotia-

Table 1: Multilateral Trade Rounds

Year	Place/Name	Subjects covered	Countries
1947	Geneva	Tariffs	23
1949	Annecy	Tariffs	13
1951	Torquay	Tariffs	38
1956	Geneva	Tariffs	26
1960–61	Dillon Round	Tariffs	26
1964–67	Kennedy Round	Tariffs and antidumping measures	62
1973–79	Tokyo Round	Tariffs, nontariff measures, "framework" agreements	102
1986–94	Uruguay Round	Creation of the WTO, tariffs, nontariff measures, rules, services, intellectual property, investment, dispute settlement, textiles, agriculture, etc.	123
2001–	Doha Round	Tariffs, nontariff measures, rules, services, intellectual property, dispute settlement, agriculture, investment, competition, government procurement, implementation, trade facilitation, etc.	161

Source: Adapted from "Understanding the WTO," available at www.wto.org/english/thewto_e/whatis_e/tif_e/fact4_e.htm.

tions began on the two in parallel. While the GATT was simply a treaty focused on reducing tariffs, the ITO charter that states ultimately agreed upon would have created an international organization and given it a much broader scope, covering issues such as full employment, fair labor standards, commodity agreements, economic development, and restrictive business practices. However, the creation of the ITO was scuttled by the US Congress, which refused to ratify the agreement, fearing incursions into US sovereignty and influenced by domestic business groups that objected to the ITO's "exceptions to free market principles" (Baldwin 2006: 679). As a result, the ITO was stillborn and the world was left instead with the GATT—a much narrower treaty focused on reducing tariffs and far weaker institutionally—to govern trade for most of the next half-century.

The multilateral trading system—the GATT and now the WTO—works to gradually dismantle barriers to the free flow of trade through successive rounds of negotiations to reduce tariffs, subsidies, and other trade barriers and strengthen a variety of trade-related rules. There have been eight multilateral trade rounds concluded to date. As Table 1 indicates, trade rounds have, over time, grown longer and more complex, as a larger number of issues and countries have become involved. The last round to be successfully concluded was the Uruguay Round (1986–94), which created the WTO in 1995.[1] The Uruguay

Round was "the largest and most complex international economic negotiation ever attempted" and brought about the biggest reform of the world trading system since the creation of the GATT (Wolfe 1998: 81). Covering a broad range of areas—including tariffs, subsidies, nontariff barriers, rules and trade remedies, services, intellectual property, investment, agriculture, textiles and clothing, and dispute settlement—the round involved approximately sixty separate agreements, annexes, decisions, and understandings and was more than thirty thousand pages long. Since the Uruguay Round, trade rounds have been structured as a "single undertaking": although there are concurrent negotiations on all different aspects of the final agreement (such as manufactured goods, services, agriculture, and intellectual property), ultimately all issues must be agreed together as one package ("nothing is agreed until everything is agreed"), making possible trade-offs across different areas of the negotiations.

Power and the Workings of the WTO

The WTO differs from other major international organizations, such as the UN, IMF, and World Bank, which have large bureaucracies and substantial administrative or programmatic functions. The WTO is centered on its 161 member states, with limited administrative or bureaucratic functions assigned to the organization. Its central function is to provide a forum for the negotiation of multilateral trade agreements among its member states and a mechanism for the settlement of disputes arising from those agreements. As Anne Krueger (1998: 14) describes, the WTO is "a rules-making and rules-enforcing organization." It includes a small Geneva-based bureaucratic secretariat that is charged with facilitating its work and providing technical and administrative assis-

Table 2: WTO Ministerial Meetings

Location	Date
Bali	Dec. 3–6, 2013
Geneva	Dec. 15–17, 2011
Geneva	Nov. 30–Dec. 2, 2009
Hong Kong	Dec. 13–18, 2005
Cancun	Sept. 10–14, 2003
Doha	Nov. 9–13, 2001
Seattle	Nov. 30–Dec. 3, 1999
Geneva	May 18–20, 1998
Singapore	Dec. 9–13, 1996

Source: Data from WTO, available at www.wto.org/english/thewto_e/minist_e/minist_e.htm.

tance.[2] Rounds of trade negotiations are punctuated by periodic meetings of trade ministers ("Ministerial Meetings" or "Ministerials"), where key decisions are often made. Most of the negotiating work takes place at the officials-level at the WTO in Geneva, where states are represented by delegations of negotiators and other trade officials.

The WTO is rare, especially among the multilateral economic institutions, in the extent to which it instantiates the principles of political liberalism and democracy at the international level. On the surface, its workings appear highly enlightened. Agreements are reached on the basis of consensus, and each state is afforded equal representation or voting power ("one-member-one-vote"). Formally, all states have an equal say in decision-making, as well as equal access to the WTO's dispute settlement procedures and equal treatment in seeking to redress their claims under its rules. This appears remarkably democratic compared with other international institutions, such as the IMF and World Bank, with their systems of weighted voting determined by a country's economic size and financial contribution, and in which the voting share of the US grants it veto power.

In the public relations materials produced by the WTO Secretariat, the WTO is held up as a paragon of democratic decision-making, with the neutrality and universality of its rules and decision-making procedures heavily emphasized. It is frequently stated, for example, that the WTO is a "member-driven organization":

That means the rules of the WTO system are agreements resulting from negotiations among member governments, the rules are ratified by members' parliaments, and decisions taken in the WTO are virtually all made by consensus among all members. In other words, decisions taken in the WTO are negotiated, accountable and democratic. (WTO 2003a)

The WTO's system of consensus-based decision-making is particularly stressed: "This means all Members are equal under the rules. It means all Members have the right to participate in decision-making. Consensus means all Members have veto power" (WTO 2001). In addition, "[I]n the WTO trading system, everyone has to follow the same rules ... [and] even a small country automatically enjoys the benefits that all WTO members grant to each other" (WTO 2003a). This rhetoric of egalitarian decision-making has played an important function in legitimizing the growing authority of the WTO.

Despite the principle of equality among states, however, the actual work-ings of the WTO and its outcomes are structured by underlying power asymme-tries. In the words of Kelly and Grant (2005: 2), "The WTO is not free of power politics . . . . the old maxim, that the strong do what they will and the weak do what they must, still applies." Richard Steinberg (2002: 342) describes the WTO's principles of consensus and sovereign equality as "procedural fictions" that ob-scure the significant power disparities that shape both negotiations and dispute settlement. In other words, the formal legal equality ascribed to states at the WTO conceals the deeper inequality in its workings. Not all states enjoy access to the full rights of membership in the WTO; instead, its rights and benefits are, to borrow from Bourdieu (2000: 77), "theoretically universal but monopolized in practice by a few."

In practice, decision-making within the GATT/WTO operates as an oligar-chy (Cox and Jacobson 1973: 433). The most important negotiations take place in small group meetings of key states (sometimes referred to as "Green Room" meetings).[3] Once an agreement is reached among this core group, it is then ex-tended out to the rest of the organization's membership. This informal insti-tutional structure allows a limited number of states to establish the negotiat-ing agenda and direct the negotiations. The composition of this elite group is determined informally, by the participants themselves or the director-general. It constitutes the inner circle of power within the WTO—those states that are recognized as the key players and exercise the most influence over the negotia-tions.

Initially, the GATT was dominated exclusively by the US; the American he-gemon held the reins of the institution and acted as both its primary initiator and vetoer (Curzon and Curzon 1973). Over time, however, power was slowly extended out to a select group of other advanced-industrialized states, with the US remaining the dominant actor. By the 1960s, as a result of the growth of European power resulting from postwar reconstruction and unification, and particularly the creation of the European Economic Community (EEC) in 1957 (the precursor to today's EU), Europe came to assume a leading role in the GATT alongside the US. Together, the US and Europe acted as "GATT's two rul-ers" (Curzon and Curzon 1973: 331). During the Kennedy Round (1964–67), for example, key meetings took place among the so-called Bridge Club—the US, EEC, and UK, hosted by the director-general. Following the rapid rise in Japan's share of world trade during the 1960s, it too was subsequently included in the inner circle—along with Canada—as junior partners forming the "Quadrilateral Group," or "the Quad." The power structure of the GATT/WTO thus evolved from pure unipolarity centered on the US to progressively incorporate other Western powers, albeit as lesser players. With the US playing the leading role, these rich countries collectively dominated the multilateral trading system.

The multilateral trading system has always contained tensions between liberalizing and protectionist impulses, giving it a somewhat schizophrenic character. The liberal economic theory that animates the GATT/WTO and provides the basis for its collective project of liberalization asserts that a country automatically gains from reducing its trade barriers (through lower prices for consumers, increased competition, and improved efficiency), regardless of whether other countries reciprocate by doing the same. In practice, however, states are eager for others to open their markets but, given the economic dislocation that liberalization inevitably produces and its associated political costs, generally reluctant to do so themselves. Although the overarching thrust of the system is to open and liberalize markets, its individual member states typically seek to minimize their own market opening and maximize that of others. At the very least, governments want to be able, at the conclusion of trade negotiations, to show their domestic constituencies that they "won" more than they "lost," or made sufficient "gains" to offset the "costs" of opening their markets. Actual bargaining between states therefore takes on a mercantilist character. Negotiations work on the basis of a reciprocal exchange of concessions—whereby countries agree to open their markets in exchange for others doing the same ("I'll agree to lower my tariffs on X, if you'll agree to lower your tariffs on Y")—and states typically try to minimize their own concessions while maximizing those of their trading partners. Importantly, the trade agreements that result are heavily shaped by the distribution of power among states: the powerful are better able to impose liberalization on the weak, while maintaining their own protectionist policies.

One consequence is that GATT/WTO agreements are "riddled with exceptions," including vague and open-ended clauses, grandfather clauses, loopholes, waivers, balance-of-payment exceptions, and exemptions and exclusions for a host of industries and products (Kennedy 1995: 685). Such mechanisms enable the states that can secure them to shield "sensitive" sectors from tariff cuts and market opening. To provide just one example among many, GATT/WTO rules allow various forms of "contingent protections," such as safeguards, that states are able to invoke by demonstrating that imports have hurt a domestic industry. Of course, this may seem puzzling given that the purported purpose of liberalizing trade through the GATT/WTO is to redirect economic activity to the most efficient producers, thereby fostering a Darwinian survival of the fittest that inevitably hurts those who cannot compete. As Messerlin and Woolcock (2012) detail, the safeguard provisions included in GATT/WTO rules originated from the US and were intended as an insurance mechanism for domestic firms unable to cope with foreign competition, allowing states to restrict imports when liberalization leads to import surges.[4] Although the GATT/WTO sets out conditions governing the use of safeguards, these conditions were actually made less restrictive with the Uruguay Round, which has led to their increased use (Messerlin and Woolcock 2012). The rules even provide "special safeguards" that are easier to invoke, for situations where the "risks" of liberalization are considered especially high, such as the special safeguard included in the conditions for China's accession to the WTO, a blatantly discriminatory measure that provided a lower threshold for invoking safeguards against China than against other countries. There is similarly a special safeguard in agriculture (the SSG), which is effectively limited by its design to being used only by developed countries, thereby functioning as a form of special and differential treatment in favor of rich countries. Exceptions and exclusions, of which safeguards are only one example, are thus as much a part of the multilateral trading system as liberalization. Such exceptions are justified as an "escape clause" or "safety valve" that enables the larger project of liberalization to move forward by smoothing areas of friction that could inhibit the process. But, inevitably, the nature of the exemptions and flexibilities provided are often skewed toward the interests of powerful states.

Power disparities influence not only multilateral trade negotiations but also dispute settlement. Historically, high-income countries have been the predominant users of the dispute settlement mechanism under both the GATT and the WTO. Notably, the US drove the creation of the WTO's more rigorous system for settling trade disputes, which essentially acts as a world trade court, and in its first five years, was the complainant in nearly one in three cases (Leitner and Lester 2015). The US was closely followed by the EU, with the two together accounting for more than half of all cases launched. Even now, in the twenty years since the creation of the WTO, the US has launched more cases than any other member, and American officials actively boast that it has won more than 95 percent of those cases (Schwab 2009). Developing countries, in contrast, have been generally disadvantaged within the WTO dispute settlement system, as many lack the financial resources, expertise, and economic leverage necessary to mobilize WTO law effectively to advance their interests (Conti 2011; Shaffer and Meléndez-Ortiz 2010). Strikingly, a least-developed country has been a complainant only once in over five hundred cases launched at the WTO (Leitner and Lester 2015).

The equality and universalism ascribed to the multilateral trading system thus belie the real workings of power within the institution. The agenda being pursued is not simply free trade, but a highly selective liberalization of trade in the interests of dominant states. As Rorden Wilkinson (2011) compellingly argues, the GATT/WTO has served an important strategic function in enabling the US and allied advanced states to open markets in core and leading-edge areas where they faced little competition and could accrue economic gain (initially primarily manufactured, semimanufactured, and capital goods, and later areas such as services and intellectual property), while preventing or forestalling liberalization in areas of political and economic sensitivity (such as agriculture, textiles, and clothing). A selective approach to liberalization has therefore been a cornerstone of the system, and the outcomes of all eight trade rounds to date have been accordingly unbalanced. GATT/WTO trade rules have worked to create market opportunities and facilitate the expansion of the US and other advanced countries in new and emerging sectors, while at the same time helping to forestall their competitive decline in mature and sunset industries. Only at the point at which the latter sectors no longer had significant economic value for the advanced economies, or their competitive preeminence was secured, did liberalization in those sectors occur (such as textiles and clothing). In this way, behind the facade of multilateralism and free trade, GATT/WTO rules have helped to perpetuate and exacerbate the advantages of the US and other advanced-industrialized states over their less powerful counterparts.

American Protectionism

Since the US has been the primary force shaping the multilateral trading system, this section turns to look more closely at the nature of American trade policy and its approach to the GATT/WTO. Although the US led the construction of the liberal trading order and its neoliberal turn, it has never been an advocate of "pure" free trade. On the contrary, American support for free trade has been highly selective, seeking open markets abroad while protecting and promoting its own firms and industries. Although the US acts with a unified voice in international negotiations, trade is a highly contentious area of American politics and policy-making and its negotiating position at the GATT/WTO is the subject of considerable domestic political debate and struggle. Consequently, US trade policy condenses the interests of diverse actors and agendas. In the simplest terms, the seemingly contradictory nature of US trade policy is rooted in tensions between internationalist and protectionist interests—that is, between outward-oriented industries that want greater access to foreign markets and import-competing sectors that want to protect the domestic one (Chorev 2008). The opening of foreign markets sought by export-oriented industries requires at least some trade-offs and concessions in opening the domestic US market as well, which are fiercely resisted by import-sensitive sectors. But what complicates matters further is the fact that many competitive, export-oriented sectors of the US economy also rely on the active support and intervention of the US government to ensure their global dominance (Porter 2005; Weiss 2005). Amid these multiple elements, the unifying feature of American trade policy is the goal of promoting US economic interests (Porter 2005). As hegemon, the US has been uniquely positioned to institutionalize its own preferences in international trade rules. While the US has driven the construction of trade rules to liberalize global markets, it has built in extensive "loopholes and escape routes" for its own policies (Weiss 2005: 724). Multilateral rules constrain US action more than in the past, but as the US played a leading role in the design of those rules—with the goal of maximizing its freedom of action while limiting that of others—they still leave the US considerable room to maneuver.

The orientation of American trade policy has evolved over time, in response to changes in the competitive position of its firms and industries. In the postwar period, there was broad support across US manufacturing sectors (though not agriculture) for the efforts of the American state to liberalize global trade. Most were not faced with any significant import competition and were eager to gain expanded market opportunities abroad (Baldwin 1987). As Baldwin (1987: 6) argues, US firms seized

competitive opportunities associated with American dominance to expand overseas market shares both through increased exports and direct foreign investment. The desire of US political leaders to strengthen noncommunist nations by opening up American markets

and providing foreign aid complemented these goals of US business, which actively supported the government's foreign policy aims.

The US fared well from its policy of fostering an open trading regime, as "American exporters and investors established substantial foreign market positions
from which they are still benefiting greatly" (Baldwin 1987: 20).

By the 1960s, however, the postwar recovery of Europe and Japan and later
the emergence of the newly industrialized countries (the "NICs," or Asian Tigers: Korea, Hong Kong, Taiwan, and Singapore) had caused significant shifts
in patterns of global competitiveness and the relative economic position of the
US. American protectionism grew as the country came to face strong import
pressure in a broad range of manufacturing industries, first in labor-intensive
areas such as textiles, apparel, and footwear, and later in more sophisticated
sectors like automobiles, semiconductors, steel, shipbuilding, machine tools,
and electronics (Baldwin 1987). Progressive liberalization under the GATT reduced the scope for tariff protections; as a result of steady liberalization, average tariff rates in advanced-industrialized countries like the US came down
substantially over the latter half of the twentieth century and are now relatively
low (approximately 5 percent) (Hoekman, Francis, and Olarreaga 2002). But,
rather than eliminating protectionism, the steady expansion of multilateral
trade rules simply channeled it into new forms. As more of its industries began losing their competitiveness and being threatened by rising imports, the
US increasingly turned to new forms of protectionism in an attempt to shield
these industries from global market forces (Baldwin 1987). Simultaneously, as
traditional production subsidies became increasingly restricted under the trading regime, the US also developed more complex and sophisticated forms of
industrial support to foster and consolidate the position of its world-leading
advanced industries (Weiss 2005).

The US has made, and continues to make, extensive use of measures to distort trade in favor of its own firms and industries, whether protecting import-
competing sectors or promoting export-oriented sectors. This has included
tariff peaks and escalation (Bacchetta and Bora 2003; Hoekman, Francis, and
Olarreaga 2002); trade defense measures to restrict import competition, including antidumping duties, countervailing duties and safeguards (Irwin 2005; Shen
and Fu 2014); voluntary export restrictions (VERs) and price undertakings, compelling other countries to "voluntarily" restrict the volume of their exports to
the US, or raise the price of their exports to make them less competitive (Mes-

serlin and Woolcock 2012); nontariff barriers, such as technical barriers to trade (TBT) and sanitary and phytosanitary measures (SPS—that is, those affecting human, plant, or animal health) (Henson and Loader 2001); agricultural subsidies (Grant 2005); impediments to the movement of labor (Cornelius 2001; Dawson 2013); restrictions on foreign ownership and investment (Globerman and Shapiro 2008; Golub 2003); barriers to foreign commercial services suppliers (EU 2007); diverse forms of subsidies and other support to industry, including R&D funding, venture capital sponsorship, intellectual property transfer, export tax credits and financing, and loan-guarantees (Weiss 2005); and discrimination in government procurement (Weiss and Thurbon 2006).

In short, while the US today lauds its "open economy" and "open investment regime" (US 2013), the reality is far more complicated. As Tony Porter (2005: 217) argues, the US has pursued a two-pronged trade strategy: on the one hand, "for commodified industries with low levels of knowledge-intensity the US government has consistently used trade policy to shield US firms from foreign competition." On the other, "for the types of knowledge-intensive industries in which most leading US multinational companies are located," the US has actively used various forms of state support, combined with its influence in shaping international trade rules, to give its industries a competitive edge and promote their global market dominance.

The American Discourse of "Unfair" Trade

As the gap between the US's free trade rhetoric and its protectionist practices become increasingly apparent starting in the late 1960s, its official trade discourse assumed a new inflection, emphasizing the need not just for "free" but "fair" trade. As Robert Baldwin (1987) describes, American policy-makers and industry groups began claiming that their protectionist policies were a necessary response to the "unfair" actions of foreign producers and governments. To quote one US official, "We are responding to unfair trade . . . . [D]efending yourself against unfair trade is not, in our opinion, protectionism" (cited in Baldwin 1987: 19). By invoking this rhetoric of unfair trade, the US has sought to reconcile its use of protectionist measures with its claims to uphold the principles of the liberal international trading regime. This new narrative has blamed the declining competitive position of the US in certain sectors on unfair foreign policies. Implicit in this is the notion that if the other side is winning in the game of global economic competitiveness, it must be because they are cheating; hence, in a "fair" game (meaning one in which the US sets the rules), the US will always win. It is, of course, a curious idea of "fairness" in which the US drives multilateral liberalization while unilaterally invoking protectionist policies. Nevertheless, the US's claim to be "leveling the playing field" has become a prime justification both for its aggressive pursuit of liberalization by other states under the GATT/WTO and its own use of trade-distorting measures (Baldwin 1987: 20).

The sense of victimhood embodied in this "fair trade" narrative pervades the contemporary discourse of US policy-makers and industry lobby groups. It is also deeply perplexing to other negotiators at the WTO, who see far more unfairness perpetuated *by* the US against its foreign competitors than the reverse.[5] There is a strange irony in the fact that the US—the world's largest and most powerful economy—considers itself the victim of the unfair trading practices of other states. But, as later chapters will demonstrate, this self-construction— the US as victim, the beleaguered nation trying to uphold the virtues of liberalism, whose willingness to open its market is unfairly abused—came to feature prominently in the later stages of the Doha Round.

The contradictions of American trade policy—between its advocacy of global trade liberalization and its own extensive use of protectionist measures—are essential to understanding the design and workings of the GATT/ WTO and, importantly, the unfolding of the neoliberal project within the multilateral trading system, to which I now turn.

The Neoliberal Project at the WTO

The WTO was established at the height of the neoliberal euphoria that gripped policy-makers in the late 1980s and early 1990s—the period in which the Washington Consensus was in its zenith. The establishment of the WTO initiated a major transformation in the governance of the world trading system, which scholars have characterized as a shift from "embedded liberalism" (Ikenberry 1992; Ruggie 1982) to "neoliberalism" (Chorev 2005; Mortensen 2006). While the GATT was a much narrower treaty with far weaker authority over participating states, the creation of the WTO involved both a deepening of the GATT and a dramatic expansion of trade rules into new areas, such as intellectual property, services, and investment. It also marked a significant shift in the trading regime away from simply reducing tariffs toward the development of rules with the potential to significantly impact domestic policies, institutional practices, and regulations (Mortensen 2006; O'Brien and Williams 2004; Williams 2005). This included a movement toward policy harmonization, in areas such as subsidies, foreign investment, and services (O'Brien and Williams 2004). In addition, the establishment of the WTO put in place a trade policy review mechanism and, perhaps most significantly, while the GATT had only limited power over its membership, the WTO came with a binding dispute settlement mechanism that gave its rules teeth. As a result, the WTO has one of the most powerful enforcement mechanisms of any international institution (Janow, Donaldson, and Yanovich 2008: 388). Finally, unlike the GATT, which was merely an international treaty, the WTO is a permanent, formal organization with a larger bureaucracy.

Under the GATT, the pursuit of economic liberalism was "embedded" in social and political constraints. The GATT promoted trade liberalization while still allowing considerable flexibility, or policy space, for states. It allowed for policies "intended to cushion the domestic sphere from the destabilizing effects produced by international market liberalization" (Mortensen 2006: 172). It provided room, for example, for states to pursue Keynesian policies directed at maintaining full employment and the postwar welfare state, as well as for developing country governments to intervene in their economies to pursue national development strategies (Chorev and Babb 2009; Ostry 2007). GATT rules primarily targeted policies "at the border" (such as tariffs) and did not interfere significantly with the autonomy of national governments and internal domestic policy-making. However, the new reach of WTO rules to "beyond the border" measures (as well as their accompanying enforcement mechanism) was intended to close off many of these prior flexibilities and deliberately constrain national policy-making.

Moreover, GATT enforcement procedures were designed to be *deliberately* weak—they were nonbinding and states could refuse to comply—thus ensuring that states were not forced to open markets unwillingly (Mortensen 2006). But whereas GATT dispute settlement relied on diplomacy, the shift to the WTO involved the "legalization" of trade disputes: its enforcement mechanism is binding and uses nonelected panels of trade experts to arbitrate disputes and impose sanctions on states. Not surprisingly, the WTO's dispute settlement system has raised significant concerns about democratic accountability. Dispute settlement panels are charged with interpreting WTO rules and arbitrating between countries, and as such enjoy tremendous authority (Mortensen 2006:

172). The power of these panels, made up of appointed trade lawyers and experts, can supersede that of democratically elected member states. Their decisions can force the reversal of national laws, and have done so in controversial cases dealing with issues such as environmental protection. The WTO's design thus entails a delegation of authority from states to a multilateral institution and its dispute settlement panels, intended to insulate the market from political forces (whether in the realm of national or interstate politics). If, then, the market was subordinated to politics under the GATT, the intent of the WTO is the reverse: to "free" the market from politics (both within and between states), by constraining the state and weakening political control over the market.[6]

The Driving Role of the United States

The neoliberal turn in the multilateral trading system manifest in the creation of the WTO was driven by the US, with the support of other advanced-industrialized states. It was the US that propelled the dramatic expansion of the scope of WTO rules into the new areas of services, intellectual property, and investment. At that time, important changes were taking place in the structure of the global economy and the geography of production. While advanced-industrialized countries of the Global North historically dominated the production and export of manufactured goods, manufacturing was increasingly shifting to the low-wage zones of the developing world. As Nitsan Chorev (2008) documents, the US was determined to address its significant trade deficit by advancing sectors in which its firms were globally competitive but faced domestic regulations and barriers in foreign markets that limited their potential growth. The US was then, and remains, the world's biggest exporter in each of the new areas (UNCTAD 2013; World Bank 2014; WTO 2012). American firms are global leaders in commercial services (such as banking and finance, transportation, telecommunications, management consulting, advertising, entertainment, education, health care provision, construction, and utilities) and, in contrast to its trade deficit in goods, this is an area in which the US has a positive trade balance. US negotiators wanted to create a more favorable climate for exporting American services abroad and make it more difficult for foreign governments to regulate or restrict the entry of American services firms. The US also sought to create more extensive intellectual property rights protections for its owners of patents, copyrights, and trademarks, such as computer, pharmaceutical, film, publishing, and apparel industries, all of which saw themselves as seriously affected by intellectual property right infringement abroad (Sell 2002). Finally, in seeking new WTO rules on investment, the US government wanted to make it more difficult for foreign governments to impose restrictions, such as local content requirements or technology-sharing arrangements, on foreign direct investment from the US. Thus, driven by changes in the structure of their economies and the nature of their competitive advantage, the US, along with the EU, aggressively pushed the expansion of trade rules into the new areas of services, intellectual property, and investment—all areas where their industries were world leaders.

It was also the US who drove the creation of the more powerful enforcement mechanism associated with the WTO. Chorev (2008) describes how, along with the expansion of WTO rules into ever more intrusive areas of jurisdiction, US negotiators sought more reliable judicial disciplines and procedures to ensure compliance with the new rules being created in its favor. The US proposal to strengthen the dispute settlement mechanism was strongly resisted by other states. The EU and Japan, for example, resented the American rule-oriented inclination and favored a more conciliatory process of negotiation to resolve disputes. However, the US forced other states to agree to the new dispute settlement mechanism by threatening aggressive unilateralism if multilateral enforcement was not improved. In 1988, in the midst of the Uruguay Round negotiations, the US Congress enhanced Section 301 of the US Trade Act of 1974, a provision that created a mechanism for the US to unilaterally take retaliatory action against foreign countries that violate international trade agreements or maintain *any* law or practice that it deems to "unjustifiably" or "unreasonably" restrict or burden US commerce (including inadequate intellectual property rights protection). The sweeping nature of Section 301—and the enhanced "Super 301"—and the arbitrary power it provided the US to impose import restrictions and close off access to the world's largest market posed a major threat to other states. This represented a powerful tool to force those states to remove trade barriers that offended the US and open their markets as it deemed appropriate. The US used the threat of aggressive unilateral action under Section 301 to pressure recalcitrant countries to swallow their opposition and go along with both the new dispute settlement mechanism and the broader provisions of the Uruguay Round. Other states capitulated and agreed to the dispute settlement mechanism in the hope of constraining American use of Section 301 by having trade actions governed by a multilateral forum and procedures rather than resulting solely from unilateral determinations on the part of the US.

When the US sought to add a more rigorous enforcement mechanism to the GATT, the EU and Canada insisted, in exchange, on the establishment of a permanent organization—the WTO—to oversee not only the dispute settlement mechanism but also the functioning of the entire system (Mortensen 2006). The decision to create the WTO was therefore the product of a negotiated compromise between the US, the EU, and Canada. Although initially needing to be convinced, American negotiators eventually came to see the creation of the WTO as highly favorable to US interests, offering an opportunity for "more direct formal transatlantic control" over the multilateral trading system (Steinberg 2002).

The Frankenstein Effect: Setting the Stage for Future Challengers

The institutional design of the GATT and later the WTO were thus strongly shaped by the desires and demands of the US, along with the EU and, to a lesser degree, other Northern states. Many of the rules, norms, and institutional practices of the WTO began as an exercise of US, and more broadly Northern, hegemony that served to mask and thereby enhance the exercise of power in, and through, the institution. Yet, in order for the WTO to be an effective mechanism for opening foreign markets to US goods and capital, it needed to be endowed with real power: its rules needed to be expansive in their scope and depth, and given teeth through a binding dispute settlement mechanism, and they also needed to be applied to all states by a neutral and impartial party in order to be recognized as legitimate. This meant, however, that the WTO's rules and enforcement mechanism could also be turned back against the US and other advanced-industrialized states. Ultimately, as I will show, several institutional features of the WTO, which originated either as an exercise of US power or a compromise to secure the participation of subordinate states—specifically, the WTO's consensus-based decision-making, single undertaking, and legalized dispute settlement system—came back to haunt the US in the context of contemporary power shifts.

First, as Richard Steinberg (2002) details, although the US initially expressed a preference for a system of weighted-voting in the WTO (thereby ensuring it the greatest vote), it nonetheless agreed to continue the GATT practice of consensus-based decision-making with each member accorded an equal vote, as a concession to secure the consent and participation of other states. The US recognized that consensus-based decision-making, rooted in the principle of sovereign equality, had powerful normative appeal and would confer greater legitimacy to outcomes within the institution. Nonetheless, the US was also confident that its underlying political and economic power would enable it to exercise sufficient influence over decision-making, rendering formal weighted-voting unnecessary. For decades, this calculation proved correct. However, when new powers began to emerge, the WTO's system of consensus-based decision-making accelerated and intensified their challenge to US dominance within the institution.

Second, in the Uruguay Round, the US introduced a new principle of the "single undertaking" to close the round, which meant that all aspects of the agreements would be binding on all members, and they were required to accept all aspects of the agreement as a package. American negotiators referred internally to the single undertaking as "the power play" and were explicit that this was a tactic used to force developing countries to sign on to the new rules on services, intellectual property, and investment, which they fiercely opposed (Steinberg 2002). The single undertaking required developing countries to accept the obligations of all the Uruguay Round agreements, rather than allowing them to effectively opt out of certain aspects as they had in previous rounds. Later, however, with changes in the distribution of power among states in the Doha Round, the single undertaking would make it far more difficult to conclude the round.

Third, in seeking a more powerful whip to enforce its trade interests under the new and expanded rules of the WTO, the US drove the creation of its powerful dispute settlement mechanism. By legalizing and judicializing the process for resolving trade disputes, rather than relying on diplomacy and negotiated solutions as under the GATT, the WTO provided a far stronger means of enforcing trade rules. Yet, at the same time, this meant that the US had also created enforcement tools that had the potential to be turned against it (Chorev 2008; Conti 2011).

The irony is that each of these elements in the institutional design of the WTO, which were tied to an assertion of US power in the previous Uruguay Round, eventually came to play a role in the unraveling of its power in the current Doha Round. As I will show, these specific institutional features have provided leverage for emerging powers, made it more difficult for the US to control the institution, and contributed to the breakdown of the Doha negotiations.

An Unfinished Project

The creation of the WTO elicited strong reactions from both sides of the ideological spectrum. Neoliberal proponents of efforts to limit the range of state intervention in the market celebrated the creation of the WTO. The secretariat, for instance, lauded the establishment of the WTO's "rules-based system" for giving "primacy to markets and not governments in determining economic outcomes" (WTO 1998). In contrast, opponents of neoliberalism expressed fierce criticism of the expanded scope and authority of the WTO. They feared that WTO rules obligated states to intervene to protect private property rights and the rights of foreign capital, while severely constraining their ability to intervene to advance social, environmental, economic, or development policy objectives. A diverse range of civil society actors voiced concerns about the effects of WTO policies and trade liberalization on issues such as human rights, inequality, the environment, labor standards, and health, and its potential conflicts with efforts to combat global poverty and foster economic and social development (Hopewell 2015b). Civil society advocacy directed at the WTO grew throughout the late-1990s and ultimately exploded onto the streets in the 1999 "Battle of Seattle"—the massive protests in opposition to efforts to launch a new round of trade negotiations. The establishment of the WTO was thus seen as a pivotal event by both the proponents and critics of neoliberalism.

Yet, the creation of the WTO was intended to be only the first step in its path toward liberalizing trade, opening markets, and restructuring the global economy along neoliberal lines—ensuring the free flow of goods, capital, and labor, protecting private property rights and the rights of foreign capital, while limiting the scope for protective social and economic policies. The actual degree of liberalization occasioned by the Uruguay Round was fairly limited; its major achievement lay in creating the basis for future negotiations and crafting structures of rules where none had existed before (such as in the new issue areas) (Hoekman 1995; Wolfe 1998). As Sauvé and Stern (2010: 2) write, the Uruguay Round was "more successful in developing trade rules than in increasing market access opportunities," but its significance came in building "a firm foundation" for future liberalization, with subsequent rounds of trade negotiations intended to move the world closer to creating a single, seamless global market. The Uruguay Round agreement even included a "built-in agenda" on agriculture and services, provisions mandating countries to immediately begin new negotiations to continue liberalization in these sectors.

An assessment of the Uruguay Round Agreement on Agriculture by the World Bank, for example, found that although the agreement did make existing trade barriers more transparent, "for *most* commodities, there will be little actual liberalization" (Ingco 1995). The Uruguay Round had two key impacts: (1) it required almost all import restrictions that did not take the form of tariffs, such as quotas, to be converted to tariffs—a process known as "tariffication," which affected more than 30 percent of products; and (2) it required countries to "bind" tariffs on all agricultural products (that is, commit not to raise their tariffs beyond a specified level). However, as a result of "dirty tariffication" (artificial inflation of base year reference points), the rates at which many countries agreed to bind their tariffs, or reduce their already bound tariffs, were significantly higher than the actual tariff rates they were currently applying. This meant that many countries did not actually have to reduce their applied tariffs at all and, in fact, could even choose to raise them later (constrained only by the maximum limit set by their bound rate). In addition, the round did not even touch many of the most extreme trade distortions, such as import subsidies, export taxes, state-trading monopolies, and domestic policies that implicitly tax agriculture. Consequently, according to the World Bank's assessment, the Uruguay Round's objective "to reverse protectionism and remove trade distortions" had not been achieved in practice, "at least not until further reductions are carried out in future rounds of negotiations" (Ingco 1995).

While the creation of the WTO as a result of the Uruguay Round represented a "quantum leap in global regulation" (Weiss 2005), it was not the realization of the neoliberal project within the realm of trade, but only its beginning. This newly constituted institution was intended to provide the forum and framework for future liberalization that would continue the construction of global neoliberalism. Thus, to summarize the argument to this point: the neoliberal project at the WTO was driven by American hegemony, but also contained elements that would come back to haunt the US and, importantly, it remained an ongoing and unfinished project.

Historical Status of Developing Countries

The remainder of the chapter looks more closely at the traditional status of developing countries within the multilateral trading system, with a particular focus on the Uruguay Round and the neoliberal turn. For nearly its entire history, from its inception in 1948 to the start of the new millennium, the GATT/

WTO operated as a "rich man's club," dominated by the US and a small group of other advanced-industrialized states (Drache 2004; Jawara and Kwa 2003; Kapoor 2006; Kelly and Grant 2005; Mortensen 2006; Raghavan 2000). Until recently, agreements were negotiated among "the Quad"—the US, EU, Canada, and Japan—and imposed upon the rest of the organization's membership effectively as a fait accompli. The rich countries carved out a trade order that suited their own interests based on their levels of development. For most of its history, GATT privileged liberalization in manufactured goods, in which these countries had a competitive advantage, while the areas of primary interest to developing countries (such as agriculture, textiles, and clothing) were effectively excluded. Developing countries were relegated to the margins of the governance of the multilateral trading system. When developing country members sought to actively engage in and shape the GATT, they were routinely barred from key negotiations, their initiatives and proposals were blocked by the dominant powers, and their interests were sidelined and ignored (Wilkinson and Scott 2008).

The compromise of embedded liberalism that characterized the "Golden Age" of capitalist expansion in the 1950s and 1960s was never fully extended to developing countries (Ruggie 1982: 413), which benefited little from the GATT or the other institutions of the postwar economic order. As Rorden Wilkinson (2011: 43) puts it, "[D]eveloping countries as a group have consistently been net losers in the multilateral trading system." With the ever-present rivalry of the Soviet Union in the context of the Cold War, the US sought to avoid alienating developing countries entirely and, combined with pressure from the developing world at the UN, this produced some small token concessions, but these were largely superficial and ineffective in addressing the concerns of developing countries. As early as 1958, the Haberler Report commissioned under the auspices of the GATT acknowledged the problems facing developing countries in international trade, yet resulted in little action (Wilkinson and Scott 2008). Over the ensuing decades, the concept of "special and differential treatment" (SDT) for developing countries slowly gained recognition within the GATT. SDT would theoretically provide an exception to the GATT principle of reciprocity by allowing for less than full reciprocity in the case of developing countries, either by granting them greater flexibility to maintain protections in their markets or improved access for their exports to developed country markets. However, as Curzon and Curzon (1973: 309) succinctly state: "[O]ne cannot get much for nothing in commercial diplomacy" and SDT provisions contained within the GATT "turned out to be largely symbolic." The minimal concessions extended to developing countries during the years of the GATT—such as the Generalized System of Preferences (GSP), a limited system of trade preferences for poor countries—were acutely inadequate to address their development needs.[7]

As early as the 1950s, concerns began emerging from the developing world that its share of world trade was declining and it was falling further behind the advanced-industrialized states. A new school of economic thought arose from the Global South centered on the dependency theory of scholars such as Brazilian sociologist Fernando Henrique Cardoso and Argentine economist Raul Prebisch (who later became the founding secretary-general of UNCTAD). These perspectives became highly influential in shaping developing country objectives in global economic governance.[8] This critical framework challenged the principle of comparative advantage central to economic liberalism and its theory of free trade, which stated that a nation should specialize in producing and exporting the goods in which it has a relative advantage compared with other states. Instead, dependency theory argued that developing countries were locked into an international economy divided into a core of developed economies producing manufactured goods and a periphery of developing countries producing primary products, with the terms of trade stacked against developing countries (who were trapped exchanging cheap primary products for expensive manufactured goods) and worsening over time. At the national level, this led many developing countries to adopt policies focused on promoting development through import-substitution industrialization (ISI). At the international level, it fueled political mobilization and activism on the part of the Third World, informed by the assessment that the structure of the global economy perpetuated underdevelopment and that fundamental structural changes in international economic relations were needed in order for poor countries to develop (Adams 1993).

With GATT tightly controlled by the advanced-industrialized countries, developing countries went outside that institution to try to pursue their objectives in other forums, specifically the United Nations, where their majority in the General Assembly from the 1960s onward gave them greater sway. They drove the creation of a new institution under the UN umbrella in 1964—the UN Commission on Trade and Development (UNCTAD)—over strong opposition from Western industrialized countries, who preferred the GATT (which they controlled) as the sole forum for managing international trade. Developing countries used UNCTAD to try to press for major changes to the international economy, and reform of the international trading regime was one of their principal objectives (Bair 2009). Since the primary products that many developing countries are dependent on exporting are vulnerable to severe price fluctuations and long periods of depressed prices, they sought intergovernmental commodity agreements (including the creation of buffer stocks) to reduce fluctuations in commodity prices and change the terms of trade between primary commodities and manufactured goods—and thereby produce an income transfer from rich to poor countries (Adams 1993). In addition, developing countries sought a system of trade preferences for their industrial exports (free entry of manufactured exports from developing countries to developed country markets for a certain period) to support their domestic strategies of infant industry protection (Adams 1993). They also pursued major financing for development, debt renegotiation and relief, and technical assistance. Developing country activism culminated in the 1970s with calls for the creation of a New International Economic Order (NIEO): "a thorough restructuring of international economic relations and for a major shift in the distribution of economic power and benefits favorable to the developing countries" (Adams 1993: 119). The principles and objectives of the NIEO included: increasing the net transfer of resources from North to South to ensure an adequate flow of real resources to developing countries (for example, through international monetary reform and grants to development), regulating the activities of multinational corporations, ensuring full sovereignty over natural resources and all economic activities within a state, guaranteeing the right to nationalization, facilitating the role of producer associations, and transferring technology from North to South (Mortimer 1984).

Not surprisingly, the US and other states of the Global North—the creators and prime beneficiaries of the existing international economic order—were fiercely opposed to such efforts at change. In the end, the efforts of developing countries to construct an NIEO were thwarted and blocked by a stalemate with the Northern powers. Then the international debt crisis began in the early 1980s, plunging many developing countries into economic crisis in which they faced major balance of payments problems, soaring inflation, and an inability to meet their international debt obligations. Amid the neoliberal revolution sweeping the globe, reshaping both ideology and policy, the crisis faced by developing countries was seen as revealing the failure of the ISI model and many developing countries were forced to resort to IMF and World Bank loans conditional on their adoption of economic reform and liberalization programs designed to eliminate state intervention in markets ("structural adjustment programs," or SAPs). In the realm of trade, this translated into the ascendance of the neoliberal trade paradigm and the negotiation of the Uruguay Round agreement. Meanwhile, UNCTAD faded to irrelevance as a political tool for developing countries. Although it continues to exist as a UN agency, it has adopted the dominant liberal trade paradigm and its role has been largely reduced to producing reports on trade and development issues from within that paradigm.[9]

The rise of neoliberalism fundamentally changed the dominant way of thinking about development and its relationship to trade (McMichael 2004). Previously, most developing countries had pursued development primarily as a national project, embracing a central and active role for the state in fostering industrialization and strong inward-looking domestic markets through policies such as import-substitution industrialization. However, from being concentrated on insulating the national economy from international trade pressures, development came to be reconceptualized as increasing a country's participation in the global economy through enhanced trade. Globalization itself became a development strategy: developing countries were told that underdevelopment was the result of insufficient integration into global markets and that trade and exports provided the path to prosperity. The solution to the development problem was thus purportedly for countries to liberalize and open their economies, removing state intervention in markets, privatizing functions previously performed by the state, and "freeing" markets to facilitate the efficient movement of goods and capital (McMichael 2004).

The Uruguay Round took place in the context of these broader ideological and policy currents and marked a key turning point in the relationship between developing countries and the multilateral trading system. The round was the first to fully incorporate developing countries into the GATT/WTO system by requiring them to undertake commitments. Of the eight trade rounds held under GATT auspices, only the final Uruguay Round was agreed to by all participants. In previous rounds, most developing countries had not been involved in the reciprocal exchange of concessions or required to undertake commitments. Countries could pick and choose which parts of the agreements they would sign on to, giving developing countries access to de facto exemptions. But with the single undertaking used for the first time in the Uruguay Round, all agreements applied to all participating countries. By signing onto the significant commitments required of them in the Uruguay Round, developing countries would supposedly reap the benefits of full integration into the global trade regime.

Impact of the Uruguay Round

Instead, asymmetries of power within the multilateral trading system reached their apogee in the Uruguay Round, which created the WTO and signaled the ascendance of neoliberalism in the realm of trade. The Uruguay Round was pushed through and concluded by a use of raw power on the part of the US (Steinberg 2002). It occurred at a historical moment in which US hegemony reached new heights: with the demise of the Soviet Union in 1991, the US emerged as the world's undisputed superpower and the center of the newly globalized capitalist economy. After being tarnished by the crises of the 1970s and amid anxiety about rising competitors such as Europe and Japan, American economic supremacy was renewed by the sustained economic boom that took off in the 1990s (Golub 2004). At the same time, though, concerns in the US about its large and growing trade deficit, and the long-term implications for its economic dominance, led to a desire to use the Uruguay negotiations to push open markets in new areas where US competitiveness was undisputed—hence the inclusion of services, intellectual property, and investment, as described earlier. While developing countries had previously been primarily ignored and excluded within the multilateral trading system, the US now turned new attention to them as a means to expand its exports and the profits of American corporations. The fall of the Soviet Union freed the US of its only real ideological and political competitor in the developing world and greatly reduced external constraints on US action. As a result, the Uruguay Round agreement was extraordinarily unbalanced—more so than any prior GATT agreement—against the interests of developing countries.

Extensive studies have shown that the Uruguay Round results disproportionately benefited developed country GDPs over those of developing countries and, moreover, that some developing countries actually suffered a net loss in GDP (Goldin, Knudsen, and van der Mensbrugghe 1993; Harrison, Rutherford, and Tarr 1996; ODI 1995; Steinberg 2002). The US, for instance, received deeper concessions than it gave, while other countries such as India gave much deeper concessions than they received (Finger, Reincke, and Castro 1999; Steinberg 2002). It is estimated that sub-Saharan Africa alone was made worse off by

$1.2 billion as a result of the Uruguay Round (UNDP 1997). The expansion of WTO rules into the new issue areas, in particular, came at significant cost to developing countries, since they are net importers of capital, technology, and services (Chorev and Babb 2009). Robert Wade (2003: 603) has likened the Uruguay Round agreements on services, investment, and intellectual property to "a slow-motion Great Train Robbery." The Agreement on Trade Related Intellectual Property (TRIPs), for example, requires the tightening of intellectual property rules in the developing world. Since most patentable intellectual property is produced by wealthy countries and almost all patent royalties (97 percent) accrue to those countries, TRIPs is projected to result in a massive transfer of resources—over $40 billion per year—from poor to rich countries when fully implemented (Gallagher 2008; Shadlen 2005; Wade 2003). This has prompted the economist Jagdish Bhagwati (2004)—a noted advocate of free trade elsewhere—to describe TRIPs as effectively creating a "tax" that developing countries must pay to developed.

In addition, and perhaps most significantly in the long-term, the new WTO rules made illegal many of the industrial policy instruments that had been historically essential to the economic development of the wealthy industrialized countries as well as successful new developers like South Korea and Taiwan (Chang 2002; Wade 2003). The WTO agreement on investment (TRIMs), for example, limits the restrictions that states can put on foreign investors, a traditional cornerstone of countries' strategies to promote economic development (Wade 2003). The TRIPs agreement prevents states from designing intellectual property rules to promote technological development (Shadlen 2005; Wade 2003). Although developing countries were strongly opposed to the expansion of WTO rules into these new areas, they were forced to consent because of significant economic and political coercion from the US and EU, including threats of unilateral trade sanctions and withdrawal of their existing access to these markets (Finger and Schuler 2000; Gallagher 2008; Porter 2005; Sell 2006; Wade 2003).

There were also less obvious costs to developing countries from the Uruguay Round. The round included extensive "beyond the border measures" intended to harmonize national regulatory and legal systems. This required most developing countries to undertake major changes and upgrading in the institutional infrastructure of their economies. Developing countries took on obligations to implement significant reforms across many areas of domestic regulation (such as technical, sanitary, and phytosanitary standards, and intellectual property law). Such regulatory and institutional changes are extremely costly in terms of both human and material resources, and many argue that developing countries grappling with major economic and social welfare challenges have better uses for their limited resources than seeking to bring their regulatory and legal systems into line with those of the advanced-industrialized states (Chang 2002; Finger and Schuler 2000).

The Uruguay Round did incorporate two areas of considerable importance to developing countries: agriculture, and textiles and clothing. However, as Sylvia Ostry has aptly stated, the supposed "grand bargain" of the Uruguay Round for developing countries—namely, the promise that they would gain improved access to the rich country markets in agriculture and textiles and clothing in exchange for agreeing to the new issues of services, intellectual property, and investment measures—was more accurately "a bum deal" (Ostry 2007). Although the Uruguay Round brought agriculture into the GATT/WTO system for the first time (it had been effectively excluded from the previous seven rounds of negotiations), this was actually driven by the US, which sought to limit EU subsidies to its agriculture sector (which had exploded in the 1980s and were undermining American competitiveness and global market share), as well as to gain better access to European markets.[10] The key terms of the new WTO Agreement on Agriculture (AoA) emerged from private negotiations between the US and EU (resulting in the so-called Blair House Accord) and consequently did little to address the concerns of developing countries. As described above, the liberalization in agriculture ultimately produced by the round was minimal— primarily because the AoA was riddled with exceptions that enabled the major powers to avoid real liberalization, making the results especially disappointing for developing countries (Bukovansky 2010). It did little to tame, for example, high rates of agricultural subsidies and tariff protection in rich countries like the US, EU, and Japan.[11] Liberalization in textiles and clothing was slightly better with a pledge to end the Multi-Fiber Agreement (MFA) in 2005, but most of the liberalization was backloaded (that is, restrictions were to be eliminated later rather than sooner), and US tariff peaks of around 15 percent on those products were not eliminated (Steinberg 2002). Moreover, for most developing countries, the elimination of the MFA was more than offset by the impact of competition from Chinese exports in textile and clothing markets around the world (Ostry 2007). The Uruguay Round outcome thus included "a serious asymmetry between North and South" (Ostry 2007); or, as one developing country official characterized it, a serious "imbalance between the obligations assumed and the benefits that accrued to developing countries."[12]

In the years following the Uruguay Round, developing countries grew increasingly dissatisfied with its outcome, as they came to recognize the full cost of the commitments they had undertaken and how little they had received in return. In the words of one developing country observer: "We felt we came out of the Round with empty pockets. We had our list of what we wanted and they had theirs. They got almost everything on theirs and we got almost none of ours."[13] Many of these problems took time to become apparent: hampered by a lack of expertise and technical capacity, many developing countries had not fully understood the implications of the agreement they were signing onto, which only became apparent when it came time to implement the commitments they had made.[14]

These disparities in countries' financial and organizational resources and the unequal distribution of knowledge and expertise were deeply consequential (Blackhurst et al. 2000; Moore 2003; De Bièvre 2006; Mortensen 2006; Sell 2006). The Uruguay Round negotiations were extraordinarily technical and complicated, even more than previous rounds, as a result of the inclusion of new issues. In the words of Sylvia Ostry (2007: 29), the complexity of WTO negotiations "requires knowledge and knowledge enhances power. The strong are stronger because of their store of knowledge and the weak are weaker because of their poverty of knowledge." As Jens Mortensen (2006: 179) describes, "Influence on WTO governance requires extensive organizational resources and legal expertise." Yet, many developing countries were severely under-resourced and suffered an acute lack of expertise and capacity (a situation that continues today for most developing countries). This lack of technical capacity contributed to the disadvantaged position of developing countries in the Uruguay Round. Technical capacity refers to a country's knowledge of trade law and economics and its ability to engage with GATT/WTO rules, legal texts, and negotiating documents, conduct legal and economic analysis, and make policy proposals in the context of negotiations and dispute settlement. As one negotiator explained, "In this game, either you have the technical capacity or people will take your wallet."[15] Many developing countries eventually came to believe that they were taken advantage of in the Uruguay Round—effectively duped into signing an agreement against their interests—in part because they lacked the expertise to fully understand what they were signing on to and its implications.[16]

Even as it was being negotiated, some developing countries had grave concerns about aspects of the Uruguay Round and worked vigorously to block all or parts of the agreement, but were ultimately unsuccessful. For instance, a coalition of developing countries—the G10, led by Brazil and India—bitterly opposed the new issues (services, intellectual property, and investment) and sought to block their inclusion in the round (Ostry 2007). However, in the end, the coalition unraveled in the face of external pressures from the US and EU. Following the Uruguay Round, when many developing countries found themselves deeply dissatisfied with the results of the round, they placed considerable blame on their inability to maintain coalition unity, which had significantly weakened their negotiating power vis-à-vis the US and EU. In the words of one negotiator, "The problem we had in the Uruguay Round was the lack of solidarity and unity of developing country members."[17] A secretariat official seconded this assessment, "One thing coalitions lacked in the past was the ability to keep people in line and not to fall prey to divide and rule tactics."[18] Their experience of the Uruguay Round thus led developing countries to place enhanced emphasis on maintaining unity in the face of the traditional powers.

After the Uruguay Round, there was much more at stake for developing countries in the multilateral trading system. As one senior developing country official stated, "The Uruguay Round changed our approach to the institution."[19] Many developing countries began to pay far more attention to the WTO, as they came to realize the significant impact it could have on their economies and policies. As one negotiator stated:

We virtually had no commitments under GATT. We had these large carve-outs that basically allowed us to do almost anything we wanted. So that meant very few people in government, in the decision-making process, had anything to do with or knew much about the GATT. Now [following the experience of the Uruguay Round] the government itself has promoted a huge amount of research and technical work. They realized its importance. The situation is very different now. We've been latecomers but now we're catching up.[20]

Moreover, while developing countries had largely been ignored under the GATT, many came to perceive themselves as victimized by the WTO and the Uruguay Round agreements. The sense of being treated unfairly, and even cheated, in the Uruguay Round has had a substantial impact on the contemporary behavior and rhetoric of developing countries at the WTO. It made developing countries as a whole far less trusting and more cynical about the intentions of the traditional powers, creating a widely held belief that the wealthier countries were hypocritical—they would bend or violate the liberal trading system's "rules of the game" when it suited their purposes. As one adviser to the Indian government stated, "We were blind men being led by some so-called wise people from the West. We agreed expecting big gains, but we didn't get them. Now we're wiser."[21] The Uruguay Round fueled widespread discontent among developing countries and growing resistance to their marginalized position within the institution. As described in the next chapter, this was something that emerging powers—Brazil and India in particular—subsequently capitalized on in seeking to increase their influence at the WTO.

Rising Developing Country Activism at the WTO

Tensions between developed and developing countries began to grow in the post-Uruguay Round period. Almost immediately after the WTO was established, the US, EU and other developed countries began pushing to expand its scope further. At the First Ministerial Meeting of the WTO in Singapore in 1996, Northern states pressed for new negotiations to begin on what would come to be known as the "Singapore Issues"—competition, investment, and government procurement—which would harmonize rules on regulating monopolies, protect foreign investors, and open up government procurement to foreign competition. For their proponents, these issues were seen as a necessary progression of the Uruguay Round. Countries from the Global North also raised the prospect of linking environmental and labor standards to existing WTO agreements. For their part, developing countries were just beginning to realize the full extent and implications of the commitments they had undertaken in the Uruguay Round and discover the difficulties they would have in implementing those commitments. They were intensely reluctant to negotiate additional agreements and instead wanted the WTO to focus on the significant problems they were identifying in the implementation of the Uruguay Round agreements. The "implementation issues" advanced by developing countries represented an attempt to rebalance the Uruguay Round "grand bargain" by, for example, extending transition periods in TRIPs and investment; increasing technical assistance; removing tariffs for the exports of the poorest countries; and providing substantially better access for textiles and clothing (Ostry 2000).

In addition, developing countries were fiercely opposed to bringing environmental and labor standards into the WTO, which they feared were a thinly disguised form of protectionism directed against their exports. At the Singapore Ministerial Meeting, developing countries expressed growing dissatisfaction that they were once again excluded from the core negotiations and decision-making process and that the Ministerial was dominated by the issues driven by the major powers to the exclusion of addressing any of their concerns regarding implementation issues.

By 1999, mounting developing country discontent translated into a heated contest over selection of the organization's next director-general, split along North-South lines. Led by the US, most Northern states pushed for appointment of Mike Moore, a New Zealander with strong pro-free trade and pro-US leanings. Most Southern states were strongly opposed; they argued instead that the organization should be led by someone from the Global South for the first time and pressed the candidacy of Supachai Panitchpakdi of Thailand. It became a lengthy and bitter dispute with the two sides deadlocked and unable to reach agreement; in an unprecedented move, the decision was ultimately made to split the six-year term of appointment between the two candidates.

The 1999 Seattle Ministerial Meeting followed shortly on the heels of this dispute. It was intended by some—the WTO Director-General Mike Moore, the secretariat, and the major developed countries—to launch a new round of negotiations, dubbed the "Millennium Round." For their part, developing countries strongly opposed beginning a new round when their problems with implementation issues from the previous round were still not addressed. Plans to launch a new round that would further expand and deepen WTO trade rules also sparked intense opposition from global civil society actors, who took to the streets of Seattle en masse in protest (Hopewell 2015b). The protesters brought together concerns about the effects of the WTO and its trade liberalization agenda on diverse issues such as human rights, inequality, the environment, labor, and health, and its potential conflicts with efforts to combat global poverty and foster economic and social development. They also criticized the decision-making process at the WTO for being exclusionary, undemocratic, and lacking in transparency and accountability. While the GATT had been virtually unknown and invisible to the general public (Murphy 2004), the "Battle in Seattle" thrust the WTO into the media spotlight and subjected it to widespread public attention and scrutiny for the first time. By calling into question the legitimacy of the institution's workings, mandate, and rules, the protests of civil society added fuel to the fire of a growing legitimacy crisis for the WTO.

The effort to launch the round at the Seattle Ministerial Meeting ultimately collapsed. Despite the attention generated by the Seattle protests, as one observer remarked, "The demonstrations in the street were the show, but the main action was what was taking place behind the show [in the negotiating rooms]."[22] The protests succeeded in disrupting the negotiations, but the primary cause of the failure to launch the round lay among the negotiating parties themselves. Once again, the traditional powers tried to proceed as they always had—driving forward with their own agenda and blithely ignoring the concerns expressed by developing countries, most of whom were not even allowed into the negotiating room. Not only did the developed countries press forward with their plans for a new round, they also continued to advance the Singapore Issues, and US President Bill Clinton made statements to the press about imposing labor standards through the WTO that provoked a massive reaction from developing countries. The Ministerial ended in collapse when virtually all developing countries walked out in protest (Ostry 2007). Nor was this the sole factor contributing to the breakdown: there were also significant divisions among the developed countries themselves, especially between the US and EU on agriculture and other issues.

The Seattle failure left a major mark on the WTO. As one close observer stated: "We were all in a state of total shock after Seattle. There was a sense of an institution adrift."[23] The WTO Secretariat, the US, and others were gravely concerned that if a new round of negotiations could not be launched, it would jeopardize the entire future of the WTO. As then-Director-General Mike Moore later wrote: "A second failure would have fatally weakened the WTO . . . . The multilateral system, not just a Round, was at stake" (Moore 2003: 111, 125). They feared that the WTO would be seen as ineffectual and become irrelevant. This fear of another failure led to intense efforts to ensure agreement on the launch of a new round at the next Ministerial Meeting in Doha, Qatar, in 2001. The director-general and the key countries pushing for a new round, the US and EU, needed to secure the support of developing countries in order to obtain the consensus required by WTO rules to launch a new round.

Developing countries remained highly resistant to begin a new round of negotiations, especially one that included the Singapore Issues, and continued to insist that the implementation issues associated with the Uruguay Round be addressed. The Tanzanian president, Benjamin Mkapa, expressed this as follows:

What is needed is not to rush into a new round, but assisting poor nations to build up a capacity that will make them participate effectively in the global trading system, as earlier pledged by developed nations. ... We do not see any logic for the urgency being placed on fresh talks by developed countries.[24]

Despite this reluctance, the timing of the Doha Ministerial—which took place in November 2001, in the immediate aftermath of the 9/11 terrorist attacks on the US—made it virtually impossible for developing countries to oppose the US. Just days before the Ministerial began, President George W. Bush uttered his infamous foreign policy dictum—"You're either with us or against us." Even American negotiators have since acknowledged that 9/11 placed significant pressure on developing countries to go along with the agreement as a show of solidarity with the US.[25] In addition, the US and EU once again used substantial arm-twisting to convince developing countries to sign on to the launch of a new round of trade negotiations that they fiercely opposed; in this case, for example, the promise of an exemption allowing the African, Caribbean, and Pacific (ACP) countries to maintain their trade preferences in the EU market—which they faced losing under existing WTO rules and would have devastated their exports—was used to force many countries to agree to the new round (Wolfe 2004).[26]

In a further attempt to overcome resistance and generate support for the round, its proponents labeled it the Doha "Development" Round. Following the Seattle breakdown, Director-General Mike Moore told his officials in a candid moment: "We've got to get this fuckin' show back on the road. And no way are we going to be seen as just bumbling along with the fuckin' built-in agenda [on agriculture and services, rather than a comprehensive new round of negotiations]. We've got to re-brand!" (quoted in Blustein 2009: 82). As Moore later publicly stated: "After Seattle, I could see how the deal could be done. I knew we had to have a development agenda which addressed developing country needs" (Moore 2003: 112). Its proponents thus used the promise of "development" to sell the Doha Round. The Doha Ministerial Declaration states that "developing countries' needs and interests" will be at "the heart" of the new round. In addition to its "development" label, the Ministerial Declaration launching the round included the words "development" and "developing" a total of sixty-three times in its ten pages and fifty-two paragraphs (Deardorff and Stern 2003).[27] As Deardorff and Stern (2003) observe, "The Doha Declaration certainly pays lip service, at least, to economic development."

This emphasis on trade liberalization as a means to foster development accorded with the neoliberal development paradigm that had by then become dominant. If development was the result of a country's increasing integration into the global economy through the removal of trade and other barriers, then multilateral institutions like the WTO that were furthering the advance of trade liberalization were suddenly recast as "development institutions." In the words of Director-General Moore (2003: 172–73):

The WTO has emerged as one of the most important international institutions for development . . . . [Developing countries] need more trade liberalization, not less . . . . Trade liberalization is key to developing countries, not just because it opens markets, but, more importantly, because it makes their own economies stronger and more efficient.

Then-US President Bush similarly lauded the start of the new round: "This bold declaration of hope by the World Trade Organization (WTO) has the potential to expand prosperity and development throughout the world and revitalize the global economy."[28] Such claims were accompanied by World Bank estimates released for the Doha Ministerial that projected massive gains from the round: it predicted that an ambitious trade deal would increase global income by as much as $830 billion in 2015, with two-thirds of the benefits going to developing countries, and lift 320 million people out of poverty (Blustein 2009: 213). These figures provided potent ammunition for politicians, trade ministers, and commentators seeking to gain support for the round. As Paul Blustein (2009: 82) has written, by seizing upon the discourse of development "the WTO could attract support from both the Left, which was sympathetic to the grievances of developing countries, and the Right, which wanted to encourage low-income nations to see trade rather than aid as their salvation."

Many of the key figures involved—including then-Director-General Mike Moore, US negotiators, and others—have since publicly acknowledged that the purported emphasis on development was primarily an exercise in branding designed to get the developing countries on board, rather than reflecting any real commitment to development or willingness to make meaningful concessions (see, for example, Blustein 2009). As former US Trade Representative Charlene Barshefsky has publicly stated: "The round was launched on essentially false pretenses" (Altman 2007). Privately, many secretariat officials and developed country negotiators confide that the development label has itself created significant problems: as one stated, "I wish we could do that one all over. It was thrown in there to sell this package and now we're stuck with it. It's completely screwed everything up. It created big expectations. And I don't think we can kill a round that's got the word 'development' on it."[29] Although originating as little more than a cynical propaganda tool, the claim that the Doha Round would foster development became one of the central justifications for the round. It also illustrated, once again, the significance of unintended consequences, as this discourse then became a lever that developing countries could use to enhance their claims vis-à-vis the traditional powers.

Conclusion

As this chapter has shown, the veil of equality and fairness in the GATT/WTO's rules and decision-making procedures has masked underlying relations of domination within these institutions. The contradictions of the multilateral trading system—the tension between its rhetoric of multilateralism and free trade and the reality of power politics and highly asymmetrical trade rules—became most acute during the Uruguay Round, which created the WTO and ushered in the neoliberal era in the realm of trade. The Uruguay Round was a pure power play on the part of the US and other advanced-industrialized states, which pushed through a highly unequal agreement to advance their interests at the expense of the developing world. But, as I will show, the Uruguay Round and the creation of the WTO also potentially represented the last gasp of American hegemony within the multilateral trading system. As the remainder of the book will illustrate, since that time, there has been a dramatic transformation in power relations at the WTO that has deeply constrained the ability of the US, along with that of other Western powers, to set the agenda and direct outcomes within that institution. Having examined historical inequalities within the global trading regime and the neoliberal turn embodied in the creation of the WTO, the following chapter turns to analyzing contemporary power shifts.

Chapter 4

Power Shift

THIS chapter examines the origins and nature of contemporary power shifts at the WTO. In a striking break with the historical exclusion and marginalization of developing countries in the multilateral trading system, I show that there has been a significant shift in power: new powers from the developing world have gained seats at the high table of decision-making within the WTO and come to play pivotal roles in shaping the Doha Round. In addition to demonstrating that such a transformation has occurred, the chapter is also centrally concerned with explaining its causes. Given the significance of recent power shifts, the issue of why and how countries such as Brazil, India, and China have come to play a more central role in global economic governance has received remarkably little attention. Instead, it is widely assumed that the rise of new powers is simply a reflection of their growing economic might (Arrighi 2007; Emmott 2008; Hung 2009; Ikenberry 2008; Jacques 2009; Wade 2011; Zakaria 2008).

One result is that attention has overwhelmingly focused on China (Arrighi 2007; Babones 2011; Beeson 2009; Breslin 2010; Emmott 2008; Hung 2009; Jacques 2009; Subramanian 2011). China is widely seen as the key rising new power and challenger to the US, based on its large economy, rapid growth rates, major role in world trade, and considerable financial power. When India and Brazil are brought into discussions of contemporary power shifts, they are typically positioned as secondary, since they possess considerably fewer of the capabilities that are seen as making China powerful. China is now the world's second largest economy, after the US, and the world's largest exporter of goods. Brazil and India's economies are only a fraction of the size of China's (with Brazil's GDP at $2.4 billion and India's at $1.9 billion, compared with China's $8.3 billion); they play a much smaller role in world trade (while China's exports represent 10 percent of world trade, Brazil and India's constitute only 1 and 2 percent, respectively); and their economic growth has been far slower (particularly in the case of Brazil, whose growth rates have averaged only 3 percent compared with 10 percent in China and 7 percent in India).[1] In economic terms, certainly, Brazil and India are lightweights compared with China.

In contrast to the predominant emphasis on their economic capabilities, however, I seek to provide a richer and more nuanced account of the rise to power and behavior of Brazil, India, and China at the WTO. I demonstrate that the forces driving the rise of new powers are more diverse and complex than suggested by a simple economic determinism and that, in fact, these countries have taken different paths to power. While China's rise has been more closely tied to its growing economic might, the rise of Brazil and India has been driven primarily by their mobilization and leadership of major developing country coalitions, which has enabled them to exercise influence far above their economic weight. Furthermore, despite its considerable economic might, even China has sought the benefits and protection of developing world alliances, although it has been a follower rather than a leader in such arrangements. My intent is not to deny the importance of economic factors, but to suggest that focusing solely on the economic provides an overly simplistic reading of contemporary power shifts.

Indeed, an account centered exclusively on the economic capabilities of states would be unable to explain much of what has occurred at the WTO in the last decade. In contrast to expectations of a dyadic shift in power from the US to China, I show that Brazil and India were the first developing countries to successfully challenge the US, emerging as major players several years before China. It was thus Brazil and India that overturned the traditional power structure at the WTO, rather than China. Moreover, although the size of their economies and roles in world trade are far smaller, Brazil and India assumed a more aggressive and activist position in WTO trade negotiations than China and, for much of the Doha Round, were far more influential in shaping the dynamics and agenda of the negotiations. Toward the endgame stage of negotiations, China ultimately came to have significant impact, but its impact was primarily as a reactive veto-power in contrast to the proactive agenda-setting role played by Brazil and India.[2]

The New Landscape of Power

The start of the Doha Round looked much like previous rounds, with the negotiations centered on "the Quad" and the US and EU firmly in the driver's seat. The launch of the round was driven by the US and EU—despite consider-able resistance from developing countries—and they played the central role in formulating the negotiating mandate. Over the course of the Doha Round, however, a significant transformation has taken place at the WTO. After 2003, the Quad vanished, replaced instead by a series of core negotiating groups centered on the US, EU, Brazil, and India. Brazil and India effectively displaced Japan and Canada from the elite inner circle of WTO negotiations: the "old Quad" was replaced by the "new Quad." These four states have been at the heart of the negotiations since then, and beginning in 2008, they were also joined by China.[3]

This change in the composition of the inner circle at the WTO is far from superficial but reflects a major change in power relations within that institution. As one secretariat official stated, "In the old days, it was a very simple game: you had the US and EU, with Canada and Japan on the sidelines. If the US and EU didn't want it to happen, it wouldn't and if they did, it would."[4] Now, however, the rise of new powers has brought an end to the US's and EU's "cartel over agenda setting and compromise brokering" (Evenett 2007). As Ostry (2000) describes, if the old GATT system was best characterized as a "bicycle built for two" with the US in the front seat and the EU in the back,

[t]he current WTO is more like a bus careening down a hill with many drivers. . . . In the past, the United States always drove the negotiations . . . . Today, even if the United States and the European Union did try to demonstrate some leadership in the Doha Round, the developing countries would not let them set the agenda and drive the negotiations. Those days are over.

Instead, Brazil, India, and China have become key players whose assent is essential to securing a Doha Round agreement: in the words of one negotiator, "Now you can't conclude any deal at the WTO without them."[5] Providing a developing country perspective, an Indian official expressed it thus: "If this was the Uruguay Round, they'd have bottled it and made you swallow it by now."[6] Far from merely symbolic, these power shifts have had a profound impact on the WTO. As the following sections will show, these three developing countries came to play a decisive role in the Doha Round negotiations. Yet the factors that propelled Brazil and India into the inner circle of power were different than in the case of China, and their behavior and impact have been equally varied.

The Rise of Brazil and India

For Brazil and India, their activist and entrepreneurial leadership of the developing world is critical to understanding their rise to power at the WTO. Unlike China, they could not rely on their economic might alone and instead had to strategically maneuver to increase their status and influence. Attributing the increased importance of Brazil and India solely to economic factors—such as the size of their economies or their rates of economic growth—would provide a limited and incomplete picture of their rise to power at the WTO and miss critical elements of the transformation that has taken place within the institution. Not coincidentally, the emergence of Brazil and India as major powers at the WTO was intertwined with a broader revolt on the part of developing countries; Brazil and India were key figures in fostering and channeling this uprising, which, in turn, played a major role in fueling their rise to power.

Emergence and Impact of the G20-T

The emergence of the Group of 20 (G20-T)—a coalition of developing countries led by Brazil and India—at the Cancun Ministerial Meeting in 2003 marked a critical turning point at the WTO that upended its traditional power structure and catapulted Brazil and India into the inner circle of power.[7] The Cancun Ministerial was intended to be an important milestone in the progress of the Doha Round; this was the stage when negotiations were to shift from vague promises of a "development" round to determining the more concrete and specific terms of the deal. In advance of Cancun, the US and EU reached an agreement between themselves and put forward a joint proposal on agriculture. This proposal prompted a strong reaction from developing countries, which saw it as an effort to force them to lower their trade barriers, while allowing the US and EU to maintain their trade distorting subsidies and tariffs. For many, this presaged a repeat of the Uruguay Round, when a private compromise between the US and EU (the Blair House Accord) served as the basis for the ultimate agreement and obliterated developing countries' hopes of making gains in the round. Now, once again, it looked like developing countries were going to get a highly unbalanced agreement.

The Cairns Group, a mixed group of developed and developing countries with export interests in agriculture led by Australia and including Canada and Brazil, had been a key negotiating group during the Uruguay Round, pushing for agricultural liberalization, and might have been expected to challenge the US-EU proposal.[8] However, Australia was then in the midst of negotiating a bilateral free trade agreement with the US, which, according to other negotiators, left it "completely neutered in dealing with the US."[9] It soon became clear that the Cairns Group was content to let the US and EU run the show in the agriculture negotiations and was not going to significantly challenge their proposal.

Prompted by the US-EU proposal, however, Brazil approached India with a plan for forming an alliance to oppose that initiative. The two countries joined forces and together succeeded in assembling a coalition of developing countries that represented more than half the world's population and two-thirds of its farmers.[10] The G20-T united not only to block the US-EU proposal but, driven primarily by Brazil, also arrived at Cancun with its own technically sophisticated counterproposal that specifically targeted US and EU agriculture subsidies. Several other developing country coalitions emerged in the process leading up to Cancun (including the Core Group, the Cotton-4, and the G33), joining existing groupings (such as the African Group, the African Caribbean and Pacific (ACP) Group, the LDC Group, and the Small and Vulnerable Economies (SVEs)), and there was significant consultation and cooperation among them (Narlikar and Tussie 2004). Amid the proliferation of developing country coalitions in the Doha Round, the G20-T played a central and pivotal role because of its proactive agenda that turned the tables on the traditional powers by going after their agriculture and trade policies, backed by a technically substantive and astute proposal. As a result, the Cancun Ministerial took shape as a dramatic battle between developed and developing countries and ultimately ended in collapse, with the G20-T's block of the US-EU proposal a central factor in the breakdown.[11]

Under the leadership of Brazil and India, the emergence of the G20-T produced, in the words of one ambassador, a "tectonic shift" at the WTO.[12] From that point onward, the US and EU realized it would be impossible to secure a Doha agreement without the assent of Brazil and India as representatives of the G20-T and the developing world more broadly. Their leadership of developing countries in opposing the US and EU launched Brazil and India into the inner circle of negotiations, as central players that were considered essential to breaking the stalemate and securing a deal. In the words of one WTO Secretariat official, the "creation of the G20-T completely imploded the Quad."[13] Despite the fact that several other states (including Japan and Canada, as well as China,

Mexico, and South Korea) had larger economies and more significant roles in world trade, Brazil and India displaced Japan and Canada from the inner circle.[14] Meanwhile, the Cairns Group, which had previously been one of the most important negotiating blocs at the WTO, was left struggling for relevance, while the "G20-T came to lead the show."[15]

In addition to shifting the balance of power at the WTO, Brazil and India's leadership of the G20-T fundamentally altered the dynamics and substance of the Doha Round. Agriculture was a central issue from the start of the round, as one of the least liberalized sectors of global trade, which was brought into the multilateral trading system only in the previous Uruguay Round. Ironically, given how the issue later came to be turned against it, the US was actually behind the move to bring agriculture under WTO disciplines. The US saw itself as a relatively free trader—compared with its key competitors at the time, the EU and Canada, as well as major export markets such as Japan—and believed that it had a genuine comparative advantage in agriculture (Wolfe 1998: 62). Agricultural production is often associated with economic backwardness, but the US is the world's largest agricultural exporter, followed by the EU. Agricultural exports are also more significant to the US economy than many would assume. Agriculture and food exports account for 10 percent of total US exports and play an important role in reducing the size of the overall US trade deficit: agriculture is one area where the US has a major trade surplus, valued at $37 billion in 2013.[16] Export markets are critical to US agriculture, consuming a large share of total production in many product categories (exceeding 70 percent in some areas).[17] Eager to increase its agricultural exports, the US entered the Doha Round with agricultural liberalization in the EU and Japan as one of its primary demands and objectives. Specifically, it sought significant improvements in market access and a phasing out of export subsidies for agricultural products.[18]

When the Doha negotiations began, they therefore centered on demands from the US and the Cairns Group of agricultural exporters that the EU and Japan eliminate their trade distorting policies (Clapp 2007). Leading up to the start of the new round, for example, the *Financial Times* (1999) identified the primary fault line in the negotiations as follows:

The US and the Cairns Group regard liberalisation of trade in agriculture as the core of the forthcoming WTO talks, expected to last about three years. They are pressing for ministers in Seattle to agree detailed market-opening objectives, including subsidy and tariff cuts, with the eventual goal of treating farm goods like any other merchandise. However, this has been strongly resisted by the European Union and Japan, backed by some other nations with high farm trade barriers.

Notably, at that time, the negotiations continued to center on the Quad, as they had historically, with developing countries still seen as relatively marginal players, while the US was in an offensive position demanding agricultural trade liberalization from other states.

Over the course of the round, however, the dynamics of the negotiations changed entirely, as a result of the emergence of the G20-T. In the words of one negotiator, "At the start of this round, the US saw itself in an offensive position. It had no idea it would be a target on agriculture. But now it has become the key focus of the negotiations."[19] There has thus been a dramatic shift in roles: for the first time, the US—historically the key aggressor in the GATT/WTO—found itself isolated and on the defensive, while developing countries assumed the role of *demandeurs* (those seeking liberalization). Agricultural subsidies in the US and other rich countries became a prime target of the Doha Round, which was transformed into a struggle between developed and developing countries, with the conflict centered on the balance of concessions to be made between the US and EU, on the one hand, and Brazil, India, and China, on the other. By 2005, the *Financial Times's* characterization of the round was almost unrecognizable from that it had provided six years before:

> The basic trade-off that would be at the heart of a successful conclusion to Doha is already clear: the rich nations—the EU, US, Japan and Canada—would reduce protection on agriculture in return for more access to the goods and services markets of the developing world, mainly big emerging market countries such as Brazil, India and China. ... [Much of the debate] has focused on the export subsidies paid by rich nations to their farmers, which depress global food prices and undercut poor countries' farmers.

The emergence of the G20-T at the Cancun Ministerial marked the end of the era in which the US and EU could drive the agenda. Under Brazil and India's leadership, the G20-T transformed the negotiations into an open battle divided along North-South lines. For the first time, developing countries had real ammunition and leverage with which to go on the offensive against the rich countries—particularly the US and EU—and target their agricultural and trade policies. Following the emergence of the G20-T, as well as the G33 (another developing country coalition led by India, discussed below), agriculture became the focal issue in the Doha Round, with progress in all other areas of the negotiations linked to it.

The coalitions led by Brazil and India have had a profound impact on the negotiating agenda, successfully putting issues such as rich country agricultural subsidies and market access, as well as special safeguards and flexibilities for developing countries (provisions advanced by the G33), at the center of the negotiations.[20] Furthermore, the negotiating texts since Cancun have substantively reflected many of their proposals. The G20-T, for example, secured the following: a tiered formula for reducing subsidies ("domestic support"), ensuring that countries which provide the most support are required to make the biggest reductions, and stiffer criteria for cutting domestic support, such as product-specific caps; substantial reductions in domestic support (compared with historical bound levels), with the EU cutting overall trade distorting support (OTDS) by 80 percent and the US by 70 percent; the elimination of export subsidies and parallel disciplines on export credit and food aid; nonextension of the Peace Clause (protecting developed countries from WTO challenges), countering the long-standing position of the US and EU; and a "tiered" formula for reducing tariffs, rather than the "blended" formula sought by the US and EU (WTO 2008b). Although the future of the Doha Round is now gravely in doubt, these coalitions significantly shaped the content of any prospective agreement. This represents a dramatic departure from the past, when developing countries had little or no influence over the shape of GATT/WTO agreements.

Brazil-India Partnership: A Marriage of Convenience

The alliance between Brazil and India that forms the basis for the G20-T is in many ways surprising. While both countries are eager to assert themselves on the international stage and gain a more prominent role in the WTO and other global institutions, their negotiating positions are very different. Having emerged as one of the world's leading agricultural exporters over the last two decades, Brazil has defined its primary interest in the Doha Round as seeking to expand markets for its agricultural exports. It is widely viewed as being among the biggest potential winners from the Round and has been one of its strongest supporters (Polaski 2006). Brazil has actively worked to construct an image of itself as a leader of developing countries, fighting to hold rich countries accountable to WTO rules and pushing them to open and liberalize their markets. In contrast, India's negotiating position more closely resembles that of most developing countries at the WTO, with major defensive interests in agriculture: it has a weak agricultural sector consisting primarily of peasant farmers, who are highly vulnerable to trade liberalization. Like Brazil, India is also widely seen as a leader of developing countries at the WTO, but in its case of their defensive concerns in seeking to resist agricultural trade liberalization.

Although they share the leadership of the G20-T, Brazil and India thus have very different interests in the agriculture negotiations and to some extent are also competing with each other for the leadership of the developing world. Yet despite their differences, both Brazil and India saw the strategic value of an alliance. Brazil came to the Doha Round seeking to make significant gains in agriculture, but it recognized that it lacked sufficient power acting alone and needed allies. As a Brazilian negotiator stated, "We needed a credible blocking coalition to start playing the game at the WTO."[21] Prior to Cancun, Brazil had begun looking for ways to construct a coalition to advance its interests, but it was biding its time and waiting for the right moment. The furor among developing countries created by the US-EU agriculture proposal gave Brazil its opportunity, as the same negotiator explained:

We began to flirt with the idea that a grouping of developing countries might have something to say. But it was not possible or viable until the opportunity had arisen and this was the joint EU-US agreement trying to replicate the Blair House deal that ended the Uruguay Round. [Prior to that] developing countries were still divided. There weren't the enabling conditions that would allow us to turn this potential of a coalition into a reality . . . . The group was only made possible by the movement of the EU and US [their agriculture proposal].[22]

Given its major export interests, however, Brazil risked being perceived as a threat by most developing countries. An alliance with India—the leading champion of the defensive interests of developing countries in agriculture— was therefore of considerable tactical importance to Brazil. In the words of one of its negotiators, "We realized that we needed to reach out to India. We saw India as a goddess that needed to be attracted in order for us to have any credibility with developing countries. For us it was a clear strategic move."[23] For Brazil, allying with India was critical to gaining credibility as a leader of developing country interests at the WTO.

The alliance was equally vital for India. India had historically been one of the most active states in resisting efforts by the advanced-industrialized countries to extract concessions from developing countries. But, in previous rounds, India had often been left isolated in its opposition to the US and other advanced-industrialized states and unable to hold out against their demands. As one negotiator stated, "The thing developing countries fear most in the negotiations is isolation."[24] Being isolated reduces a state's power and leaves it vulnerable. The US has frequently sought to isolate India and paint it as the lone "troublemaker" objecting to and blocking agreement. This is an unenviable position since, to quote an ambassador, "No country wants to take responsibility for the round falling apart. Nobody wants to be fingered as killing the round."[25] In the past, such pressure has forced India to cave in and consent to agreements with which it was profoundly dissatisfied. Given its sensitivities in agriculture, combined with its experience of previous trade rounds, India knew that it needed a strong coalition of allies to effectively defend its interests in the Doha Round, particularly against the US. Consequently, for India, to quote one of its former negotiators, "The G20-T was a compulsion. They knew they had to do something but they knew they couldn't do it alone."[26] A negotiator from a rival state opined that, for India, the opportunity created by the coalition was "a god's gift."[27] Although the initial impetus behind the G20-T and its subsidy reduction agenda came from Brazil, India embraced and became equally aggressive in pursuing this agenda as a means of advancing its own strategic interests. The G20-T would not have been feasible without India, whose active participation and leadership were essential to securing the support of developing countries.

It was the underlying partnership between Brazil and India that made the G20-T possible, but privately the two countries are forthright in acknowledging the tensions in their relationship. As a Brazilian negotiator acknowledged,

It was sheer personal interests forcing Brazil and India to get into a coalition. We knew there were difficulties in trying to form a long-term coalition with the Indians given their difficulties in agriculture. Our relationship with India is like a kind of very delicate embrace where you cannot leave each other.[28]

An Indian negotiator concurred:

It's a coalition of the unwilling, let me admit. But at the same time, we know we can't have any kind of illusion of our status being equivalent to the G2 [the US and EU]. Even China has greater status than us. But we know between the two of us [India and Brazil] there's a formidable force that the G2 can't ignore.[29]

Given their lesser economic weight, compared with either the traditional powers or China, neither Brazil nor India could rely on economic might alone. Instead, they needed to ally together and secure the backing of the developing world more broadly to enhance their power and effectively counter the US and EU.

India's Plan B: The G33

At the same time, concerns about the durability of its alliance with Brazil led India to diversify its strategy beyond the G20-T. India is acutely aware of the differences in their interests and far from confident about the long-term loyalty or reliability of Brazil. During the Uruguay Round, India and Brazil created and led a coalition—the G10—to oppose the inclusion of services, investment, and intellectual property in the round. This coalition eventually collapsed, as its members were bought off with carrots and sticks from the US and other Northern powers; India was left the last one standing after Brazil conceded and was consequently forced to consent itself. Contemporary Indian negotiators have a strong sense that the country was abandoned by Brazil, leaving it isolated and powerless to defend its interests. To quote one Indian trade official, "Brazil can't be trusted—they have a history of abandoning developing country positions."[30] Brazil, for its part, is highly conscious of this construction of its previous behavior and, in the words of a third country negotiator, has worked hard over the course of the Doha Round to ensure that it does not "give India the opportunity to say Brazil sold us out."[31] Yet India's fears that it would not be able to count on Brazil in the later stages of the Doha negotiations motivated it to invest in developing other alliances.[32]

In addition to the G20-T, India has been a leading force behind the G33, a second coalition that emerged at Cancun and has had a significant impact on the Doha negotiations. The G33 is a large coalition of developing countries— currently composed of forty-six states—with defensive concerns in agriculture, whose objective is to limit the degree of market opening required of developing countries.[33] It has specifically advocated the creation of a "special products" (SPs) exemption that would allow developing countries to shield some products from tariff cuts, as well as a "special safeguard mechanism" (SSM) that would allow them to raise tariffs in response to an import surge. The stated intent of both instruments is to protect food security, rural livelihoods, and rural development. These were new initiatives, with an innovative rationale, and of considerable consequence: combined with weaker tariff reduction formulas, the special products exemption would reduce the extent of liberalization required of developing countries in the round, while the SSM design advocated by India would allow developing countries to breach their pre-Doha commitments, thus potentially rolling back liberalization undertaken in the previous round. Although these measures were defensively oriented, this was a proactive agenda involving the creation of new negotiation issues that generated substantial opposition from the US, EU, and other developed countries. Despite this opposition, India and the G33 not only succeeded in putting special products and the SSM onto the negotiating agenda but also secured the commitment that they will be part of any final Doha agreement (Eagleton-Pierce 2012; Margulis 2013). India led the charge for an expansive definition and operationalization of these measures and, as discussed below, conflict over the design of the SSM ultimately became a central issue in the breakdown of the 2008 Ministerial Meeting.

Under the auspices of the G33, India also led an initiative to secure changes to existing WTO subsidy rules to enable developing countries to engage in public food stockholding for food security purposes (Wilkinson, Hannah, and Scott 2014). India sought such changes in order to protect a landmark new food security program it enacted in 2013—which provides subsidized food to the poor and guarantees minimum price supports for farmers—from WTO challenges. Hotly contested by the US, this became the "make or break" issue at the 2013 Bali Ministerial and in its aftermath (*Bridges Weekly* 2013). Despite American opposition, India secured the needed exemption, an interim due restraint mechanism, or "peace clause," that made its food security program immune from legal challenges while states negotiate a permanent solution.

Broader Leadership of the Developing World

Brazil and India's leadership of developing countries—and their impact on the negotiating agenda—has extended beyond the G20-T and the G33. Through the Core Group, India mobilized developing country opposition to the Singapore Issues (competition, investment, and government procurement) and succeeded in forcing those issues off the negotiating table.[34] This represented a major victory for developing countries in the Doha Round. Brazil and India (along with South Africa) have also led developing countries in scoring important victories in the area of intellectual property and access to medicines: despite strong opposition from the US and EU and their pharmaceutical corporations, developing countries secured an agreement in 2001 exempting essential medicines (such as HIV/AIDS drugs) from WTO intellectual property rules (the "TRIPs Agreement") and declaring that such rules could not be used to prevent governments from acting to protect public health, as well as a waiver in 2003 allowing the export of generic drugs to developing countries that lack domestic pharmaceutical manufacturing capacity. In pursuing these initiatives, India was driven not only by public health considerations but also by the major commercial significance of the TRIPs waiver and declaration to its generic pharmaceutical industry, which played an important role in this fight (Roemer-Mahler 2012). Importantly, the intense opposition to TRIPs also prevented the US and EU from seeking expanded intellectual property protections ("TRIPs-Plus") in the Doha Round. In addition, Brazil and India have been key figures in the NAMA-11 coalition of developing countries in the negotiations on manufactured goods ("nonagricultural market access" or NAMA).[35] Under their leadership, developing countries secured major "special and differential treatment" (SDT) provisions, including weaker tariff-reduction formulas and substantial flexibilities in both agriculture and manufactured goods (WTO 2008a; WTO 2008b).

Beyond specific coalitions, Brazil and India have engaged in extensive coordination and alliance-building across the developing world. At the 2005 Hong Kong Ministerial, for example, they led a mass coalition of developing countries (the G110), representing the majority of the WTO's membership, when the G20-T and G33 came together and allied with other groupings of developing countries—the African Group, the African Caribbean and Pacific (ACP) Group, the LDC Group, and the Small and Vulnerable Economies (SVEs)—to oppose the agenda being pushed by the advanced-industrialized states. Through a combination of formal coalitions and more informal leadership, Brazil and India organized a significant portion of the organization's membership behind them, which they used to play a major agenda-setting role and significantly shape the direction of the Doha Round.

Building Effective Coalitions

There had been previous efforts by developing countries to form coalitions to increase their bargaining power at the WTO. Developing countries began experimenting more actively with forming coalitions during the Uruguay Round and leading up to Doha (such as the Informal Group, G10, and Like Minded Group), with Brazil and India playing a central role. However, as Amrita Narlikar (2003) has documented, these early coalitions were largely ineffective, hampered by the absence of a strong issue-specific focus, a lack of expertise (particularly the capacity to advance specific proposals and engage in the technical aspect of the negotiations), and an inability to maintain unity and resist collapse in the face of pressures from the dominant powers. These factors considerably reduced their power as a negotiating force, and the collapse of their coalitions proved extremely costly for developing countries, which were left with the unfavorable results of the Uruguay Round.

An important question is thus why Brazil and India's coalition-building efforts in the Doha Round were successful when previous such efforts had failed. As Narlikar and coauthors (Hurrell and Narlikar 2006; Narlikar and Tussie 2004) convincingly argue, these new coalitions were the product of almost two decades of experimentation, learning, and adaptation by developing countries. Led by Brazil and India, they were able to learn from their previous mistakes in order to build stronger and more effective coalitions in this round. Perhaps most important, coming out of their experiences in the Uruguay Round and the lead-up to Doha, developing countries were keenly aware of the danger of political isolation and the costs of failing to maintain unity (de Lima and Hirst 2006). Developing countries had a renewed and strengthened commitment to coalitions but needed effective leadership, which Brazil and India provided.

The G20-T alliance forged by Brazil and India was the real game changer at the WTO and marked a break with previous coalitions in several important ways. In light of the diverse (and potentially conflicting) interests of developing countries, building and maintaining coalitions at the WTO is no easy feat. Given their previous experiences, Brazil and India were acutely aware of the problem of maintaining unity. By constructing the agenda of the G20-T around the issue of rich country agricultural subsidies, Brazil and India found a means to overcome differences and unite developing countries. Indeed, its leaders acknowledge that subsidies provided perhaps "the *only* issue to unite the G20-T behind."[36]

With their attack on rich country agricultural subsidies, the G20-T struck a major Achilles heel of US (and more broadly Northern) trade policy. Agriculture is arguably one of the areas where the most egregious violations of the spirit (if not the laws) of the liberal international trading system by the US and other advanced-industrialized countries are to be found. It is an area where state intervention to cushion producers from market forces is extensive, particularly by rich countries, which have the greatest resources to provide subsidies. And in developing countries, the economic importance of agriculture remains enormous, employing large parts of the population in many countries. The G20-T argued that rich country subsidies distort trade by allowing farmers in the Global North to sell their products at artificially low prices, giving them an unfair advantage over producers from the Global South, while lowering global prices and the incomes of poor farmers.

The subsidies issue provided a compelling narrative that accorded with the liberalization mandate of the WTO and thus increased the legitimacy of the G20-T's claims (see also Eagleton-Pierce 2012). Moreover, while developing countries have repeatedly been on the defensive in WTO negotiations, the subsidies issue provided an opportunity to turn the tables and go on the offensive against the developed countries. In keeping with the adage that "the best defense is a good offense," this offered important strategic advantages for developing countries. The G20-T turned the rhetoric of free trade and liberalization back on the major powers and highlighted their hypocrisy (Bukovansky 2010; Taylor 2007). In the process, this significantly strengthened the position of developing countries vis-à-vis the US and EU across the negotiations, including their ability to defend protections in their own markets.

Diplomatic and technical capacity were critical to the ability of Brazil and India to create and manage the G20-T and other coalitions that could provide a credible challenge to the US and EU. In the lead-up to the Doha Round, Brazil and India both invested heavily in staff and resources dedicated to the WTO (Shaffer, Sanchez, and Rosenberg 2008; Sinha 2007). They now have among the largest delegations in Geneva, supported by highly trained officials in their capitals, and their negotiating teams are among the most skilled, active, and knowledgeable at the WTO. Brazil and India used their considerable diplomatic skill to coordinate the positions of developing countries; provide strategy, talking points, and messaging; and produce compelling negotiating proposals backed by research and analysis. Both countries were able to provide the highly sophisticated expertise and technical capacity (that is, the ability to run econometric analysis, assess the impacts of specific commitments, and generate negotiating proposals) that most other developing countries lacked. This marked an important departure from previous developing country coalitions and made it possible for them to respond to and counter the US and EU.

Desperate for a coalition that would enable them to push back against pressures from the US and EU, the formation and success of the G20-T "electrified" the ranks of developing countries, in the words of one negotiator.[37] A representative of Indian industry expressed it thus: "There is a strong sense developing countries were bulldozed in GATT/WTO agreements in the past." Now, however, Brazil and India were "standing up to the bulldozer and a lot of other developing countries were happy to stand back and let them do this job for them."[38] Given the diverse interests of developing countries, the G20-T, the G33, and other broader alliances have not been without inherent tensions, and the US has made concerted efforts to spit these developing country coalitions and undermine support for the emerging powers (Burges 2013; Hopewell 2015a). However, coalition members are keenly aware that, as one G20-T member stated, "Our strength lies in the group."[39] The knowledge that their bargaining leverage would be substantially weakened without these coalitions has served to reinforce coalition unity and support for Brazil and India's leadership.

Gaining Power through Leadership

The emphasis on Brazil and India's coalition-building is not to dismiss the importance of their economic capabilities or to suggest that such capabilities have played no role in their increased stature at the WTO. Economic weight and coalition strength are, of course, far from independent. Their newfound economic might has undoubtedly helped Brazil and India to build stronger and more effective coalitions. Possessing far greater economic capabilities than most developing countries, their economic success has played an important role in legitimizing Brazil and India's leadership of the developing world and provided the resources to build the technical and diplomatic capacity that has been critical to the success of their coalitions. Yet clearly, if Brazil and India had been able to rely on economic might alone, they would not have needed to invest so heavily in constructing coalitions.

It was Brazil and India's leadership of developing country coalitions—particularly the G20-T and G33—that catalyzed power shifts at the WTO and propelled them into the inner circle of power. As one negotiator stated, "The US and EU aren't talking to India because India is India. They do it because India is seen as a leader of the G20-T and the G33, and if they don't get an agreement with India, it's not just India that will withdraw its support, it's all of those countries."[40] A Brazilian negotiator concurred:

There are various ways to be admitted [to the inner circle]. You need interests large enough and that are capable of screaming enough if their needs are not met—you can do it alone or in a coalition, but it's better to do it in a coalition. For us, the G20-T served as a stepping stone to consolidate our access to the most exclusive negotiating forum [at the WTO].[41]

Lacking the economic heft of other major powers, the mobilization of developing country coalitions was critical in enabling Brazil and India to boost their status and influence at the WTO.

The Rise of China

China's rise to power has differed greatly from that of Brazil and India. China joined the WTO only in 2001, after an arduous accession process that took more than fifteen years of negotiations and required China to undertake substantial concessions and domestic reforms. Its accession corresponded with the launch of the Doha Round and many predicted it would assume a central role in the negotiations, given its prominent role in world trade. Instead however, for much of the Doha Round, China has been a relatively marginal player on the sidelines of the real action and decision-making. As late as 2007, for example, the *Economist* (2007) could report that "four powers hold the key to Doha"—the US, EU, Brazil, and India—and make not a single mention of China. While Brazil and India joined the inner circle at the WTO following Cancun in 2003, it was not until the Ministerial Meeting in July 2008 that China was included in this core group and assumed a more significant role in the negotiations. Furthermore, whereas Brazil and India fought their way into the inner circle, China was brought in—and it was brought in largely because Brazil and India had already been so successful in fundamentally changing the dynamics of the negotiations.

A Quiet Presence

If Brazil and India sought the spotlight at the WTO, China sought to avoid it. Although it is an important member of the G20-T and the G33, with its economic stature adding considerable weight to these coalitions, China made no effort to establish itself as a leader of developing countries, as Brazil and India did. Indeed, when asked in interviews, Chinese negotiators bristled and grew visibly uncomfortable at the suggestion that China might assume a role as a leader of developing countries and quickly moved to dismiss it, stating: "China is not a leader and China does not want to be a leader."[42] A negotiator explained: "We would have to take the spotlight, and that is against China's philosophy to be quiet, low profile, modest."[43] Such a strategy is in keeping with Deng Xiaoping's famous directive of *taoguang yanghui*, that the country should "observe developments soberly, maintain our position, meet challenges calmly, hide our capabilities and bide our time, remain free of ambition, and never claim leadership." As a rival negotiator stated: "China doesn't want a following .... China's not like an India or a Brazil. They stay behind and do not take on a prominent position at the forefront. We were surprised even that they joined the G20-T and the G33."[44] Instead, China has been remarkably quite and assumed a low-profile in the negotiations, with other negotiators describing it as "a little on the outside of things."[45] Unlike Brazil and India, China has sought to deflect attention and avoid any obvious projection of its power. Rather, China's behavior at the WTO has been more akin to an elephant acting like a mouse.

China's quietude is often attributed to the newness of its membership in the organization (Scott and Wilkinson 2013), and certainly China itself has sought to foster this interpretation. But after fifteen years of intense accession negotiations and subsequently over a decade of membership in the WTO, China's efforts to portray itself as new and inexperienced and still learning the ropes within the institution warrant skepticism. As discussed further in Chapter 6, China has important strategic reasons for its comparatively quiet behavior in the negotiations. As a highly competitive exporter whose explosive economic growth and development have been driven by exports, China clearly has a great deal at stake in WTO negotiations. Yet its position at the WTO is a complicated one. On the one hand, China's large and rapidly growing economy make it a prime target at the WTO, with other states eager to improve their access to its market. And, on the other, many countries are threatened by China's industrial export capacity. These factors combine to create significant vulnerabilities for China, as it potentially faces both demands that it open its market and efforts to constrain its exports. In consequence, China has sought to appear nonthreatening, fly under the radar as much as possible, and avoid drawing unwelcome attention to itself. It has therefore avoided taking a leadership role or proactively trying to shape the agenda of the negotiations.

When the Doha Round began, it was widely expected that China would side with the advanced-industrialized states, given that China's interests are primarily export-oriented and, in many ways, its economic profile is much closer to the advanced-industrialized states than to developing countries (see, for example, Pearson 2006). As the round progressed, however, precisely the opposite occurred, as China increasingly allied itself with the developing world. In the words of one US trade official: "In many ways, at the WTO, China has the same interests as developed countries: market access to large emerging economies, developing countries. It could have gone two ways: we could have co-opted China, but instead Brazil and India did."[46] The particular demands on China have oriented its approach to picking allies. While the country faces potential pressure from all sides, China has determined that the primary threat it faces is from the advanced-industrialized states—especially the US. A Chinese negotiator explained:

It is our position that the greatest source of pressure on China in this round will come from the rich OECD countries. So our strategy has been to pay more attention to how our unity with developing countries could be strengthened.[47]

Another Chinese official put this even more bluntly:

[China needs coalitions] because of our bitter experience of negotiating bilaterally with the US [for China's WTO accession]. The US always got what it wanted. Our prospects of winning are higher if we are with other developing countries and not alone. The US is still the superpower—the world's biggest economy. In a one-on-one setting, the US will most always win, because we are counting on the US market. It is a question of markets: we export goods to the US; we have to please the US because they are buying our goods. Multilaterally, it is a different picture: then it is no longer one-to-one, but the US versus a group of countries. The US is the big elephant, but we now have a group of wolves—then we have a chance.[48]

The threat posed by the US and other traditional powers has therefore led China to energetically stress its developing country status and to join developing country coalitions in order to strengthen its defenses and avoid being singled out as a target. As a rival negotiator stated, "They are aware of the risk and do everything they need to avoid it."[49] China's participation in the G20-T and G33, along with its more informal solidarity and alliances with the developing world, have been critical to its efforts not only to counter pressure from the US and other rich countries but also to prevent challenges from other developing countries. Thus, even for China, developing country coalitions have played a vital role in its strategy at the WTO.

Consequently, as a member of the G20-T and the G33, China has allowed itself to be led and represented by Brazil and India. As one official observed,

"China has made a simple calculation that it's not in their interests to get out in front, because then they would draw more critique. I'm sure they think there is enough China-bashing already. So they are happy to leave the leadership role to India and Brazil."[50] Seeking the protection of developing country alliances and with Brazil and India advancing an agenda broadly in accord with its own interests, China was disposed to let those two countries lead the fight against the traditional powers. As one negotiator commented, "They see that as long as India and Brazil are fighting for what they want, why should they say anything."[51] A secretariat official seconded this assessment: "They don't waste capital if they have others that will do it for them."[52] The result is that, as another official stated, Brazil and India "managed to drag around China" and China "effectively let Brazil and India run their participation" at the WTO.[53]

China's Entry to the Inner Circle

It was not until the July 2008 Mini-Ministerial Meeting in Geneva that China was included in the inner circle and began to assume a more important role in the negotiations.[54] As usual at the Ministerial, the center of the action was the Green Room, where a small, elite group of trade ministers gathered for negotiations. For the first time, however, China was invited to join the core group, which at this meeting consisted of the US, EU, Brazil, India, Australia, and Japan.[55] What had changed to prompt the inclusion of China? The decision was driven by the US and the WTO's director-general. Their motives were two-fold. First, four years of negotiations centered on the US, EU, Brazil, and India had produced a standstill—as the breakdown of the previous Ministerial meeting the year before in Potsdam had shown. Faced with an impasse—between the US and EU, on one side, and Brazil and India, on the other, split over the issues of agricultural subsidies and market access in the North and industrial tariffs in the South—there was a sense that it was necessary to re-jig the players in the group to try to break the standstill. The US in particular—as well as others seeking a conclusion to the round—thought that China would side with them and help to counter India, which the US blamed for holding up the deal. As one official commented: "The US believed that China would be more of an ally than an adversary in these meetings. It made a calculation that because of China's relatively passive approach to being the biggest developing country here and letting others run with the agenda, it would be an ally."[56] Similarly, another negotiator stated, "China has a lot to gain, so people thought bringing it to the table will help get a deal. They thought it would put added pressure on India by having China in the room."[57]

The US also had a second motivation for including China. While the US is interested in gaining improved access to the Chinese market through the Doha Round, China's absence from the Green Room for most of the round indicates that the US expected to be able to secure these gains without directly engaging China. The US believed that it needed only to strike a deal with Brazil and India, which would set the terms of its access to developing country markets, including China. However, by 2008, Brazil and India had been so successful in resisting the pressures of the US and its allies and securing their own demands that the negotiations had moved toward a prospective agreement that provoked protest from powerful actors in the US Congress and its business and farm lobby groups. They contended that the US was not making sufficient gains in expanding access for its exports, particularly to the large and rapidly growing Chinese market as well as those of other emerging economies, to justify its concessions on agriculture subsidies and other areas.

In response, US negotiators determined that the best way to improve the package and sell it to their domestic constituencies would be to secure special concessions from China, beyond the formal terms of the agreement that was emerging. The US sought an informal commitment from China that it would agree to limit the use of its flexibilities in agriculture, by keeping commodities in which the US is a leading exporter (such as cotton, wheat, and corn) off its list of special products that are subject to less liberalization. It also sought agreement from China that it would participate in "sectorals"—proposed initiatives under which participating countries would aggressively cut tariffs to zero or close to zero across entire industrial sectors—in two areas of American competitiveness, chemicals and industrial machinery. Thus, by the 2008 Ministerial, as one negotiator stated, "The main demands of the US and EU could not be addressed without getting a "yes" from China. The US needed China to be there."[58]

There were thus two key factors driving the decision to bring China into the Green Room: one was strategic—the US thought it could use China to put pressure on Brazil and India—the other was that because Brazil and India had been so successful in negotiating a favorable deal for developing countries and had backed the US into a corner, it needed to be able to secure extra concessions from China in order to sell the deal back home. Unfortunately for the US, however, this strategy backfired. Negotiations in the Green Room came to center on the design of the SSM championed by India. Rather than joining with the US, China—which also has significant defensive agricultural interests arising from its large peasant population—supported India on the SSM. Moreover, China refused to simply give away the additional commitments the US was demanding on agricultural special products and industrial sectorals, which it saw as unjustified relative to the concessions the US was willing to make and beyond the scope of the terms already agreed to. Ultimately, the Ministerial broke down with recriminations on all sides.

On its face, the breakdown was due to conflict over the SSM, but the deeper issue was the US desire to "rebalance" the deal by securing greater access for its agriculture and manufactured goods to the markets of the large emerging economies, particularly China (US 2011). If China had conceded to the US and agreed to grant the additional concessions it was seeking, the Doha Round may well have been concluded in 2008. Certainly, the US has a long track record in multilateral trade negotiations of successfully overpowering developing countries and securing their assent for its initiatives. Instead, however, China stood firm, refused to cave to the US and rebuffed its demands for additional market opening. Thus, when pushed, China showed that it is willing and able to assert itself and defend its interests against the US. Given its economic heft and the importance of its market, by blocking the US initiative to "rebalance" the round, China effectively exercised a veto that contributed directly to the current breakdown and stalemate in the Doha Round.

With the 2008 Ministerial, China was almost involuntarily pulled into the spotlight. Even since being admitted to the inner circle in 2008, negotiators report that China has still tried to slip back into its comparatively quiet and low-profile role in the negotiations. Its attempts to do so have been less successful than in the past because of the US emphasis on gaining further opening in China's market and those of other large emerging economies. Yet China did not suddenly assume an activist role like that of Brazil and India.

The World Turned Upside Down

The Doha Round has come to be defined by a clash between the old powers—the US and EU—and the new—Brazil, India, and China—that signals a substantial change in power relations within the multilateral trading system. The influence of the new powers is evident in their success in both blocking the traditional powers and advancing their own initiatives. First, as a result of the newfound power of Brazil, India, and China, as well as broader activism on the part of the developing world, the US and other Northern powers have been repeatedly thwarted in many of the key objectives they sought to obtain from the Doha Round, including the following: labor and environmental standards (a priority of the US going into the current round of negotiations, which developing countries strongly opposed as a disguised form of protectionism intended to limit their exports), the Singapore Issues (competition, investment, and government procurement, which were intended to continue the expansion of the scope of WTO rules), expanded TRIPs-Plus intellectual property protections, sectoral negotiations on manufactured goods, and efforts to force the large emerging economies to undertake more aggressive liberalization. Second, Brazil and India, in particular, emerged as a major source of initiative in the Doha Round, succeeding in putting issues of importance to developing countries— such as agriculture subsidies, special products, the special safeguard mechanism, food stockholding, TRIPs and public health, and extensive special and differential treatment (SDT) provisions for developing countries—at the center of the negotiations and winning substantial concessions. With regard to special and differential treatment, in both the agriculture and manufactured goods negotiations, the emerging powers have helped to secure considerably weaker tariff-reduction formulas for developing countries than for developed countries, along with substantial flexibilities to enable developing countries to further protect their markets. As a result, the tariff reduction commitments—and thus the degree of liberalization—that would be required of developing countries from the Doha Round are extremely limited. Indeed, one observer described them as "nearly inconsequential" (Dadush 2009: 4). Developing countries have therefore been able to carve out significant policy space within a prospective Doha agreement to enable them to pursue their economic development objectives; indeed, provisions related to the special safeguard mechanism that would allow them to breach their commitments made in the Uruguay Round could allow them to claw back and expand policy space they had previously lost in the international trading system. At the same time, developing countries would nonetheless enjoy improved access to developed country markets because of the stricter formula and fewer flexibilities that would force those countries to make meaningful cuts in their tariffs.

Compared with the Uruguay Round—when developing countries were railroaded into an agreement that trampled their interests—the change in the

Doha Round has been profound. Collectively, Brazil, India, and China have now demonstrated the power to resist an unbalanced deal as well as to successfully make meaningful demands of developed countries. If anything, the new powers—specifically Brazil and India—have seized the reins and been driving the agenda at the WTO. Since Cancun, the US and other advanced-industrialized states have been largely reactive—they have repeatedly been on the back foot, trying to respond to the demands of developing countries, while having little success in advancing their own. As one secretariat official stated, "The US has not been leading this organization in quite a while."[59] This rebalancing of power has shifted the terms of a prospective WTO agreement; it has changed the nature of the bargain to be struck and the balance of concessions among states necessary to secure a deal. The US and other Northern states can no longer impose and extract what they want at will from the developing world. They can no longer impose the type of deeply imbalanced deal that they did in the Uruguay Round, for example, and are now being forced to extract less from the Global South and being called upon to make real concessions of their own. As a result, this has significantly reduced the potential gains to the US from the round and has increased the costs.

The tables have turned: the US—particularly Congress and its business and farm lobby groups—is now the one complaining that the proposed Doha Round agreement is unfair and unbalanced *against the US*. Based on the way the deal has taken shape—with what it perceives to be weak tariff-reduction formulas and excessive flexibilities for the large emerging economies—the US has come to believe that the terms of the agreement have turned against it and that, from its perspective, the costs of the agreement could outweigh the gains. According to the US ambassador to the WTO, for example, "[T]he round is currently imbalanced" (*Bridges Weekly* 2010a). The US National Manufacturers Association expressed the following criticism of the draft agreement on manufactured goods ("NAMA"):

The "Swiss Formula" that advanced developing countries are entitled to use is so full of holes it is more properly called "The Swiss Cheese Formula." It severely imbalances the NAMA negotiations for the United States, requiring major cuts in US tariffs but only minor cuts in the applied rates of the advance developing countries. (NAM 2008)

Similarly, the head of the American Farm Bureau has complained that, while the US is being made to reduce its subsidies, its hopes for market access in agriculture "have been continually whittled away" (quoted in Blustein 2009). In a 2008 letter to then-President Bush, leaders from both parties in the House and Senate committees responsible for trade stated that "the negotiating texts currently on the table would provide little or no access for US goods" (US Congress 2008).

The deal that has taken shape is one that these actors find profoundly unsatisfactory. From their perspective, the US would be required to significantly cut its tariffs on industrial and agricultural goods and agricultural subsidies, while gaining insufficient new access to foreign markets for its exports. As one US negotiator put it, "We'd be giving everything and getting nothing."[60] The core complaint of the US is that the prospective agreement does not require enough of the large emerging economies—China, India, and Brazil—who benefit from the special and differential treatment (SDT) that they played a major role in securing for developing countries, which provides for weaker tariff-reduction formulas and extensive flexibilities (US 2011).

As a result, particularly since the 2008 Ministerial, the US has sought to increase its potential gains from the round by aggressively pushing for China, India, and Brazil to grant additional concessions. Its efforts have centered on pressing these countries to participate in sectorals in key areas of manufacturing interest to the US (including chemicals, information technology, and industrial machinery). Sectorals are effectively an add-on to the core agreement that have been pushed primarily by the US and other developed countries in order to enable them to extract additional market opening from the large emerging economies. In addition, the US has also pressed the emerging economies to commit to not using their flexibilities in agriculture—which would shield designated products from full tariff cuts—against specific products of export interest to the US, in order to guarantee the US market access gains in those areas. From their newfound position of power, however, the new powers have been able to successfully withstand US demands, which they view as incommensurate with the commitments the US itself is willing to undertake.

While the EU more quickly adapted to the new power balance at the WTO—and shifted to "negotiating with diminished expectations" (Young 2007)—the US has fiercely resisted this new reality. It has worked hard to "rebalance" the deal—to make it more favorable from its perspective—by trying to force the large emerging economies to undertake greater liberalization commitments. In this effort, the US has had the tacit support of other advanced-industrialized countries, such as the EU, Canada, and Australia, but these countries have been far more subdued in their criticism of the large emerging economies. While acting as quiet allies behind the scenes, these countries have left the US largely on its own to lead the charge against the emerging economies.[61] One business representative, for example, complained, "The EU has been rather secondary because the US has been doing it [fighting the new powers] for them."[62] Negotiators suggest that the EU—a major target at the start of the round—is relieved that pressure has shifted to the US.[63] The US has been backed into a corner: confronted with an agreement with which it is dissatisfied, it has been left isolated and on the defensive. In contrast, many developing countries appear satisfied with the prospective agreement—even India, historically one of the round's most vocal critics. As an Indian official stated, "There is already enough on the table for developing countries and LDCs. Our concerns have been taken care of."[64] In a marked departure from the past, the US has found itself a key target of blame for the impasse in the Doha Round and widely seen as "the main stumbling block" to the conclusion of the round (*Bridges Weekly* 2009).

The persistence of this impasse has caused the Doha negotiations to collapse. Some take the fact that the new powers have ultimately been unable to secure their objectives through conclusion of the round as an indication that they lack power (Narlikar 2010; Schirm 2010). I would argue, however, that this is an excessively high standard by which to evaluate the power of Brazil, India, and China. By this criterion even the US could not be considered powerful, since it also has not been able to conclude the round and achieve its preferred objectives. A more realistic standard of power at the WTO is to evaluate the impact that countries have had on the round. By this measure, though the natures of their behavior and impact differ, Brazil, India, and China have undoubtedly arrived as major powers.

In addition, beyond the Doha Round, the new developing country powers have also become among the most active and frequent users of the WTO dispute settlement system, which they have used to discipline the trade policies of the traditional powers and advance their own commercial interests. Among the most high profile and widely publicized cases were the landmark disputes that Brazil won against US cotton subsidies and EU sugar export subsidies in 2005 (detailed in Chapter 5). In another remarkable example, India used the threat of a WTO dispute to force a reversal of EU intellectual property policy—which had been used to restrict the movement of Indian generic pharmaceuticals through European ports—in 2010.[65] The EU had been confiscating generic pharmaceuticals from India in transit through European ports on their way to other developing countries, on the grounds that the drugs were infringing on the IP rights of its pharmaceutical companies and in violation of EU patent laws. The drugs were patented in Europe but not in the sending and receiving countries, and thus the EU was using its position as a global transport hub to extraterritorially impose its IP regime on foreign goods passing through its ports. India's recourse to the WTO, however, arguing that the EU was in violation of its obligations under WTO rules to provide freedom of transit to goods passing its territory, forced the EU to back down and allow Indian pharmaceuticals to travel freely through its ports (*Bridges Weekly* 2010b). Even China is now making similarly extensive use of the WTO's rules and enforcement mechanism to challenge efforts by the traditional powers to restrict its exports. Together, Brazil, India, and China have initiated a combined total of twenty-eight cases against the US and nineteen against the EU. They have challenged a wide range of trade and other policies, including trade remedies (safeguards, antidumping, and countervailing duties), sanitary and phytosanitary (SPS) standards, rules of origin, customs rules, environmental regulations, TRIPs, patent rules, excise taxes, subsidies, the enforcement of intellectual property rules, import duties, and tariff preferences.[66]

Conclusion

As this chapter has shown, a real and significant shift in power has indeed taken place at the WTO. The rise of Brazil, India, and China has destabilized the traditional power structure within the institution, brought an end to the dominance of the US, EU, and other advanced-industrialized states in both negotiations and dispute settlement, and placed their trade policies under scrutiny in the Doha Round. Yet an analysis of developments at the WTO challenges the conventional wisdom that the rise of new powers in global economic governance is merely a function of their growing economic might. Instead, I have argued that the forces driving their rise are more diverse and complex than suggested by a simple economic determinism and that these countries have taken different paths to power. Although China's rise has been more closely tied to its economic weight, for Brazil and India alliance-building and leadership have been critical to enhancing their power at the WTO. My purpose has not been to deny the role of economic change in contemporary power shifts, but to suggest that an exclusive focus on economic capabilities risks missing important aspects of the rise of new powers in global economic governance.

These differences in their sources of power have also had important implications for the strategies and behavior of these countries at the WTO. Brazil and India worked to position themselves as leaders of the developing world and assumed a confrontational stance in relation to the US and EU as a means to elevate their own status and influence. Highly vocal and assertive, Brazil and India have been a major source of initiative and played a central role in shaping the agenda of the Doha negotiations. In contrast, China has been reluctant to throw its weight around. While it has sought the protection afforded by developing country coalitions, it has explicitly avoided the leadership role eagerly cultivated by Brazil and India. China has been assertive only in a defensive and reactive manner and has not sought to be an initiator or agenda-setter; yet China nonetheless came to have a significant impact in the later stages of the round, when it refused to accede to US demands. Analysis of the WTO thus suggests the need to look beyond raw economic power to understand emerging challenges to the dominance of the US and other Northern states in global economic governance.

Chapter 5

Brazil: New Drivers of Liberalization

$\mathbf{H}$AVING analyzed the power shift that has taken place at the WTO and the new landscape of power within the institution, the following chapters examine the agendas being pursued by the emerging powers. To understand the origins of their negotiating positions at the WTO, it is necessary to extend the analysis to encompass the emerging powers' domestic political economies, examining the internal dynamics and actors shaping their trade policy. For it is here that we find an answer to the question of why the rise of new powers from the developing world has not posed a direct challenge to the neoliberal agenda of the WTO. The political economies of Brazil, India, and China have all been profoundly transformed in recent decades, with growing integration into global markets and dependence on exports for economic growth and stability. All three countries have developed powerful commercial interests eager to maintain and expand their access to foreign markets through global trade liberalization. Consequently, each of the emerging powers has a significant stake in the liberal international trading order.

I begin, in this chapter, by focusing on Brazil. Brazil is particularly important as the driving force behind the G20-T, which—as described in the preceding chapters—was a prime catalyst in upsetting the traditional power structure of the WTO. Brazil's leadership of the G20-T and its role in trade disputes launched against the US and EU have been widely hailed as a major victory for developing countries and have attracted a tremendous amount of interest from academics, policy-makers, activists, and the media. The G20-T, for example, is frequently characterized as a highly successful example of contemporary South-South cooperation being used to project the interests and development concerns of the Global South onto the international stage; in the words of one observer, "[T]he South fighting for the South"(Ruiz-Diaz 2005). Many view it as a progressive force with echoes of the sort of developing country activism not seen since the efforts of the G77 and the Nonaligned Movement to construct a New International Economic Order (NIEO) in the 1960s and 1970s. However, I contend that these accounts of Brazil's recent activism at the WTO miss one of its central components: the critical role played by business actors, specifically Brazil's agribusiness sector.

In this chapter, I analyze Brazil's objectives at the WTO and its influence on negotiations and dispute settlement. I argue that far from challenging the neoliberal agenda of the WTO, Brazil has emerged as one of the most vocal advocates of free market globalization and the push to expand and liberalize global markets. I show that Brazil's stance has been driven by the rise of its sophisticated and highly competitive agribusiness sector, which has emerged as an influential force in Brazilian trade policy and at the WTO. Brazil has adopted an aggressive position at the WTO, seeking to make use of both its strong dispute settlement mechanism and the Doha Round negotiations to advance the commercial interests of its agribusiness sector. In the process, it has posed a serious challenge to the policies of the US, EU, and other developed countries. Brazil has gained considerable support for its agenda by strategically mobilizing the politics of the North-South divide, and it has been highly effective in portraying the commercial interests of its agribusiness sector as part of the Global South's struggle for development and social justice. Yet, as I demonstrate, agriculture subsidies were not a natural or inevitable target for developing countries and, in actuality, the reduction in rich country agriculture subsidies advocated by Brazil could negatively affect the welfare and food security of some developing countries.

Brazil's Emergence as an Agroexport Powerhouse

As in many developing countries, the Brazilian economy, for much of its history, centered on the export of tropical agricultural products, such as coffee and rubber, to rich country markets in Europe and the US. Motivated by the desire to move the country away from its dependence on agricultural exports and foster the development of manufacturing industries, the state embarked on a program of import-substitution industrialization (ISI) beginning in the 1930s and accelerating from the 1950s and 1960s (Evans 1979). Economic policy during this period emphasized the subordination of agricultural to industrial development, and Brazil's ISI policies achieved considerable success in fostering economic development by increasing manufacturing and fueling relatively high rates of economic growth (de Holanda Barbosa 1999). However, the international debt crisis that afflicted many developing countries in the early 1980s plunged Brazil into an economic crisis, faced with major balance of payments problems, soaring inflation, and an inability to meet its international debt obligations. Policy-makers determined that the old model of an inward-looking economy with substantial state intervention to promote industrial development was no longer sustainable and embarked on a program of economic reform and liberalization. Until then, Brazil's agricultural sector had been based primarily on large plantations producing tropical products for export, small family farms supplying the domestic market, and peasants engaged in subsistence production. As a result of the success of Brazil's ISI policies, over much of the twentieth century the importance of agriculture in the national economy declined as that of manufacturing increased. In fact, as recently as the 1970s, Brazil was a net-agricultural importer and, until the 1960s, it systematically received food donations from abroad (Martha, Contini, and Alves 2013).

In response to economic crisis in the 1980s and 1990s, Brazil introduced dramatic market-oriented economic reforms that included aggressive inflation fighting to stabilize the macroeconomic environment, the elimination of foreign trade restrictions and barriers to foreign investment, and reducing state intervention in markets (which in agriculture, for instance, included privatizing state enterprises, reducing subsidies, and eliminating government purchases, marketing boards, and minimum support prices). Liberalization dramatically transformed the Brazilian economy, and it had an explosive effect on the growth of Brazil's agribusiness sector and its exports. This should not, however, be read simply as a story of the triumph of neoliberal economic reforms prompting a flourishing of private enterprise. In fact, the origins of Brazil's agricultural export boom lay in extensive state-directed investment in research and development initiated in the 1970s, under the auspices of a new national agricultural research institute, EMBRAPA (Empresa Brasileira de Pesquisa Agropecuária). In addition to significantly increasing the productivity and competitiveness of Brazilian agriculture, the innovations produced by EMBRAPA enabled Brazil to move away from the tropical products typically exported by developing countries (coffee, tea, sugar, bananas, and the like) to producing and exporting commodities (soybeans, cotton, beef, chicken, pork, and so on) that directly compete with those of the world's dominant agricultural exporters—the US, EU, and other countries of the Global North (Gold-smith and Hirsch 2006).

The combination of technological innovation and economic liberalization produced a boom in Brazilian agricultural production and exports, with exports growing at rates as high as 20 percent per year (Valdes 2006; Wilkinson 2009a). Massive investment and consolidation fueled the expansion of corporate farm-ing, including the emergence of "mega farms"—large, professionally managed corporate farm groups, often with planted areas in excess of 1 million hectares. Brazil now has one of the world's most sophisticated agroindustrial sectors, based on massive economies of scale and highly mechanized, capital-intensive, vertically integrated production. It has become one of the most competitive ag-ricultural producers in the world and is a leading exporter of a large and grow-ing number of products (including beef, poultry, sugar, ethanol, orange juice, coffee, soybeans, corn, pork, and cotton).[1] Brazil is now the world's third largest agricultural exporter, after the US and EU, and the country with the largest agri-cultural trade surplus. Moreover, its exports are expected to continue to expand rapidly, putting it in a position to potentially overtake the US and EU.

Although foreign multinationals have a significant presence in Brazil's ag-ricultural sector, as they do nearly all over the world, it would be inaccurate to characterize the sector as dominated by foreign corporations. In the last two decades, there has been a dramatic expansion of Brazilian firms. Of the forty leading agribusiness companies now operating in Brazil, thirty-five are Brazil-ian in origin.[2] There are approximately twenty agribusiness companies in Brazil with annual sales of more than US$1 billion and many others poised to reach this level soon (EIU 2010b). Brazilian firms have also diversified and moved up the value chain into higher value-added activities, such as trading, processing (including biofuels production), and transport. Furthermore, many Brazilian companies have transformed themselves into global players, through aggressive campaigns of foreign investment and acquisitions (Wilkinson 2009a). Brazil's JBS, for example, has become the world's largest meatpacker, with annual rev-enues of more than $40 billion. Following acquisitions of many of the biggest beef, pork, and chicken processing companies in the US and Europe, it operates 150 plants around the world, with 190,000 employees, and exports to 110 coun-tries.[3] BRF-Brasil Foods is now among the largest processed food producers in the world, operating in 110 countries, with $14 billion in annual revenues and 130,000 employees.[4] Brazilian firms have thus sought to capture the opportunities offered by global markets by transnationalizing their activities, expanding their production and distribution facilities around the world, and becoming among the world's largest firms in several sectors. Here, too, the Brazilian state has played an important role, with the National Development Bank (BNDES, Banco de Desenvolvimento Econômico e Social) financing the expansion and internationalization of Brazilian agribusiness by supplying low-cost loans for investment and foreign acquisitions (Hochstetler 2014a; Hochstetler and Montero 2013). The remarkable growth of Brazil's agroindustrial exports and firms has thus been propelled by a combination of market liberalizing reforms and activist state policies.

The Influence of Agribusiness on
Brazil's Objectives at the WTO

The rise of Brazil's agribusiness sector has had a significant impact on its trade policy. Although Brazil has been governed by the left-wing Workers' Party (PT) since 2002, first under President Lula da Silva and then Dilma Rousseff, the state has maintained neoliberal macroeconomic and trade policies. This has included privileging agribusiness expansion, driven by the conviction that Brazil must "export or die" (Karriem 2009). The agribusiness sector contributes 28 percent of GDP and is a vital engine of growth in the Brazilian economy (Damico and Nassar 2007; USDA 2009; Valdes 2006). Agribusiness exports are also seen as a critical means of generating foreign exchange and avoiding the balance-of-payments problems that historically have plagued the country: they are responsible for more than 40 percent of exports and 97 percent of the country's balance of trade surplus (OECD 2009). As one Brazilian trade official put it, "My sympathies are with agro-business. Just look at the figures—my macro stability depends on agribusiness."[5] The agribusiness sector is also well represented within the state—with many senior-level government appointments filled by representatives of the agroindustrial sector—and there is close collaboration between agribusiness representatives and government officials (Hopewell 2014).

While the state is subject to multiple and competing pressures and there continues to be contestation over the direction of economic and trade policy, agribusiness exports constitute an important pillar of the current development model being pursued by the Brazilian state. That strategy has involved pursuing export-led growth combined with social welfare and redistributive policies.

Alongside the expansion of the agroexport sector, the Brazilian economy grew rapidly, with falling unemployment, rising wages, and a growing middle class. The Lula government raised the minimum wage and expanded social welfare policies through programs such as the *Bolsa Familia*, an income transfer to poor households, and Zero Hunger (*Fome Zero*), a program to combat food insecurity and extreme poverty. These policies have achieved significant reductions in poverty, especially extreme poverty, and inequality: the proportion of the population living in poverty fell from 30 percent in 1990 to 11 percent in 2009, and Brazil's GINI coefficient (a common measure of income distribution, with higher scores representing greater inequality) fell from 0.60 in 2001 to 0.55 in 2009.[6]

Of course, Brazil's economic model has not been without criticism. Its economic growth has been buoyed by booming commodity prices—involving agriculture as well as natural resources (such as iron ore), which Brazil has in abundance—driven by demand from China and other large emerging economies. There has been a reorientation of Brazil's trade toward China, with China overtaking the US as Brazil's most important trading partner: Brazilian exports to China experienced a remarkable increase from $1.1 billion in 2000 to $21 billion in 2009, overwhelmingly dominated by commodities, while its imports from China, primarily of manufactured goods, also increased substantially, from $1.2 billion to $15.9 billion.[7] The growing penetration of the Brazilian market by Chinese manufactured goods, as well as intense competition in third country markets that were once important destinations for Brazil's manufactured exports, have stoked fears of deindustrialization and reprimarization of the Brazilian economy (Jenkins and Barbosa 2012). There are concerns that Brazil is excessively dependent on the export of raw materials to China, while consuming imports of Chinese manufactured goods, thus potentially re-creating colonial patterns of dependency (Furtado 2008; Pereira and Neves 2011). And the long-term sustainability of Brazil's economic boom is also in question, given its dependence on high commodity prices and the Chinese market. Brazil's growth rates, which peaked at about 8 percent at the height of the commodity price boom, have slowed more recently.

Despite Brazil's gains in reducing poverty and inequality, 22 million people continue to live on less than $2 per day, with poverty especially prevalent in rural areas, and Brazil remains one of the most unequal countries in the world. Furthermore, the benefits of Brazil's commodity-export model have not been universally shared. The upper tiers of the income strata have profited handsomely from the country's economic boom, and the so-called new middle class—the approximately 38 million people who have been lifted out of poverty—have gained from the government's redistributive policies. At the same time, however, the "traditional middle class" has been hollowed out—the approximately 20 million people composing this category have felt the effects of rising unemployment resulting from the elimination of manufacturing jobs, inflation and higher prices that have eroded their real incomes, and higher interest rates that have increased their cost of borrowing (Leahy 2011). Brazil's agribusiness and resource extraction development model has also been associated with destruction of the Amazon rainforest and the ecologically fragile *Cerrado* (tropical savanna) region, as well as violence against peasants, landless workers, and land reform activists (Branford and Rocha 2002; Rodrigues 2009). There has been vocal criticism from social movements about the social and environmental costs of Brazil's intensive commodity-export model (see, for example, MST 2009), yet such concerns have not substantially disrupted the direction of Brazilian agricultural or trade policy.

The goal of increasing agribusiness exports has been given primacy in determining Brazil's trade policy and its position at the WTO. Agribusiness has become a powerful force in Brazilian politics and has considerable influence in shaping government policy, particularly in the realm of trade. But this is more complicated than simply a case of the state being captured by a powerful domestic interest group; the Brazilian state is not merely an instrument controlled by agribusiness. Instead, the relationship between the state and agribusiness is better understood as an alliance or partnership, based on common interests and ideology. Given the centrality of agribusiness exports to the Brazilian economy, expanding exports is a shared objective of both the state and agribusiness.

Historically, Brazil's trade policy was inward-looking—centered on protecting domestic industries from foreign competition—and it played only a minor role in multilateral trade negotiations (de Lima and Hirst 2006). However, as the export-oriented agribusiness sector developed, it pressed the state to take a more aggressive position at the WTO. Brazilian agribusiness identified the Doha Round as an opportunity to reduce trade barriers and other market distortions; its interests centered particularly on improving market access and reducing subsidies in developed countries, such as the US and EU, which depress world prices and impede the growth of Brazilian exports. The pro–free trade stance of agribusiness has met with opposition from a variety of domestic actors—including social movements, NGOs, trade unions, small farmers and peasants (including the Landless Workers Movement, MST), and manufacturing sectors threatened by foreign competition—who have urged the Brazilian state to resist trade liberalization at the WTO. However, in determining Brazil's trade policy, the opponents of trade liberalization have been largely outweighed by the potential benefits for Brazil's agribusiness sector and its exports (Veiga 2007).

Brazil is widely seen as one of the biggest potential winners from the Doha Round and has been one of its most active and vocal supporters. Brazil has defined its primary strategic interest as enhancing the competitive position of its agribusiness sector in global markets.[8] Brazilian officials and its agribusiness sector believe that if its key competitors are forced to reduce their subsidies, Brazil could surpass the US as the world's leading agricultural exporter. As one Brazilian negotiator stated: "Now, in the US today, agriculture is inefficient, addicted to subsidies and seriously flawed. In the US, it's subsidies that are making them inefficient. It's the law of survival—you either survive by being competitive or die."[9] Driven by the rise of its agribusiness sector, Brazil has thus adopted an aggressive position at the WTO, bringing two high-profile disputes against the US and EU and leading the G20-T in pushing for agricultural trade liberalization.

Trade Disputes: The Cotton and Sugar Cases

In September 2002, Brazil launched two groundbreaking dispute settlement cases against US cotton subsidies and EU sugar export subsidies.[10] The cotton and sugar agribusiness associations, ABRAPA and UNICA, financed the cases and provided outside legal counsel. When Brazil won both cases in 2005 (WTO 2005a; WTO 2005b), their impact was profound.[11] They marked the first time that a developing country had successfully challenged developed country agricultural subsidies. As a result, the EU was forced to reform its sugar support programs to eliminate the offending export subsidies. The US eliminated its most egregious cotton subsidies and was required to pay Brazilian farmers $147 million per year until it fully reformed its cotton subsidy programs; failing to do so, Brazil was granted the right to impose more than $800 million in retaliatory trade sanctions against US goods, pharmaceuticals, and software. The dispute was finally ended in 2014 with an agreement that required the US to pay Brazil

$300 million in compensation, as well as to substantially modify its system of export credit guarantees (which were identified as a prohibited export subsidy), in addition to reforms to its cotton subsidies legislated in the Farm Bill (which sets US agriculture policy for the next decade) passed that year (*Bridges Weekly* 2014a). Moreover, Brazil's victories were of broader significance beyond the specific commodities they addressed, as they revealed major inconsistencies between US and EU agriculture policies and WTO rules. As one US congressional report stated, "A review of current US farm programs measured against these criteria suggests that all major US program crops are potentially vulnerable to WTO challenges" (Congressional Research Service 2006). Brazil's success in the disputes demonstrated the vulnerability of developed country farm programs and raised the prospect that they could be subject to a wave of WTO dispute settlement challenges.

The cases thus had significant material implications, and they also had important symbolic effects. The disputes gave Brazil significant ammunition for fighting US and EU subsidies in the Doha Round negotiations (Conti 2011: 92). Brazil was able to use the disputes to construct a David-and-Goliath-like image of itself as a hero of the developing world taking on the traditional powers. Despite Brazil's major agroindustrial interests in cotton, for example, the issue came to be framed as a struggle of poor, developing country cotton farmers against the US. NGO campaigns, led by Oxfam and the IDEAS Centre, helped to link the Brazil cotton case with the plight of poor West African cotton farmers—with Benin and Chad joining the case as third parties—and rally public support against US subsidies.[12] Brazil actively cultivated this association, seeking to convince African countries to join the case and attaching a statement from Oxfam regarding the impact of subsidies on West African cotton producers to its own legal submission. Media accounts heralded the cotton case as opening the door to "an unprecedented assault by some of the world's poorest countries on the agricultural policies of its richest"(Wallis and Williams 2002). The cases came to be widely seen as a "litmus test" of whether the WTO and the international trading system could "work for the poor" (Milligan 2004), and Brazil's victories were portrayed as "a triumph for developing countries" (*Bridges Weekly* 2004). As one Brazilian official indicated, "The disputes were symbolically very important in strengthening our position. They served as very friendly propaganda."[13] The cotton and sugar cases had a major impact in shaping NGO, media, and public opinion on agriculture subsidies, and they also served to unite the developing world behind Brazil, helping it to gain political leadership of the developing countries and create the G20-T.

Doha Round Negotiations and the G20-T

In addition to dispute settlement, Brazil's second vehicle for advancing the interests of its agribusiness sector has been the G20-T. While India and China were important members of the coalition, Brazil was the driving force behind the G20-T: it created and coordinated the group, provided its strategy and communications, organized and ran its meetings, and produced the majority of its research and technical analysis and its negotiating proposals. In the words of several negotiators—both members of the G20-T and countries across the negotiating table—Brazil did the "heavy lifting" for the group.[14] In turn, its agribusiness sector played a powerful and influential role behind Brazil's negotiating team and strategy in Geneva.

Determined to make significant gains in the Doha Round, in early 2003 Brazil's major agribusiness associations invested in creating a specialized trade policy institute, the Institute for International Trade Negotiations (ICONE), dedicated to producing sophisticated technical work to support the Brazilian government in the negotiations.[15] In the words of one representative, "It was like industry contracted out their trade policy work to ICONE, who were the experts and worked on their behalf."[16] Brazilian negotiators evaluate their work as "at the level of the best research in the world."[17] But ICONE is forthright about its orientation: as one representative stated plainly, "We work for agribusiness; we are free traders."[18] ICONE came to have a central role in formulating Brazil's negotiating position in the Doha Round.

Despite efforts to increase its own capacity, the Brazilian government was unable to do much of the highly technical work needed for the Doha negotiations on its own and instead relied significantly on agribusiness, through ICONE.[19] Immediately after the founding of ICONE, the government created an informal technical working group to support the work of its negotiators in Geneva.[20] Although the group included all relevant government ministries and stakeholders, participants report that the real players were the Ministry of Foreign Affairs (Itamaraty), the Ministry of Agriculture, and ICONE.[21] Concerned about the appearance of working so closely with agribusiness, Itamaraty intentionally kept the working group "off the books," in the words of one negotiator, such that it was never given an official name, had no official role in decision-making, and produced no official documents.[22] But it was in this group that Brazil's negotiating position, and ultimately most of the negotiating proposals put forward by the G20-T, originated.

The informal working group began meeting in the months prior to Cancun. It started by conducting an extensive analysis of the US-EU agriculture proposal and preparing a response and counterproposal. This work was taken directly from Brasilia to Geneva, where it became the basis for the G20-T proposal at Cancun and remains the core of its platform. The same process continued as the negotiations moved forward. The informal group functioned as a technical working group at the officials level, with participants engaged in marking up and drafting proposals together. During some periods, it would meet as frequently as every week, working for days at a time. ICONE played a central role: it generated the majority of the technical work, providing technical studies of domestic and export subsidies, tariffs and nontariff barriers, and other issues in the negotiations; running econometric analyses of the impact of different tariff and subsidy reduction proposals; and generating proposals that were given to Brazilian negotiators and from there to the G20-T. Between 2003 and 2007, ICONE prepared sixty-two confidential technical papers and simulations for the Brazilian government (ICONE 2007a). ICONE's analyses were instrumental for the development of Brazil's, and consequently the G20-T's, negotiating positions.[23] Detailed negotiating proposals based on the work of ICONE would be formulated in the internal working group; Brazil would then take them to the G20-T membership, where they would be modified slightly, and subsequently presented at the WTO as the official G20-T position. ICONE also had an active presence in Geneva: it attended G20-T meetings and strategy sessions (notably, the only nonstate actor to do so) and accompanied the Brazilian negotiating team to formal meetings and negotiating sessions at the WTO.[24]

As the key source of technical inputs for the G20-T, ICONE was an instrumental force in the group. As one Brazilian negotiator stated, "To explain the G20-T you have to talk about ICONE."[25] A participant at Cancun explained:

Cancun was the first time Brazil came to the table with strong technical support; they had ICONE—they were the guys with the numbers—so it was very private sector driven. It showed Brazil had the numbers, the capacity of putting together a proposal that was technically sound, solid. That was the driving force for the G20-T—it was a technically-driven, market-driven initiative.[26]

Brazil's technical capacity—its ability to produce complex, technically sophisticated proposals and counterproposals, with compelling rationales—provided a significant draw for other developing countries. The lack of technical capacity has historically contributed to the disadvantaged position of developing countries at the WTO, and the need for technical knowledge and expertise is particularly acute in the agriculture negotiations, which are highly complicated.

Under the leadership of Brazil, and backed by ICONE, the G20-T provided the technical expertise critical for countries to engage in WTO negotiations and respond effectively to dominant countries like the US and EU. As one negotiator explained:

For the first time, a developing country group proved to be technically effective. We weren't just saying "no" but "no, and this is how we think it should be done" and we were producing technically sophisticated proposals with a solid rationale. Now, when the US, Japan, or whoever comes to the table with sheets of paper saying "we need something", we can prove their arguments are bogus—that they're hiding aspects of their policies or ours—and put it on the table. For example, in one meeting on market access, we had computers going and could immediately check the consequences of their proposals—we had tables, databases we could run instantly. We knew right away it would have the effect of shielding x and y and z and wouldn't work for us.[27]

This technical capacity was critical to the G20-T's success. As another negotiator stated, "How to explain the success of the G20-T? It was the technical capacity of Brazil—that technical capacity was the miracle making it possible for us to make proposals and convince people."[28] The G20-T's technical capacity—including the majority of its analysis and proposals—originated overwhelmingly from Brazil, and specifically from its agribusiness sector through ICONE.[29]

Brazil's—and hence ICONE's—technical dominance, relative to other members of group, gave it significant influence. A participant described the dynamic in the G20-T meetings as follows:

In agriculture, Brazil had way more technical work than anyone else, so it was easy to present a position and have other countries accept it. Many other countries had no idea of what the impact would be. Sometimes the meetings were like a class on how subsidies work, how each country should calculate its position, what the impact of subsidy reduction would be. And agriculture is very technical, so it was easy to be influenced by countries that were more technically prepared.[30]

This technical expertise was a key reason that other developing countries were willing to get behind Brazil, but it also gave Brazil—and its agribusiness sector—considerable sway over the orientation and agenda of the group.

Brazil's leadership of the G20-T has been based on its technical capacity and the political effectiveness of its negotiators in steering the coalition, as well as its ability to advance a powerful narrative to support its agenda. Brazil's willingness to challenge the US and EU and its success in securing a number of important victories for developing countries—not only in the cotton and sugar cases, but also in the fight to ensure that WTO intellectual property rules (the TRIPs Agreement) did not impede access to essential medicines (such as HIV/AIDS drugs) in developing countries—lent it credibility as a leader of the developing world and helped it to gain broad support. Brazil also actively made use of President Lula's image as an advocate for the poor to build support for its leadership: Foreign Minister Celso Amorim's statement at the Cancun Ministerial, for example, referenced Lula's commitment to "social justice" and "the plight of the poor," before stating that "none of the other issues in these negotiations remotely compares to the impact that the reform of agriculture can have on the alleviation of poverty and the promotion of development" (WTO 2003b). Brazil portrayed the G20-T as "the voice of developing countries" and its agenda of reducing subsidies as a central part of the shared struggle of poor countries for development (Amorim 2003). Discourses of developing country solidarity and North-South struggle served as a potent integrating frame for the G20-T, and its ability to mobilize a discourse of development—along with an agenda of subsidy reduction that accorded with the dominant free trade principles of the WTO—added considerable power to the G20-T and Brazil's leadership.

Framing Developing Country Concerns in the Doha Round

Rich country agriculture subsidies served as the central unifying demand of the G20-T, and developing countries more broadly, at the WTO.[31] Today, many view this as a natural issue for developing countries to ally themselves around, based on the argument that subsidies depress global prices and undermine the competitiveness and livelihoods of poor farmers. But a closer analysis shows that this is largely a product of how successful Brazil and ICONE—through the G20-T—have been in framing the issue. The present conception of agriculture subsidies as a development issue—and indeed, the pre-eminent development issue in the Doha Round—was not pre-given, but constructed by the G20-T, in the sense that it drove the understanding of the issue that has now become dominant.[32] The current framing of the agricultural subsidies issue has become so deeply embedded—taken for granted and effectively naturalized—that it is easy to forget that it is actually relatively recent. In fact, at the start of round, agriculture subsidies were seen very differently—primarily as a fight between the US and the EU, with the US and other agricultural exporters on the offensive in pressing the EU to reduce its subsidies (see, for example, *Financial Times* 1999). Typical accounts of the agriculture subsidies issue at the time made no mention of "development" or developing countries (for example, WTO 2001), and many assessments of developing country interests at the WTO did not even mention subsidies (instead emphasizing only tariffs and market access) (for example, World Bank 1998).

Over the course of the Doha Round, the framing of the issue changed completely, as Brazil and the G20-T re-constructed agricultural subsidies as a critical development and global poverty issue, in which developing countries were pitted in a struggle against rich countries like the US and EU. Agriculture subsidies became a cause célèbre, generating widespread public and media attention, even from quarters that typically paid little attention to the WTO, as they came to be portrayed as a significant cause of global poverty and among the most important and most pressing concerns of the developing world. The demand was not to fundamentally alter the principles of the multilateral trading system but to make them "fairer" to developing countries by disciplining agriculture subsidies in order to create "a level playing field" on which all countries could compete "equally" (G20 2003). In the process, the G20-T helped to make agriculture the central focus of the Doha Round—as one Brazilian negotiator stated, "This round is an agriculture round."[33] The agricultural subsidies issue became a key justification and source of momentum for the entire round, with claims that WTO-mandated trade liberalization is vital to international development and that developing countries will be hurt the most if the Doha Round is not concluded.

In presenting agricultural subsidies as a development issue, Brazil and the G20-T were aided by other actors, with major international NGOs playing a prominent role. Many civil society actors had initially opposed the launch of the Doha Round, but their efforts had failed. Once the round was underway, many NGOs made a pragmatic decision to shift their strategy to trying to find ways to advance the interests of developing countries within the negotiations and help them secure the best possible deal (Hopewell 2015b). NGOs were constrained by the fact that the general framework for the negotiations—the issues and areas that were being negotiated—had already been laid out. Furthermore, many had tried advocating on issues that presented a more radical challenge to the international trading system, such as those that would restrict market liberalization, but had found there was no appetite for this sort of change at the WTO and that it was not within their reach. As a result, many NGOs decided that they needed "to focus on where change is likely to happen."[34] The subsidies issue was particularly attractive because it appealed to the proliberalization narrative of the WTO—an expedient alignment that one NGO representative acknowledged "helps to push the issue up on the agenda."[35] NGOs also saw the issue as a means to draw attention to the unfairness built into the existing rules of the international trading system and the disadvantaged position of developing countries—in the words of Oxfam (2002), the "rigged rules and double standards" of the international trading system. In addition, many NGOs had bought into the prevailing economic orthodoxy that exports are a tool for developing countries to achieve economic growth and reduce poverty and, therefore, that helping poor countries gain greater access to global markets by removing market distortions would aid development and poverty reduction (see, for example, Oxfam 2002). As a result, they genuinely believed that reducing rich country agricultural subsidies was a way in which the Doha Round could benefit developing countries. Oxfam was only among the most prominent of many NGOs—including the Institute for Agriculture and Trade Policy (IATP), CUTS International, IDEAS Centre, International Center for Trade and Sustainable Development (ICTSD), Action Aid, Quaker United Nations Organization (QUNO), Agency for Co-operation and Research in Development (ACORD), and Third World Network—to adopt the issue of agricultural subsidies and market access as a central aspect of their advocacy campaigns at the WTO.

Aware of their influence in shaping public and media opinion on the issue, Brazil actively cultivated relationships with international NGOs, particularly those based in the US and EU (such as Oxfam and IATP), which helped to increase the pressure on those states. Brazilian negotiators met frequently with NGOs in Geneva, giving them "a free pass" to the Brazilian mission and sharing strategy, analysis, talking points, and messaging.[36] Lacking technical capacity themselves, NGOs relied on Brazil for assistance with their economic analyses (and those of the West African cotton-producing countries they were supporting).[37] Brazilian negotiators believe that these relationships paid off, with one stating: "The way we handled international public opinion was responsible for a lot of the success of our strategy and NGOs were quite an important weapon in the public opinion battle."[38]

Beyond NGOs, Brazil and the G20-T were also indirectly aided by a number of other actors. Although officially neutral in the Doha negotiations, the WTO Secretariat was eager for justifications for both the organization's mandate and the Doha Round, and actively sought to foster the association of subsidy reduction with development, particularly through the speeches and public remarks of the director-general (see, for example, WTO 2007). The World Bank jumped on agriculture subsidies as an "urgent" development issue, with claims that "subsidies are crippling Africa's chance to export its way out of poverty" (World Bank 2002). Free market think tanks and antitax lobby groups in the US, such as the American Enterprise Institute and the Cato Institute, which oppose the tax burden and market distortions created by subsidies, adopted development as a further argument against subsidies (American Enterprise Institute 2005). The issue thus brought together an unusual mix of allies in opposition to agricultural subsidies (Margulis 2010), described by Brazil's foreign minister as "a virtuous alliance among those who support free trade and economic development throughout the globe"(Amorim 2003).

The G20-T was portrayed as projecting the interests of the Global South into the international arena: according to Brazil's ambassador, "Developing countries expressing their interests as one."[39] Yet there is reason to question this purported concurrence of interests and how well the G20-T truly represents the interests of developing countries. For Brazil—the driving force behind the G20-T—the group has been useful, in the words of one of its negotiators,

because it provides credibility, and in trade negotiations to some extent you have to disguise the fact that you're a greedy bastard. So you put lofty ideas in your presentation, you show a willingness to partner in coalitions and disguise that you're going for the kill. Pardon my language, my frankness, but I think people tend to hide these things too much.[40]

With the G20-T, the subsidies issue was tied to the "lofty ideas" of development, developing country solidarity and empowerment, and righting imbalances at the WTO. However, these notions also served to disguise whose commercial interests were truly at play.

Reducing rich country agriculture subsidies came to be framed as a shared interest of developing countries, with even President Lula (cited in Cason and Power 2009), for example, claiming that it would "bring better living conditions to billions of farmers around the world." But the reality is far more complicated. Only a small proportion of developing countries are globally competitive with the export capacity to benefit from liberalization in agricultural markets and subsidy reduction. In contrast to Brazil's large-scale and highly competitive industrialized agricultural sector, the vast majority of developing countries have weak agricultural sectors consisting primarily of vulnerable peasant farmers. Gains from the Doha Round are thus expected to go to only a few countries, with Brazil being one of the biggest beneficiaries, while for most developing countries, the costs associated with the round could well outweigh any potential gains (Polaski 2006). Most poor countries are net importers of food that is heavily subsidized by rich countries, meaning that these subsidies effectively function as an income transfer from tax payers in the Global North to consumers in the Global South (McMillan, Zwane, and Ashraf 2006; Valdes and McCalla 1999). For these countries, the net effect of reducing rich country agricultural subsidies may, in fact, be harmful: to the extent that it achieves its intended objective of raising global agricultural prices, it would actually increase their cost of food (Bhagwati 2005; Birdsall, Rodrik, and Subramanian 2005; Panagariya 2005; Polaski 2006; World Bank 2008). Many of these countries are facing high rates of poverty and already struggling to feed their populations in the face of elevated food prices and growing global food insecurity (Margulis 2013). The unqualified assertion that removing subsidies in rich countries will bring net gains to developing countries as a whole is therefore highly questionable (FAO 2008). At the very least, the ultimate implications for developing countries and the poor are complex and uncertain.

Another element of complexity that has been lost in the current framing of the subsidies debate, which has tended toward a broad condemnation of subsidies, is that many developing countries are themselves subsidizers, and this constitutes a key part of their development and food security policies. Although the level of support to producers in the developing world is relatively low compared with that provided by the US, EU, and other developed countries, many developing countries do make use of subsidies, and support is often concentrated in certain commodities. In China, for instance, such subsidies have been increasing as the country grows richer and seeks to redistribute some of those gains and improve rural households' income (OECD 2009); producer subsidies now constitute approximately 15 percent of gross farm receipts.[41] To focus on the example of cotton, although US subsidies have drawn nearly all of the attention, several developing countries also provide significant direct assistance to their cotton producers and many others apply import tariffs (World Bank 2008). In China, direct subsidies to farmers constitute more than 40 percent of their income from growing cotton; even in Brazil, cotton subsidies constitute between 20 and 30 percent of gross farm receipts (OECD 2009). Subsidies, along with other interventionist policy tools such as price supports, state trading enterprises, and tariffs, are increasingly seen as important for developing countries to improve food security and rural incomes, particularly in light of the recent global food crisis (Margulis 2014). However, this nuance is lost in the sweeping condemnation of subsidies.[42]

Despite the intense focus on agricultural subsidies, there are alternative policies that could be of greater importance to the interests of many developing countries, and especially their most vulnerable agricultural producers and consumers. These include, for example, policies to address high levels of market concentration by a small number of massive global trading companies, as well as price volatility generated by commodity speculation, commodity agreements to improve prices for developing country producers, and trade rules to allow governments to create food reserves and engage in supply management (both to boost prices for producers and prevent food crises). Such ideas have occasionally been floated—by states, NGOs, and other actors—in the milieu of the WTO but received less favorable attention than the agricultural subsidies issue. For Brazil and its agribusiness sector, which have been so influential in driving the developing country agenda at the WTO, such policies have no appeal, as they would mark a move away from opening markets. As one Brazilian negotiator explained: "No, we don't like them. The most competitive country is the one who would be paying for that—we'd be paying for others to acquire their capacity. Our argument is just open markets." Given the roots of its policy in agribusiness, Brazil has a vested interest in pushing the negotiations in a specific direction: toward the liberalization necessary to benefit its exporters.

The G20-T and the cotton and sugar cases helped to project the interests of Brazilian agribusiness—and a handful of other competitive agricultural exporters—as the interests of the Global South. Over the course of the Doha Round, its "development" dimension has been progressively boiled down to a focus almost exclusively on agricultural liberalization (Wilkinson 2007). The influence of Brazil and its agribusiness sector is critical to explaining why agriculture has become such a central part of the round. It has also significantly shaped the direction that developing country "activism" has taken in the current round, with a narrow focus on liberalizing agriculture markets through the removal of subsidies, rather than advocating policies that would mark a more radical departure from the WTO's traditional neoliberal trade paradigm.

Conclusion

The influence of Brazil and its agribusiness sector in the G20-T, which has played such a pivotal role in driving contemporary power shifts within the WTO, is a key part of explaining why these power shifts have not resulted in a more fundamental challenge to the dominant neoliberal trade paradigm. Brazil's emergence as a global agribusiness powerhouse reoriented its international trade policy from inward-looking to focused on exports as a key source of economic growth and development. In the process, Brazil has become a new champion of liberalization, seeking to use the WTO's dispute settlement system and negotiations to pry open and expand markets for its exports, and especially demanding market liberalizing reforms from the US and other advanced-industrialized states.

In seeking to advance its agenda, Brazil has wrapped its self-interested motives in an altruistic guise of Third World solidarity and struggle and gained considerable support by portraying its particularistic interests as the universal, shared interests of the Global South. Brazil's Third Worldist discourse has served to mask and advance the narrow commercial interests of its agribusiness sector. But far from representing a challenge or alternative to the liberal international economic order, Brazil's agenda is entirely in keeping with the neoliberal orthodoxy of WTO; Brazil has embraced the rules, norms, and principles of the multilateral trading system as a means to advance its significant export interests. Moreover, its ability to simultaneously mobilize these two previously opposing discourses—a discourse of Third World struggle, alongside a protrade discourse that resonates with the dominant norms of the WTO—has added considerable ideological force to Brazil's position.

This analysis sheds light on why the ascension of developing countries into the elite inner circle of power at the WTO has not resulted in a direct challenge to its neoliberal agenda. The case of Brazil illustrates how the emergence of a highly competitive export-oriented agribusiness sector prompted the expansion and internationalization of domestic capital, creating an independent, private sector lobby with considerable influence on the state. Driven by the rise of the agribusiness sector, the state and capital allied together to aggressively pursue the expansion of markets for Brazilian exports through dispute settlement and negotiations at the WTO. Similar dynamics have been at work in the other emerging powers. Because of the nature of their integration into the world economy, Brazil, India, and China all have significant interests in liberalizing trade. Each has experienced the emergence of a highly competitive export sector directed toward global markets—Brazil in agriculture, India in services, and China in manufacturing—that has fueled their economic growth and an outward reorientation of their economies. The following chapters turn to examining China and India in more detail.

Chapter 6

China: A Delicate Dance

T<small>HIS</small> chapter shifts the focus to China and the agenda it has pursued at the WTO, in order to illustrate the constraints on the new powers. Recognizing the nature of the constraints operating on the emerging powers is essential, I contend, for properly understanding and interpreting their behavior at the WTO. The chapter begins by analyzing China's remarkable economic transformation and its process of accession to the WTO. As I show, China is highly dependent on exports of manufactured goods and, therefore, like Brazil, it is heavily invested in the WTO's project of reducing barriers to trade and expanding global markets. Far from being opposed to the WTO's project of market liberalization, China endured major costs to join the WTO and gain access to its tools and protections and the opportunity to advance its trade interests through future trade rounds; it also strategically used the WTO to further its own project of domestic economic reform. Furthermore, although its exports have grown remarkably, China continues to face significant trade barriers around the world. The WTO and its dispute settlement system provide an important means for China to challenge barriers to its exports, when they are imposed in violation of multilateral trade rules, and may work to pre-empt or discourage other states from taking protectionist actions against it in the first place. And as the third largest contributor after the US and Europe, China now pays a substantial part of the WTO budget.[1]

China thus has a keen interest in using the Doha Round negotiations to reduce trade barriers and improve its access to foreign markets as a means to facilitate the continued growth of its exports. Yet China has been less aggressive than many expected in pursuing its offensive trade interests in the Doha Round. This behavior, I argue, is a reflection of the delicate dance of the emerging powers, as they attempt to manage, without disrupting, their continued economic and political rise. China's position in the Doha negotiations is constrained by the risk of provoking a backlash that could jeopardize its export opportunities and economic growth. Acutely aware of the sensitivities attached to its position as the world's leading exporter and second largest market, China simultaneously occupies a position of strength and vulnerability in the multilateral trading system and has tailored its behavior at the WTO accordingly. In addition, China and the other emerging powers also face constraints stemming from the need to maintain their alliances with other developing countries.

China's Economic Transformation

In the last three decades, China's economy has been profoundly transformed by a program of economic reform and liberalization. Following the success of its communist revolution in 1949, China's foreign economic policy became semiautarkic (Reardon 2002): China delinked from the capitalist global economy and the state intentionally chose to limit its foreign economic exchange. Trade was highly restricted, except for small amounts of food aid and the export of raw materials to provide necessary foreign exchange (Jiang 2012). Modeled after Soviet-style industrialization, China adopted an extreme version of the import-substitution strategies employed by many developing countries at that time (Lardy 1993). Imports were limited primarily to industrial machinery from the Soviet Union needed to enable industrialization. By the late 1970s, however, a number of factors created pressures for reform, including the deterioration of its relationship with the Soviet Union; the disastrous state of the national economy following years of poor economic management and the turmoil of the Cultural Revolution; and the fact that China was falling far behind its smaller neighbors—the newly industrialized countries, such as South Korea, Taiwan, Hong Kong, and Singapore—whose economies were taking off as a result of their export-oriented development strategies (Feng 2006; Jiang 2012).

In 1978, Deng Xiaoping introduced China's "reform and opening up" plan, initiating what became a massive reorientation of economic policy. The reforms involved introducing market mechanisms and competition into the domestic economy in order to improve efficiency in the allocation of resources, while slowly opening up to the outside world ("open-door policy") to gain access to foreign investment and technology. The initial goals and scope of reforms were fairly modest: in the realm of external economic policy, Deng sought to modernize the Chinese economy through the import of foreign capital and technology, which required foreign exchange, something China could generate through export-processing, benefiting from its comparative advantage in low-wage labor. China's economic liberalization built steadily over subsequent decades and came to encompass wide-ranging reforms, including dissolving the commune system; allowing Township and Village Enterprises (TVEs) to engage in market-oriented production; creating Special Economic Zones (SEZs) offering preferential policies to attract foreign investment and process goods for export; lifting price controls; increasing space for the operation of private firms; privatizing state-owned enterprises; opening to and encouraging foreign investment (while closely regulating the entry of foreign firms to channel investment toward national development objectives, by fostering joint ventures with Chinese firms and the transfer of technology); and encouraging foreign trade by reducing tariffs and other trade barriers (especially in the lead-up to its WTO accession). By the mid-1980s, export promotion had largely replaced import substitution as the driver of China's trade and foreign economic policy (Jiang 2012).

Liberalization and export promotion produced a rapid expansion of China's exports. In a remarkably short period of time, China has become the "workshop of the world"—a hub for the production and export of manufactured goods. While its exports were initially concentrated in cheap manufactured goods (such as apparel and footwear), China has steadily moved up the value chain to more sophisticated and higher value-added manufactured products (such as electronics, machinery, and equipment) (Amiti and Freund 2007). Its production and export profile is increasingly shifting toward the high-tech sector, presaging direct competition with core industries in advanced-industrialized states like the US and EU (Bussiere and Mehl 2008). And its export growth has only accelerated since gaining WTO membership in 2001, following a lengthy process of negotiating the terms of its accession. As Berger and Martin (2011) detail, between 2000 and 2007, the value of Chinese exports more than quadrupled and rose from 20 percent to 35 percent of GDP. In 2000, China's exports, measured in dollars, were a third of those of the United States and around half of those of Japan and Germany. By 2009, China had become the largest exporter in the world.

China's manufacturing exports have been the engine of its astonishing economic growth, at rates averaging close to 10 percent for nearly thirty years. In some years, exports and investment associated with building capacity for exports have accounted for more than 60 percent of China's economic growth (compared, for example, with 15 percent in the G7) (Guo and N'Diaye 2009).

Exports have transformed China from a poor and largely peasant-based agrarian economy into an industrial powerhouse. In 2010 it surpassed Japan as the second largest economy in the world, behind only the US, at market exchange rates; and in 2014, it surpassed the US as the world's largest economy when measured in terms of purchasing power parity (PPP).[2] China has amassed the world's largest foreign exchange reserve, in excess of US$4 trillion, and become a major creditor to the rest of the world and especially the US (with China the largest holder of US debt). It is now producing its own globally competitive multinational corporations, which are engaged in investments and acquisitions around the world, and is thus a major exporter of capital and FDI. Indeed, China has become a critical motor of the entire global economy. In the 2000s, its seemingly insatiable demand for inputs to feed its factories and burgeoning infrastructure made it the world's largest importer of many natural resources (including oil, coal, iron ore, and soy) and set off a commodity price boom that fueled economic growth for resource-exporting countries across the developing world, from Africa to Latin America, and in developed countries like Canada and Australia. Since the 2008 global financial crisis, China—one of the few countries to avoid a major economic slowdown—has accounted for more than 35 percent of all global economic growth (Guerrero 2014). Domestically, the social effects of China's economic transformation have been profound: fueled by export-led growth, per capita incomes have tripled and poverty rates have declined from 85 percent to 27 percent, lifting over half a billion people out of poverty (World Bank 2009).

Crucially, however, China's "economic miracle" is not simply a neoliberal story of markets flourishing once unleashed from the fetters of the state. On the contrary, unlike the "shock therapy" pursued in Russia, China's transition from a centrally planned, socialist economy to capitalism involved a gradualist program of economic opening and reform that reserved a major role for the state in steering economic growth and development (Whyte 2009). In addition, China's prereform socialist economic policies provided the foundation for its economic takeoff in the 1980s, by providing an industrial infrastructure, high levels of social capital based on universal health care and primary education, and widespread access to land that provided a safety net for much of its population during transition (Guerrero 2014).

China's success in generating economic growth and increased standards of living are without historical precedent. Yet China continues to face significant economic challenges. First and foremost, China's per capita income lags far behind developed countries (US$6,807 in real terms, compared, for example, with US$53,143 in the United States), and China ranks only 91 (of 187 countries) on the UN Human Development Index.[3] Poverty remains a problem on an enormous scale: more than 350 million people continue to live in poverty (27 percent of the population) and over 150 million in extreme poverty (12 percent).[4] China houses 13 percent of the world's poor, making it, after India, the country with the second largest number of poor people (World Bank 2013). Poverty is particularly acute in rural areas, fueling massive rural to urban migration. Prior to reforms, China had very low levels of income inequality, with a GINI of 0.277 in the early 1980s, making it one of the most equal countries in the world; by 2006, however, China's GINI had risen to 0.496, surpassing the level of inequality in the US (Andreas 2008).[5] Continued poverty in the face of rising inequality, particularly between rural and urban areas, has raised the potential for social unrest, a prime concern for the Communist Party intent on maintaining its grip on power.

Moreover, China's economic future is far from certain. Global demand for China's goods was substantially disrupted by the 2008 global financial crisis and ensuing recession. The Chinese yuan has appreciated by roughly 35 percent against the dollar since 2005, undermining the competitiveness of China's exports (*Economist* 2013). There are concerns about a growing real estate asset bubble and the accumulation of nonperforming loans in its banking system, which could substantially disrupt the domestic economy (Lardy 2012). China faces a host of other development challenges, including limited agricultural land and water resources to meet the needs of its massive population and fuel its continuing growth; growing environmental problems such as heavily polluted air and water; and extensive corruption (Guerrero 2014). The state is centrally preoccupied with maintaining political stability and the control of the Communist Party. Yet there are signs of brewing popular discontent with increasing protests over issues such as wages and working conditions for workers in factories; health and environmental issues and food safety; and human rights and democracy in Hong Kong (Ngai, Chi Chan, and Chan 2009).

In order to continue to reduce poverty, as well as to face the dual challenge of absorbing an ever-growing mass of migrant workers from rural areas and urban unemployment stemming from the restructuring of state-owned enterprises, the consensus among policy-makers is that China must grow at rates of at least 7–8 percent per year (Li 2009). Although the Chinese state has made efforts to reduce its dependence on foreign markets by engineering a transition to a less-trade dependent and more inwardly oriented economy, such efforts have been hampered in part by persistently low rates of domestic consumption resulting from extremely high savings rates (an outgrowth of China's underdeveloped pension and health care systems, both of which lead individuals to self-insure through savings) (Guo and N'Diaye 2009; Lardy 2012). It has proven extremely difficult to reorient the economy toward domestic consumption rather than exports; despite efforts to stimulate domestic demand in the wake of the global financial crisis, China's economic growth remains heavily dependent on exports. China therefore faces considerable pressure to sustain and expand its exports. This is further compounded by concerns that it may "grow old before it grows rich" (Goldman Sachs 2006)—that looming demographic changes (a rapidly aging population combined with the effects of the one-child policy) may impede its future growth prospects, putting additional pressure on China to ensure rapid growth in the near term. There are also concerns that China may become stuck in a "middle-income trap," or at the very least that high rates of growth are becoming considerably more difficult to achieve as the country becomes wealthier and more developed (Babones 2011).

Given the nature of China's political system, the relationship between the state and private sector differs from that of Brazil, described in the last chapter. In contrast to Brazil and India, both democracies, China is a strong authoritarian state in which state-business relations remain closely intertwined, with the arms of the state extending deeply into the private sector. The boundaries between the state and domestic capital are far less well defined in China, and there appears to be little sign of an independent business lobby emerging to exert influence on the state in the realm of trade policy, as in Brazil and India.[6] Yet, even if private sector actors are not actively driving trade policy, exports have been an equally important, if not more important, source of growth and dynamism for the Chinese economy; therefore, maintaining and expanding access to foreign export markets are powerful motivations for the Chinese state, just as they are for Brazil and India.

Subramanian and Kessler (2013) describe China, now the world's largest exporter and importer of manufactured goods, as a "mega-trader." As Mattoo and Subramanian (2012: 1744) point out: "China's openness, measured in terms of trade outcomes, is far greater than anything achieved by the US in the post-war period and resembles the levels of openness achieved by Britain at the height of empire." The ratio of trade to GDP for the US rarely exceeded 15 percent during Pax Americana (Mattoo and Subramanian (2012: 1744). In contrast, China's trade to GDP ratio reached an astonishing 71 percent at its highest point in 2006, and post-2008 it still rests at above 50 percent.[7] The Chinese economy is thus extraordinarily dependent on trade. This makes the country's economic rise precarious, because it is based on exports to foreign markets and therefore vulnerable to external disruption.

China's Accession to the WTO

Brazil, India, and China were each among the original twenty-three signatories to the GATT in 1948. Yet while Brazil and India continued to be active—though frequently overpowered—members of the institution in the ensuing decades, China effectively dropped out following its revolution in 1949. China is thus a comparatively recent participant in the multilateral trade regime, having joined the WTO only in 2001, after more than fifteen years of contentious negotiations over the terms of its accession.

The US had both economic and strategic motivations for supporting China's accession to the WTO. First, the US was concerned about its large and steadily growing trade deficit with China and viewed the accession negotiation as a golden opportunity to redress this. By the 1990s it was already becoming clear that China represented a huge market access opportunity, and American policy-makers believed that by using China's WTO accession to force a reduction in its tariffs and other trade barriers, the US would see a dramatic increase in its exports to China (Feng 2006; Mattoo and Subramanian 2012). The US was not alone, as many other advanced-industrialized countries shared the same view and objectives. Second, with the fall of the Soviet Union and China's ongoing market-oriented reforms, the US was eager to push forward its process of liberalization and market opening and bring China into the fold of the capitalist global economy.

For its part, China sought membership in the WTO as a means to gain access to the benefits and protections of its rules and dispute settlement system, which Chinese leaders expected would enable the country to defend its trade interests more effectively and engage in trade diplomacy (Jiang 2012). WTO membership would grant China automatic most-favored nation (MFN) status with its trading partners, as well as enable it to gain access to the progressive global reduction of tariff levels and nontariff barriers to come through future rounds of negotiations, beginning with the Doha Round. This would allow for deeper participation in global production and investment networks, and China expected to gain an expansion of foreign trade and direct investment to help fuel its continued economic growth (Feng 2006). In addition, in the midst of an ongoing elite struggle within the Communist Party, reformers—who were prevalent at the top of the party—sought to use WTO membership and its associated requirements to overcome anti-reform factions (such as the so-called ultra-Leftists and those with economic interests tied to China's declining state-owned enterprises) and other internal obstacles to reform. WTO accession helped to propel and lock in domestic economic reforms, by "allowing reformers to cite international agreements as a way of countering domestic anti-reform political pressures" (Dayaratna-Banda and Whalley 2007), and "made China's opening up policy and export-orientation strategy more irreversible" (Feng 2006: 65).

In order to gain membership in the WTO, China was required to make deep, wide-ranging, and often painful concessions to liberalize its market and reduce its trade barriers. Accession centers on negotiating what concessions a country will be required to undertake in exchange for becoming a WTO member. The process is inherently asymmetrical and stacked against the acceding state. A country seeking to join the WTO is forced to negotiate the terms of its accession multilaterally with the WTO membership as a whole, as well as bilaterally with any individual member who wants concessions from it. While regular negotiations at the WTO take place on the basis of a reciprocal exchange of concessions, during an accession process the concessions are solely unilateral. A country wanting into the club has relatively little bargaining power, allowing existing members to set the "membership fee" very high. This situation enabled American officials, for example, to celebrate the extensive "one-way trade concessions" they were able to extract from China (US 2000). In fact, the commitments new members now make in order to join the WTO are higher than those any existing member has made in *all* successive rounds of GATT/WTO agreements combined. Consequently, China's current obligations under the WTO go far beyond those of any other state. Its accession required major reforms of virtually all aspects of its economic and trade policy, including substantially reducing its barriers in industry, agriculture, and services (Kong 2000; Qin 2007; Scott and Wilkinson 2013). The terms of China's accession generated considerable domestic resentment at the seeming unfairness of the process. It also fueled expectations that China should and would eventually be compensated by significant gains in future trade rounds.

Still, despite this asymmetry, the consequences of China's accession were far from what the US and other advanced-industrialized states intended. In pursuing China's accession, the rich countries were motivated by a desire to boost their exports and improve their trade balances. Instead, however, despite the harsh obligations imposed by the US and others, China's accession to the WTO had an explosive effect on its export growth and accelerated the movement of global manufacturing production to China. As Zeng and Liang (2010) document, US imports from China experienced a threefold expansion from 2001 to 2007, increasing from $103 billion in 2001 to $340 billion in 2007. Meanwhile, the US trade deficit with China ballooned during the same period, growing from $84 billion in 2001 to $274 billion in 2007. Similarly, China's share in the EU's imports nearly doubled (Jenkins and Barbosa 2012).

China's Stance in the Doha Round

China came into the Doha Round expecting to see significant market opening from other states—something it saw as necessary to balance and justify the high costs it incurred during its accession. China has major offensive interests in the Doha Round. As one of the world's largest producers and exporters, China has a keen interest in reducing trade barriers and further opening markets to its exports, particularly in manufactured goods, where it is most competitive. China would also benefit from the strengthening of multilateral trade rules intended to come from this round (such as rules governing the use of antidumping measures and other mechanisms that countries use to block its exports). In fact, many predict that China would be one of the biggest winners from the Doha Round (Polaski 2006). Several negotiators from rival states grudgingly suggested that "the Doha Round is a round for China."[8]

As noted above, because of the terms of its accession, the existing WTO disciplines imposed on China far exceed those of any other member. Given the biting costs of its accession, China entered the Doha Round with little appetite to assume substantial new obligations itself and an expectation that it was now China's turn to reap the benefits of further liberalization by other states. China has a defensive interest in minimizing its new commitments in this round, fearing domestic political fallout from being forced to incur more costs so soon after its accession. Furthermore, as a result of China's accession commitments, it now has relatively low tariff levels compared with many other countries. In addition, the difference between China's bound and applied tariffs is very small. In WTO negotiations, states agree to limits on their maximum tariff rates ("tariff bindings" or "tariff ceilings"); yet a country's actual tariff rates ("applied tariff rates") may be considerably lower than the limits to which it has committed. There are multiple possible reasons for this: when making commitments in previous WTO agreements, a state may have wanted to leave itself room to increase its tariffs, or it may have subsequently engaged in unilateral action to lower its tariff rates, beyond the commitments made in WTO agreements. The difference between a country's bound and applied tariff rates is referred to as "water" or "binding overhang." Since many countries have considerable water in their tariffs, reducing their bound rates at the WTO will not necessarily require cuts to their applied rates. However, for China—whose bound and applied rates are generally very close or identical (that is, little or no water in its tariff structure)—nearly any cut in bound rates would result in real cuts to its applied rates. This means that even a relatively small reduction in tariff bindings occasioned by the Doha Round will have a significant and real impact on China's already low tariffs, and thus its ability to protect its market from foreign competition. In light of the significant liberalization commitments undertaken in its accession, China sought additional flexibilities in the Doha Round for "recently acceded members" (RAMs), such as itself; in the end, it secured longer implementation periods to phase in new tariff reduction commitments.[9] Nevertheless, given the importance of the Chinese market and the fact it has little water in its tariffs, in the words of a rival negotiator: "More than anyone else, China is going to be the biggest contributor to the round."[10]

It is important to appreciate the significance of China's offensive trade interests at the WTO. Despite the impressive growth of its exports to date, China continues to face trade barriers—in both developed and developing country markets—that hamper the growth of its manufacturing exports. Its economic rise to date has been heavily dependent on exports to developed countries, particularly the US and EU, which each accounts for more than 23 percent of its exports.[11] Developed countries as a group receive two-thirds of China's exports. Yet, within these markets China continues to face high tariffs (tariff peaks) for its key export products (such as textiles and clothing and footwear) and extensive nontariff barriers. Furthermore, many of China's main competitors enjoy duty-free access to these markets through preferential trade arrangements targeted at least-developed countries (LDCs), which leaves Chinese exporters at a competitive disadvantage.[12] As the locus of global economic growth shifts to the global south, developing countries—particularly the most rapidly growing large emerging economies—represent increasingly important markets for China. Yet most of these countries have high rates of tariff protection on manufactured goods, with an average tariff rate of 34 percent (Chang 2002).

In addition, both developed and developing countries make extensive use of so-called trade remedies such as antidumping, countervailing duty, and safeguard measures to block Chinese exports. China is by far the most frequent target of such measures: between 1995 and 2013, China was subject to 989 antidumping investigations globally (over three times more than the next most targeted economy, Korea).[13] Of those, nearly 75 percent resulted in the imposition of antidumping tariffs on imports from China.[14] China's exports face the greatest number of contingent protections in foreign markets, and discrimination against China's exporters is increasing (Bown 2010; Bown 2011). In some years, China has accounted for over 40 percent of new antidumping measures imposed in foreign markets.[15] China has become the biggest target, for example, of US antidumping actions, accounting for more than 60 percent of US antidumping investigations in 2008 (Zeng and Liang 2010). The US also imposes higher antidumping duties on products from China than other states: according to the findings of a study by the US Government Accountability Office (2006: 1), between 1980 and 2004 the average duty rate applied against China was approximately 98 percent, more than 60 percentage points higher than the average 37 percent rate applied to other market economy exporters of the same products. Other developing countries are actually the most frequent users of antidumping measures against China,[16] but those imposed by the US and EU have the biggest impact (Li and Whalley 2010). Antidumping, countervailing duty, and safeguard investigations are costly and create substantial insecurity and uncertainty in China's access to foreign markets. The use of trade defense measures against China has resulted in significant losses to its export sector, reducing firm numbers, output, employment, profits, and exports, and even forcing some Chinese firms to close down and exit the market (Li and Whalley 2010).

Moreover, far from being protected by its WTO membership, the use of antidumping and other contingent protections against Chinese exports has accelerated since its accession in 2001 (Bown 2011). This is due, in part, to the fact that

China's WTO accession protocol included provisions that allowed for blatant discrimination against its exports: China was designated a "nonmarket economy," a special category making it easier for other states to apply antidumping measures against its exports and impose higher duties for up to fifteen years after its accession (Zeng and Liang 2010).[17] Entering the Doha Round, China thus had a significant interest in seeking to tighten WTO rules to restrict the use of antidumping measures, as well as to remove its nonmarket economy status and receive equal treatment as other states.

The barriers China faces in foreign markets—both contingent and permanent—represent a violation of the spirit of economic liberalism that animates the WTO and has been eagerly propounded by the US and other rich countries for decades. Moreover, the importance of these barriers should not be underestimated. China is extraordinarily trade dependent, its per capita incomes remain very low, and the domestic political legitimacy of the government rests on its ability to continue to achieve extremely high rates of growth. China's exports are concentrated in many of the most heavily protected sectors of global trade, and many of its exports are in areas where profit margins and competition are extremely tight—reducing tariffs via the WTO could thus make a big difference to China's relative competitiveness. These barriers are starting to matter more than ever. China has faced rising labor costs (resulting from a combination of labor supply tightening and increasing labor activism), increased transportation costs, and international pressure to appreciate its currency—all of which undermine its competitive advantage, especially in labor-intensive, low-wage production. With China's massive population, maintaining labor-intensive industries capable of supplying large numbers of jobs—such as textiles and clothing—is essential. But, because of rising costs, China is already seeing (1) the movement of production to lower wage countries (such as Vietnam, Sri Lanka, Bangladesh, Cambodia, and Pakistan; Vietnam's textile and clothing exports to the US, for example, have increased 38 percent since 2010) (Reuters 2014; Textile Outlook 2014); and (2) the movement of some manufacturing activities back to the US (*Wall Street Journal* 2013). In textiles and clothing, for example, China's share of the US and EU markets—the world's biggest—is already declining (Reuters 2014; Textile Outlook 2014). In such a cost-sensitive sector, tariff rates have a significant impact. The vast majority of China's exports are covered by the "most-favored nation" (MNF) tariff rates stipulated under WTO rules, which means that they are subject to high MFN tariffs imposed on textiles and clothing in core markets such as the United States and the EU (Hayashi 2007). These tariffs add as much as one-third to the price of Chinese goods. In contrast, many of its closest competitors enjoy preferential duty-free access for textiles and clothing in these markets, yielding them a considerable advantage (Hayashi 2007; ICTSD 2009). As Mattoo and Subramanian (2012: 1737) write: "[W]ith some exaggeration one might say that the MFN tariff of countries is really a China tariff, or the China tariff is really the 'least-favored-nation' tariff." Thus, reducing MFN rates via the Doha Round is of substantial consequence to China.

Given its high degree of dependence on exports and the considerable trade barriers China continues to face, it has substantial interests in ensuring the security of its access to foreign markets, reducing the discrimination faced by its exports, and improving its market access. One would expect that China would, therefore, be aggressive in seeking to use the WTO to reduce the barriers it faces around the world in order to maximize the continued growth of its exports. Yet this has not been the case. Instead, China has been far less proactive in the Doha Round than Brazil or India and has, in fact, held back from aggressively pushing for market opening in its areas of export interest. As one negotiator succinctly stated, "China is not out there as a *demandeur*, aggressively seeking market access concessions."[18] In the negotiations on manufactured goods, for instance, China could have pushed for a stiffer tariff-reduction formula,[19] with fewer flexibilities for developing countries, as well as additional sector-specific negotiations to reduce tariffs even more aggressively ("sectorals"). The industrial goods agreement being negotiated will allow developing countries to undertake a lower level of tariff cuts and provide them with significant additional flexibilities. Many of these flexibilities are expected to be used against products from China, yet China has not pushed against them. Nor has China sought sectorals in its areas of export interest, although as the world's most competitive producer in several manufacturing sectors, many predict that it could be one of the largest beneficiaries from such negotiations.

This is not to imply that China has been completely passive in the Doha negotiations. It has, for example, as the largest single target of antidumping actions globally, pressed for a tightening of WTO rules governing the use of such measures. China has often aligned with the "Friends of Antidumping Negotiations" (FAN), a mixed group of developed and developing countries calling for reforms to make the use of contingent protections more restrictive. China has challenged, in particular, US practices such as "zeroing" and "sunset reviews," which serve to inflate dumping margins and prolong the imposition of duties. It has also actively sought to have its nonmarket economy (NME) treatment revoked and be granted market economy status, pressing the WTO to review the NME clause in the Anti-dumping Agreement (Zeng and Liang 2010). Yet despite these areas of activity, China has been far less aggressive than Brazil or India in seeking to advance its trade interests in the Doha Round.

A Primary Threat and Target

Although China has clear offensive interests in the round, it also has compelling reasons to be cautious and not appear too aggressive in the negotiations. Paradoxically, the very same factors that make it economically powerful also make it vulnerable in international economic forums, especially those related to trade. China is in the distinct position of being perceived by other states as both a prime threat and target at the WTO.

As an export powerhouse in an organization designed to open markets, China is in a highly sensitive position. In the words of one WTO official, "Everyone is more or less frightened by their industrial capacity" and competition from China.[20] For many countries—both developed and developing—competition from Chinese imports has already wiped out major parts of their manufacturing sectors. Developing countries, for example, have lost market share to China both in their own domestic markets as well as in third-country markets (such as the US and EU), especially but not exclusively in low-end manufacturing sectors (Jenkins, Peters, and Moreira 2008). Examples abound: while Mexico's textile exports to the US initially boomed as a result of NAFTA and the growth of its export-processing Maquiladora industry, China came to surpass Mexico's exports to the US by 2003 as lower costs prompted many multinational firms to relocate production to China, causing mass layoffs and plant closures in Mexico (Jenkins, Peters, and Moreira 2008; Utar and Ruiz 2013). Similarly, nearly all of Brazil's shoe- and toy-making sectors have been wiped out by lower-cost products from China: "It's impossible to compete against China in these sectors," according to a Brazilian industry leader (*Economist* 2008). Under pressure from Chinese competition, Turkey lost 10 percent of the jobs in its textile sector in just two years (Bloomberg 2007). Africa is estimated to have lost more than 250,000 jobs in its textile and clothing sector (UN 2006). In 2009, India slapped a temporary ban on toy imports from China to protect its domestic industry, with its trade minister stating: "Look, we don't mind you exporting to India, but not to an extent that can kill my domestic industry" (Reuters 2009).

As a result, much of the resistance states have to further opening their markets in the Doha Round stems from concerns about competition from China's exports. Since China's exports are concentrated in the most highly protected sectors of global trade, "liberalization under the Doha agenda, especially in the politically charged, high-tariff sectors, is increasingly about other countries opening their markets to Chinese exports" (Mattoo and Subramanian 2012: 1737). This is something both developed and developing countries are reluctant to do. As an EU negotiator stated: "We think the really poor countries should have full access to our market. But the others [China and the other large emerging economies] are not traditional developing countries—they're growing rapidly and they'll take over from us. That's the future."[21] The advanced-industrialized states want to use the Doha Round to lock in whatever remaining advantage they have and give their industries a competitive edge versus China, by maintaining protections for key industries and gaining greater access to the Chinese market. Likewise, even many developing countries acknowledge that their greatest competitive threat is not from the US or other industrialized countries, but from China. According to one developing country negotiator, "We're at the frontline of an onslaught of Chinese imports; our industries have been very badly affected," and that, he indicated, was the primary cause of their reluctance to lower their tariffs in the NAMA negotiations.[22] Similarly, as a senior Indian trade official openly acknowledged in explaining their opposition to sectorals: "We need protections for certain sectors, because otherwise they would be wiped out by China."[23]

Furthermore, given the competitive threat that it poses, China faces the risk that other countries could attempt to use the WTO to constrain its exports. Textiles and clothing provide a prime example. Developing and less developed countries, in particular, were highly concerned about the elimination of the textiles and clothing quota system, which governed trade in the sector for decades and had, in recent years, provided them with a degree of protection from Chinese competition. Under the Uruguay Round Agreement on Textiles and Clothing (ATC), this system of quotas was phased out and eliminated by 2005. When quotas for textiles and clothing began to be phased out with implementation of the ATC, a broad-based coalition of industry groups from both developed and developing countries launched a major campaign lobbying their national delegations at the WTO to push for an extension of the quota system. More recently, many developing and less developed countries have feared that further liberalization of the textile and clothing markets in rich countries through the Doha Round will erode their preferential access to these markets (which often allows their products to enter duty-free while China's are subject to high MFN tariff rates) and leave them unable to compete against China. A group of developing countries and LDCs, led by Turkey, called for a special work program in the Doha Round on textiles and clothing—to include a monitoring mechanism and the use of special safeguards to block Chinese exports—and later sought a carve-out that would separate textiles and clothing from the regular negotiations on industrial goods, remove them from the general tariff reduction formula, and slow liberalization in this sector. Although China was able to prevent these particular initiatives, they contributed to the pressure that ultimately forced China to agree to "voluntarily" restrict the growth of its textile and clothing exports to the US, EU, and a host of other countries—something Dayaratna-Banda and Whalley (2007) characterize as "China Containment Agreements." Situations such as these, in which other countries attempt—through the WTO or otherwise—to contain competition from its exports, represent a potentially significant threat to China.

At the same time, China's large and rapidly growing economy makes it a major target for countries seeking access to its market. It faces concerted efforts to force it to undertake more onerous liberalization commitments, coming primarily from the US and its advanced-industrialized allies. This is particularly problematic for China as it seeks to continue its economic growth by moving up the value-chain into producing and exporting more sophisticated goods. To undertake such industrial upgrading, it needs to be able to protect these nascent industries until they are sufficiently mature to compete in global markets. As one of its negotiators stated, "Because China has one of the biggest markets in the world, people are more concentrated on our market, so we have to do things very carefully."[24]

This is most striking in efforts by the US and other developed economies to restrict China's access to the special and differential treatment afforded to developing countries in the Doha Round and subject it, instead, to stricter liberalization obligations. Within the round, the rich countries have been aggressive in seeking greater liberalization from the advanced developing countries than other developing countries (known as "differentiation"). China is the primary target of such efforts, given that it is by far the biggest developing country market and the most significant competitive threat to the developed countries. As one Chinese negotiator stated, "A lot of countries take China as their big target in the negotiations," but "China just wants the same treatment as other developing countries."[25] The principle that developing countries should be granted "special and differential treatment" (SDT) has long been formally enshrined in the GATT/WTO (even if its realization in practice has been disappointing). In the Doha Round, SDT is supposed to be incorporated across multiple areas of the negotiations, potentially in forms such as reduced liberalization commitments, greater flexibilities and exemptions, and longer implementation periods to phase in reforms. For its part, China has actively sought to avoid differentiation and secure the same level of special and differential treatment afforded to other developing countries. It has typically done so not by being out in front advancing its interests but by trying to blend in and hide itself among other developing countries and ride the coattails of their initiatives to gain SDT.

The negotiations on fisheries subsidies, which are identified as a special area for intensive negotiations in the Doha Round, provide an illustration. The negotiations are intended to impose disciplines upon and dramatically reduce levels of fisheries subsidies worldwide, based both on commercial considerations as well as the negative environmental impacts of such subsidies in encouraging overfishing and the depletion of global fish stocks.[26] Part of the negotiations have involved the issue of providing SDT to developing countries, motivated by a desire to ensure that poor and vulnerable populations dependent on small-scale, subsistence-based fisheries (which have no significant environmental impact) are not harmed by the new rules. As a developing country, China has been seeking to gain access to this SDT and claim the same treatment as other developing countries. But China has a massive industrial fishery: it is one of the world's biggest producers and exporters, with a large-scale and highly industrialized fishing fleet (Blomeyer et al. 2012). Allowing China the same special and differential treatment as other developing countries would allow it to continue to heavily subsidize its fish sector; this would not only undermine the environmental objective of the negotiations but also give China a significant commercial advantage over developed countries such as the US, EU, and Japan, which would no longer be allowed to freely subsidize their own industries. According to a negotiator for a rival state: "China tries to be really quiet, because they know they are the target. . . . They waited for India and Indonesia to come forward with broad carve outs [for developing countries], then they slid onto that."[27]

Other developing countries recognize China's strategy and are not necessarily supportive. At one meeting of negotiators on fish subsidies, for example, the Chinese negotiator claimed to be speaking "on behalf of developing countries" and argued against the imposition of fisheries management conditionalities on developing countries. However, the Argentine negotiator promptly responded by challenging China, stating: "We don't share your view, so I suggest next time you speak on behalf of China, not developing countries." This sparked a heated exchange involving multiple delegations.

The issue of sectorals in the negotiations on manufactured goods provides an illustration of how these twin tensions—between perceptions of China as a threat and a target, leading to simultaneous efforts by other states to contain China's export threat and gain access to its market—operate to constrain China's negotiating position. Manufactured goods is an area where China clearly has a competitive advantage, and the purpose of sectorals is to drive aggressive liberalization in certain sectors; hence, we would expect China to be active in pursuing its offensive interests in this area. Instead, in the later stages of the round, it is the US who has become the primary proponent of sectoral negotiations, while China has allied with other large emerging economies such as India and Brazil to oppose sectorals. On sectorals, China finds itself caught in a no-win position. On the one hand, the US has aggressively pushed for sectorals in the areas where its industries are globally competitive (such as chemicals and machinery), but China is still trying to build its own domestic industries. For the US, doing so would provide expanded market opportunities for its industries and, by disrupting China's efforts at industrial upgrading, lock in America's competitive advantage in the long term. Given their importance to China's development strategy, these represent important defensive interests; China can only lose from sectorals in these areas. On the other hand, China could potentially reap significant gains from sectorals in areas where it is most competitive, such as textiles and clothing, footwear, and electronics; yet, given the sensitivities in these areas, noted above, fighting for sectorals in its own areas of export interest would be far too controversial, alienate the developing countries that are its sole allies at the WTO, and likely backfire by producing negative repercussions. As a rival negotiator indicated, speaking of the prospective benefit to China of a sectoral in textiles and clothing, "But China hasn't put that on the table. It's the US and EU who are the *demandeurs* [for sectorals]. They [China] are much smarter politically. It would be unwise for them to call for a sectoral in that area."[28] Since it cannot push for sectorals in the areas of its own competitiveness and offensive interest, and can only lose from sectorals in the areas of interest to the US and other rich countries, China has taken a stance of opposing sectorals.

The China Paradox

China walks a delicate line at the WTO. It is highly dependent on export markets for its continued economic growth and development; it has an interest in reducing global protectionism and barriers that threaten the stability of its exports and impede their future growth. Yet any sign of assertiveness or aggression on its part risks generating a backlash that could ultimately jeopardize its access to the foreign markets it depends upon. Such a backlash could take the form of reducing its existing access to foreign markets or foreclosing the possibility of expanding that access in future. China has therefore exercised a form of pre-emptive restraint. Rather than actively pursuing additional liberalization or market access, China has sought to appear as nonthreatening as possible and fly below the radar at the WTO. A developing country negotiator explained why China has not aggressively pursued liberalization in the Doha Round as follows:

China is too wise for this. They are the largest exporter in lots of areas, even with existing market access barriers. If they ask for more, they are only going to get problems. That is precisely why they are not asking for more market access.[29]

This strategy has been immensely frustrating to rich country negotiators. According to an EU negotiator:

China—how they operate in the negotiations—it's amazing. They're the second exporter in the world behind Germany, before the US. And they're not pulling their weight. They're acting like a banana republic. They never take the floor and when they do, it's in a negative way. They don't want to scare. They would love a textile sectoral, but don't say that publicly—they fear it would be counterproductive. They're acting as though they're a weak, poor developing country with defensive interests when it's so clear in any analysis that they're the biggest winner from Doha.[30]

Or, as an industry representative more succinctly put it: China is "not about to risk its skin."[31] Although it has a keen interest in the continued liberalization of global markets, China's cautious behavior is shaped by fears of provoking a counter-reaction were it to aggressively demand greater access to other countries' markets.

The China paradox is that its economic power—its massive exports and large domestic market—renders it vulnerable at the WTO and imposes significant constraints on its behavior, preventing it from aggressively pursuing its interests in global trade liberalization. For China, standing out and taking an aggressive stance in pushing countries to further open their markets runs the risk of generating a powerful backlash, not only against China but also potentially against the entire multilateral trading system and its goal of liberalizing trade. China cannot risk rocking the boat: as a result, it has taken a comparatively passive role, and been far less aggressive than expected in pursuing its offensive trade interests at the WTO.

The Constraints of Alliances

Finally, in addition to the risk of backlash, a further constraint operating on China, as well as the other emerging powers, arises from their developing world alliances. While such alliances have been critical to the success of Brazil, India, and China in advancing their interests and evading the pressures and threats they face at the WTO, they have also come at a cost, by requiring the sacrifice of their market access ambitions directed at other developing countries.

As the world's leading exporter of manufactured goods, China, for example, would be one of the biggest beneficiaries of increased access to developing country markets, where average tariff rates are highest. Yet China has been willing to accept a weak tariff reduction formula for developing countries along with major exemptions, which would significantly limit the amount of market opening and new export opportunities available to it. The costs to competitive exporters like China are readily apparent. As one negotiator stated, "The idea that increased flexibilities [in the industrial goods negotiations] are good for developing countries in general is bullshit. Those carve-outs hurt us [competitive producers] .... We'd be happier if the additional carve-outs were kept in check."[32] Nonetheless, this is something China has determined it must accept. As a Chinese negotiator explained:

We face divide and rule strategies of the developed countries. China has been adhering to this principle of unity. China could have been more aggressive in seeking market access to developing countries, but our strategy has been to show solidarity with other developing countries.[33]

Consequently, even when pursuing a specific trade issue, China and the other emerging powers have refrained from pressing other developing countries for liberalization. The negotiations to strengthen rules governing antidumping measures, one of the areas where China has been relatively assertive, provide an illustration of the careful line it walks. China has framed the issue principally as a struggle against the US, although in reality other developing countries such as India are bigger users of antidumping actions against China.[34] By framing the issue as though the US were the exclusive problem, China thereby avoids explicitly targeting other developing countries, enabling them to unite against US antidumping practices.

This is not unique to China. Beyond reducing rich country agriculture subsidies, Brazil also has a significant interest in reducing tariff barriers globally, especially in developing country markets. In fact, Brazil has identified developing country markets as the key source of its future export growth (particularly large emerging economies like India and China). Yet it has held back from seeking improved market access in the developing world, as that would jeopardize the unity of the G20-T and broader developing world support for its leadership.[35] This was a strategic trade-off: in order to gain the allies it needed to target rich country agriculture subsidies, Brazil was forced to make significant compromises, including reducing its market access demands and agreeing in principle to some kind of SSM and SPs for developing countries. As one of its negotiators stated, "Yes, on market access we definitely hit the brakes hard."[36] Instead, Brazil has been willing to accept a relatively weak tariff reduction formula and extensive flexibilities for developing countries, which significantly reduce or eliminate any potential gains it could make in those markets. Thus, while Brazil has been able to aggressively challenge US and EU agriculture subsidies—its key competitors in third country markets—it has nonetheless been limited in its ability to press for expanded access to the developing country markets that are the key destination for its exports.

Rather than pushing for increased market access and limits on the flexibilities allowed to various other developing countries themselves, Brazil, India, and China have held back and hoped that other actors—specifically the US, EU, and other developed countries—will aggressively pursue the opening of those markets. In the words of a representative of Indian industry, "It doesn't make sense to pursue market access to developing countries because that's the block that's going to stand with you against the industrialized countries."[36] Likewise, as one negotiator stated:

We can't go around demanding increased market access to developing countries for political reasons. We happen to be on the same side of the table [as the US and others seeking more market access] but unlike the US, we can't say anything about it. We have to keep quiet and tie ourselves to the US' coattails and hope they get more market access that we can benefit from.[38]

Thus, while developing world alliances have been an important source of strength and protection to the emerging powers, such alliances have also constrained the ability of the emerging powers to pursue their offensive trade interests at the WTO.

Conclusion

This chapter has concentrated on analyzing China's agenda at the WTO, as a marked illustration of the constraints on the emerging powers. It has argued that despite their significant interests in trade liberalization, the emerging powers nevertheless face constraints on their ability to aggressively pursue their export interests at the WTO—whether arising from the need to exercise caution to avoid provoking a backlash, or maintain the support and backing of their allies. For China, in particular, contrary to what we might expect, its considerable export success creates vulnerabilities that restrict its behavior in WTO negotiations. As a result, the risk of a backlash that could endanger its current and future trade opportunities has prevented China from aggressively pursuing the liberalization of global markets at the WTO. Thus while Brazil, India, and China have gaining considerable power in multilateral trade governance, this does not imply complete freedom of action; on the contrary, the rising powers are constrained in important ways with regard to how they can behave and what they can push for in the context of WTO negotiations.

Chapter 7

India: Balancing Complex Trade Interests

A S the Doha Round stalled and it became clear that the US and other traditional powers would not be able to secure their desired outcomes, they eagerly directed blame at the emerging powers. American negotiators have characterized the rising powers as irresponsible and unwilling to pull their weight in the negotiations by making sufficient concessions to the US and other advanced-industrialized states. Of the three rising powers, India has been the prime target of Western ire: it is frequently identified as a threat to the liberal agenda and principles of the trading system, because of its stance on agriculture, and cast as a troublemaker and disruptive force impeding conclusion of the Doha Round. As chronicled in earlier chapters, India has long been a thorn in the side of the US and allied advanced-industrialized states, strident and persistent in standing up to and resisting their dominance—whether, for example, in opposing the new issues in the Uruguay Round, the launch of Doha without attention to outstanding implementation issues, or the inclusion of the Singapore Issues in the round, or more recently, refusing to back down on securing flexibilities for developing countries in agriculture.

Among Western negotiators, trade experts, and media, India has often been made a scapegoat for the repeated breakdown of the round, and India-bashing has become common practice. Following the 2008 Ministerial, some Western delegates took to referring to India's trade minister, Kamal Nath, as "Mr. No."[1] Many are highly dismissive of India's negotiating position, as well as the arguments advanced to support its agenda. Several Western negotiators, for example, rolled their eyes in interviews when discussing India's stance in the agriculture negotiations and its "suicidal farmers," with one explicitly stating, "To be honest, I can't stand India."[2] The *Economist* magazine (2014a), in an article on the state of the Doha Round, attributed blame for the latest breakdown to India and featured a cartoon drawing depicting negotiators from other states frantically trying to stop a giant elephant from crushing an egg representing the WTO. As Efstathopoulos and Kelly (2014) describe, the depiction of India as a "malcontent" in multilateral trade negotiations "emerges from the perception that it has 'long harbored deep antipathy toward the global trading system.'"

This conception of India's trade policy, I contend, is at the very least outdated: in recent decades, India's orientation toward the multilateral trading regime has undergone a fundamental shift as a result of the country's own economic reforms and liberalization. I challenge the conventional portrayal among Western commentators of India as a recalcitrant spoiler, arguing that this characterization is more a reflection of the political agenda of the traditional powers than of India's actual negotiating position in the round. Like Brazil and China, India has seen the development of a globally competitive, export-oriented industry with significant interests in trade liberalization in foreign markets—in its case, not in agriculture or manufacturing but in services. As a result, India's negotiating position has taken a 180-degree turn, as India has gone from being the primary opponent of services trade liberalization in the Uruguay Round to one of its leading advocates in the Doha Round. Indeed, from its own perspective, India's stance in the Doha Round has been considerably more liberal than that of the US. At the same time, India also has defensive concerns in agriculture arising from its massive and heavily impoverished peasant population. In other words, just like the traditional powers, the emerging powers must balance a complex mix of offensive and defensive trade interests. I show that the efforts of the new powers to protect their vulnerable sectors are no different from those of the US, EU, and others, which have long been accommodated and built into the fabric of previous GATT/WTO agreements.

As with the preceding analyses of Brazil and China, this chapter delves into the realm of India's domestic political economy in order to better understand its agenda at the WTO. The chapter begins by examining India's economic liberalization program and the emergence of its services export sector. It then proceeds to analyze how India's changing economic interests have influenced its negotiating stance in the Doha Round, leading India to emerge as a major driver of the push to liberalize global services trade. The final section of the chapter addresses the origins and nature of India's defensive interests in agriculture; it demonstrates that, far from being exceptional, obstructionist, and illiberal as the US and others contend, India's behavior and objectives are firmly in keeping with the norms and practices of the multilateral trading system.

India's Burgeoning Services Exports

Along with that of the other emerging powers, India's economy has been transformed by a program of economic reform over the last several decades. Following independence from British rule in 1947, India's economic policy was heavily shaped by its experience of colonialism. It focused on cultivating national economic development through extensive state intervention and import substitution industrialization. However, the country experienced a serious deterioration of its external economic position during the 1980s, with worsening trade imbalances and rising external debt (from $20 billion in 1980 to $72 billion by 1991) and debt servicing costs (Choudhury and Khanna 2014). The situation was brought to a head in 1990–91, when the Gulf War caused India's oil import bill to rise dramatically, exacerbating its trade deficit and prompting a withdrawal of investment and credit. This created an acute balance-of-payments crisis: India's foreign exchange reserves were reduced to such an extent that it was on the verge of being unable to finance its imports, and the government was close to default. India found itself with a mere $1.1 billion in hard currency reserves, enough for only two weeks of imports, and was forced to turn to the IMF for emergency aid (Choudhury and Khanna 2014). Needing more than $5 billion from the IMF to meet its immediate obligations, India was forced to airlift its gold reserves to London as collateral for the loan. With its echoes of the colonial era, this produced a national outcry, which caused the government to fall. The 1991 crisis, along with an IMF-mandated structural adjustment program, led India to chart a course of liberalization still ongoing two decades later. India's economic reforms have included opening the country to foreign trade (removing import restrictions and reducing tariffs) and investment, deregulation, privatization, tax reform, and inflation-control measures.

Over the past two decades, India has emerged as one of the fastest growing economies in the world, with growth rates as high as 10 percent in some years.[3] While China's economic growth has been driven by its export-oriented manufacturing sector, and Brazil's by its agriculture and natural resource exports, India's impressive economic performance has been fueled primarily by the rapid growth of its services sector (Downes 2009; Raman and Chadee 2011). India has found its niche in the global economy in the provision of tradable services, with the emergence of a cutting-edge services export sector. India's services exports have grown faster than those any other country in the world, at rates reaching 35 percent per year (World Bank 2004; WTO 2009). Its export growth has been led by information technology (IT), IT-enabled services (ITES), and business process outsourcing (BPO), which have expanded at an average annual rate of around 50 percent since 1993 (EIU 2008). India has been at the forefront of a transformation of the global services economy occasioned by the explosion of offshoring and outsourcing of functions previously performed in-house by corporations in the US and other advanced-industrialized states to lower-cost producers, often in the developing world (including software development, call centers, payroll and accounting services, medical transcription, radiology, financial industry research and analysis, legal research and writing, engineering, and research and development). India is by far the world's single dominant player in this field, having captured more than half of the global IT-BPO services offshoring market. Its IT-BPO sector is now a $100 billion industry (*Economic Times* 2013). Indian firms provide services to more than half of all Fortune 500 companies (Chadee, Raman, and Michailova 2011). As one of India's negotiators at the WTO stated, in the provision of IT-BPO services, "No one else is as competitive as we are."[4] The growth in Indian services trade has been identified as one of the most significant global trade trends in recent decades (Alejandro et al. 2010).

Services now constitute over 35 percent of India's total exports (WTO 2010), with 26 percent alone coming from the IT-BPO sector (NASSCOM 2010). The IT-BPO sector is the best performing in the Indian economy; its contribution to national GDP has grown from 1.2 percent in 1998 to 8.1 percent in 2014.[5] Relative to other large emerging economies, India is not a major trader: it supplies only a small fraction of world merchandise exports (just over 1 percent) and has a significant deficit in trade in goods (WTO 2010). Yet India's services exports have grown far more rapidly than its merchandise exports and have generated a large services trade surplus of $27 billion (Chanda and Sasidaran 2007; Mukherjee and Malone 2011; WTO 2013). India's services exports consequently make a critical contribution to its foreign exchange earnings and balance-of-payments position, as well as increasing tax revenues, stimulating domestic demand, and creating positive spillover effects in the wider economy (Alejandro et al. 2010). The industry sees opportunity for significant future expansion (NASSCOM 2010), and services exports are expected to continue to grow rapidly (approximately 20 percent per year), serving as a key source of dynamism in the Indian economy (EIU 2010).

India's "services revolution" (World Bank 2004) has been propelled by several different factors. As Alejandro et al. (2010) document, India has a competitive advantage in services derived from its large pool of skilled, English-speaking workers available at relatively low wages. In 2010, the estimated salary range for Indian software developers was about $5,300 to $9,700, compared with $53,000 to $80,000 in the US. Public and private educational institutions in India—including the highly esteemed Indian Institutes of Technology, Indian Institute of Science, Indian Institutes of Management, regional public engineering schools, and public-private partnership institutions—produce approximately 2.5 million university graduates each year, the second largest annual number of science and engineering graduates after the US. India was therefore well positioned to benefit from rapid advances in technology that dramatically reduced the costs of telecommunications and increasingly enabled spatial fragmentation in the production of services, with more and more services becoming tradable across borders. In addition, in its nascent stages, India's IT-BPO services industry gained a significant boost from events such as the Y2K millennium bug and euro conversion, which created large-scale demand for basic IT services and helped fuel the takeoff of the Indian industry and its exports (Kapur and Ramamurti 2001).

Attributing the explosive growth of India's services export sector simply to economic liberalization and the "unleashing of market forces" would be erroneous. On the contrary, the state and its policies played an important role in the creation and expansion of the IT-BPO services industry. First, the previous import substitution policies invested heavily in elite national higher education and research institutions and provided a critical level of technological endowments (Patibandla and Petersen 2002). This substantial investment in human capital and technological capabilities created the essential foundation for the emergence and development of India's services export sector.

Second, several of India's leading IT services firms originated, or grew out of large conglomerates that were founded or fostered during India's ISI period (for example, Wipro, Infosys, Tata Consultancy Services, Tech Mahindra). This is not coincidental: state policy directly contributed to the development of the Indian IT sector. The Indian state began promoting software exports as early as 1970 (Raman and Chadee 2011). More important, however, in the 1970s, the state introduced significant restrictions on foreign direct investment in an effort to limit the dominance of foreign multinationals in the national market and promote indigenous industries and domestic entrepreneurs. The Foreign Exchange Regulation Act (FERA) of 1974 capped allowable foreign ownership at 40 percent of equity, thus requiring partial Indian ownership of all entities operating in the domestic market. Foreign companies already operating in India were required to dilute their shareholdings to meet the new rules. The Indian government was motivated by concerns that foreign MNCs were reaping excessively high profits in their market and repatriating the capital in the form of earnings, which was putting a serious drain on India's scarce foreign exchange reserves without transferring any sophisticated technology to India or helping to foster the development of its domestic industry (Negandhi and Palia 1987). In response, many foreign multinationals, including IBM, closed up shop and left India in the mid- to late-1970s. IBM had entered India in the 1950s and came to dominate the market for computers and computer services. The departure of IBM created a vacuum that Indian firms soon filled, serving the domestic market as well as supplying high-value services to multinational firms (Alejandro et al. 2010; Negandhi and Palia 1987). As Kapur and Ramamurti (2001: 25) write, "[M]any Indian software firms cut their teeth in the domestic market after IBM left India." These firms benefited from a form of infant-industry protection based not on tariffs but foreign investment restrictions.

The emergence of India's IT services sector can thus be seen as a direct—and highly successful—result of the import substitution policies of the Indian state. As a result of its restrictive FDI policies, India effectively pushed out foreign multinationals in the 1970s, later reopening with liberalization in the 1990s (Choudhury and Khanna 2014). The intervening period created space in the domestic market that made possible the initial development of Indian firms and allowed them to gain a foothold, just as the computer market was growing rapidly in India and around the world during the 1980s. Subsequent opening to FDI with neoliberal reforms then provided capital and channels for Indian service exports to access foreign markets; this opening occurred fortuitously at the moment when Indian firms were poised to take advantage of the new opportunities emerging to export services to global markets.

Third, state policies in the post-reform era have also been directed at promoting IT services exports. In the 1990s, the state established Software Technology Parks—special zones designated for export-oriented activities—that provided firms with high-quality infrastructure and exemptions from taxes on export profits, customs and excise duties, and service and sales taxes, and permitted up to 100 percent FDI (Alejandro et al. 2010). The state thus played a significant role in enabling and fostering India's services export boom.

India's IT-BPO expansion was initially fueled by lower-skilled and lower-value activities, such as insurance claim processing, call centers, and software installation and support, but its most competitive producers are quickly moving up the value chain and expanding into more sophisticated and higher value-added, knowledge-intensive, tradable services (Hoekman and Mattoo 2007). These include software development, finance, law, procurement, human resources, media, entertainment, and healthcare, as well as engineering, research and development, and product testing and design for industries such as telecommunications, semiconductors, automotives, aerospace, consumer electronics, medical devices, and energy. Software provides a striking example of the sophistication achieved by the Indian services industry: more than half of the software development centers in the world with Carnegie Mellon University's CMM highest Level-5 rating (a capability measure) are located in India (Kapur and Ramamurti 2001). To quote a report from management consultancy A. T. Kearney (2009: 8):

India started as a low-cost location that provided routine tasks for American IT companies, and it still retains a competitive advantage in this area. At the same time, it has moved up the value chain. Today, virtually any offshoring service can be performed in India, and new areas are constantly being invented.

The growth of the IT-BPO sector in India was fueled in part by considerable foreign direct investment (Srivastava 2006), with foreign firms relocating aspects of their operations to India. Foreign firms began investing in creating facilities in India as early as the 1980s. By 2001, US companies that had opened software development centers in India included Cisco, Hewlett-Packard, IBM, Lucent, Microsoft, Motorola, Oracle, and Sun Microsystems (Alejandro et al. 2010). General Electric (GE), for example, invested $260 million in Bangalore to build its largest R&D lab in the world, employing more than six thousand engineers and scientists.[6] IBM now employs more workers in India than the US (Choudhury and Khanna 2014). NASDAQ—the American stock exchange heavily oriented toward technology and Internet-related companies—opened its third foreign office in Bangalore (Kapur and Ramamurti 2001: 24).

Despite the presence of foreign investment and firms, as with agribusiness in Brazil, Indian firms have played a central role in the development of the sector and its growth has fueled a dramatic expansion and internationalization of Indian capital. The largest Indian firms have become significant international players (A. T. Kearney 2009). To provide just a few examples: Wipro generates more than $7 billion in annual revenues, with nearly 150,000 employees globally; Infosys has $8 billion in revenues and 160,000 employees; and Tata Consultancy Services has revenues of $13 billion and over 300,000 IT consultants in more than forty-six countries.[7] Indian services firms have engaged in substantial acquisitions and outward foreign direct investment. Domestically, Indian firms have bought up foreign IT enterprises in India: Tata Consultancy Services, for example, purchased Citibank's India-based operations (employing twelve thousand people) in 2008, with an agreement that it would continue to supply Citibank (A. T. Kearney 2009: 3). Internationally, Indian firms like Wipro and Infosys have opened offices in the US and elsewhere, facilitated in part by changes in Indian government policy to promote the international expansion of Indian firms by easing restrictions on raising capital abroad and making foreign acquisitions (Kapur and Ramamurti 2001: 26).[8] Since the implementation of these reforms, Indian firms have made increasingly high value acquisitions in the US and other foreign markets, such as the acquisition by VSNL (now Tata Communications Limited) of the US firm Teleglobe International Holdings for $254 million in 2005 (Nayyar 2008: 121). India has become a hub for the entire global offshoring industry and, as its firms move up the value chain, they are pushing its expansion to new geographic locales. Tata Consultancy Services, for instance, has expanded its operations to Argentina, Brazil, China, Hungary, Mexico, Singapore, the US, and Uruguay (A. T. Kearney 2009: 8).

As with the agribusiness sector in Brazil, as the Indian IT-BPO sector developed, its firms bypassed old industry associations and corporatist structures in order to form a new and independent private sector lobby, the National Association of Software and Services Companies (NASSCOM) to represent their interests vis-à-vis the state. Given its importance for the Indian economy, the sector exerts considerable influence on trade and economic policy. Fueled by the rise of the Indian IT services sector, the state and national capital have allied together to project their export interests abroad.[9] At the WTO, Indian negotiators have worked closely with the country's services export sector throughout the Doha Round. According to Indian negotiators, NASSCOM in particular has been "very active," followed by other industry associations such as the Confederation of Indian Industry (CII) and the Federation of Indian Chambers of

Commerce and Industry (FICCI), providing the state with inputs and contributing to the formulation of India's negotiating position on services.[10] As industry representatives stated, "Whatever inputs we have given to the government, they have taken them," and "Their negotiating position more or less reflects our own position."[11] This is a reflection of the fact that the Indian state sees services exports as essential to the country's economic stability—including its balance of payments—and growth.

While the services export sector now constitutes a critical part of the Indian economy, there are important questions about how widely the gains it generates are being shared. Among other factors, there are important limitations to the employment-generating capacity of India's services exports (Mukherjee 2013). The sector touches a relatively small portion of the overall population and has not translated into widespread employment gains. It currently employs 2.8 million people, with indirect job creation estimated at an additional 8 million (NASSCOM 2009; *Economic Times* 2013). In most countries, this would be an enormous figure, but for India, with a workforce of nearly half a billion, IT-BPO remains a relatively small employer in the economy overall. The professional, highly educated and skilled workers it employs represent a small elite, far removed from the low-skilled workers who make up the bulk of the Indian workforce. India's services-led growth is thus frequently described as "jobless growth" (Gordon and Gupta 2004); this differs notably from China's economic growth, which has been fueled by low-skill, labor-intensive manufacturing, and has generated mass employment.

In contrast, the gains from India's impressive economic growth have largely "bypassed the poor," with its economic ascendance benefiting "mainly the affluent upper classes of this populous nation, with very little if any trickling down to the rural poor who make up roughly two-thirds of the country's 1.2 billion people" (Wright and Gupta 2011). India continues to have among the poorest human development indicators in the world, with the majority of its population dependent on subsistence agriculture and extremely high rates of poverty (Jha et al. 2006). Although it is now the world's third largest economy, India ranks 135 (of 187 countries) on the UN's Human Development Index.[12] Nearly 70 percent of the population lives in poverty (less than $2 a day), and 33 percent lives in extreme poverty (less than $1.25 a day).[13] While this represents an improvement—from its poverty rate of 82 percent in 1994—it still leaves more than 800 million people in poverty. One-third of the world's poor are in India

(World Bank 2013). With child malnutrition at 48 percent, India has one of the highest rates of underweight children in the world, higher than most countries in sub-Saharan Africa (*Economist* 2010b). Although GDP has more than doubled since 1991, malnutrition has decreased by only a few percentage points (*Economist* 2010b). By comparison, in China child malnutrition has fallen to 7 percent (McMichael 2012: 15). Despite the success of its elite institutions in producing highly skilled graduates, basic education is poor and the adult literacy rate is only 66 percent (compared with 93 percent in China) (*Economist* 2010a). The vast majority of the workforce—80 percent—is found in vulnerable employment.[14] Just half of the country's roads are paved, only 75 percent of the population has access to electricity, and much of the population lacks access to safe drinking water. The gains from India's services export sector have thus benefited a relatively small elite, while the vast majority of the population—primarily the rural poor—have been left behind (Shahi 2014).

India in the Doha Services Negotiations

The Indian government has made the services export sector a top priority in its economic and trade policy. Historically, India's stance in the multilateral trading system has been overwhelmingly and consistently defensive, seeking freedom for its policies to restrict trade and promote the growth of its domestic (primarily manufacturing) industries during the ISI period. Yet, this changed with economic liberalization, and especially the growth of India's services export sector. Trade is now a key part of India's economic strategy. The state has made an economic growth rate of 8 percent one of its primary objectives. As described in India's chief policy planning document, achieving and sustaining its economic growth target "cannot take place without tapping on the opportunities offered by the international economy."[15] This has, in turn, shaped its orientation to the WTO, as the same document explains:

Until recently, the strategy has been largely defensive. Such defensive and status-quoist [*sic*] position, while appropriate for an inward looking development strategy, is not so now, and so has to give way to a more aggressive and proactive position. . . . The Indian interventions at the Doha Ministerial demonstrate the much more active and aggressive position that is being taken by India.[16]

Ironically, given that India was a vocal and strident opponent of services liberalization in the Uruguay Round and led the (ultimately unsuccessful) campaign to block the incorporation of services in the multilateral trading regime, liberalization of trade in services has become one of India's key priorities in the Doha Round.[17] In a relatively brief period of time, India's economic position, and consequently its stance on services trade liberalization, have thus changed dramatically. As one of its former negotiators stated, India's position on the liberalization of trade has undergone a "paradigm shift" since the Uruguay Round.[18] India is now one of the key proponents of services liberalization at the WTO. Indeed, as its negotiators report, "We became possibly even more keen on services than the US."[19]

Although services have become an increasingly important part of the global economy, now accounting for nearly two-thirds of global output (Javalgi et al. 2011), cross-border trade in services is generally no more than 20 percent of all trade for most countries (Hoekman and Mattoo 2011; Javalgi et al. 2011). This low share of services in international trade is in large part the direct result of high barriers to trade and investment in the services sector. The global economy remains far less open to trade in services than goods (Winters et al. 2003), and efforts to liberalize services trade have lagged far behind those involving goods. Services came under multilateral trade disciplines only in the Uruguay Round (as the General Agreement on Trade in Services, or GATS) and that round included little real liberalization—its primary achievement being the establishment of a set of rules and framework for future liberalization (to begin with as part of the "built-in agenda" for additional negotiations following the Uruguay Round) (Dawson 2013). From the perspective of the multilateral trading system, trade in services is no different than trade in goods. Given the high barriers to services trade, economists argue that there is great scope to expand trade and reap economic gains through liberalization in this area (Winters et al. 2003). The Doha Round was widely seen as offering an instrument to reduce such barriers (Hoekman and Mattoo 2011).

Services do not fit the model many people have in mind when they think of trade, as material goods moving across borders, regulated by tariff or quota restrictions (and more recently various forms of nontariff barriers). Instead, services trade often involves foreign direct investment or the movement of people across borders. The GATS categorizes services into four types or "modes" of supply: *Mode 1: Cross-border supply*, the cross-border supply of services from the territory of one state to another (that is, "outsourcing"); *Mode 2: Consumption abroad*, a service consumer entering another country to obtain a service (for example, tourism, foreign students, or individuals traveling abroad to receive healthcare services); *Mode 3: Commercial presence*, a company from one country establishing operations in another country to supply a service; and *Mode 4: Presence of natural persons*, the temporary movement of persons across borders to supply services.

The GATS agreement that resulted from the Uruguay Round reflected prevailing power asymmetries at that time. The negotiations centered on the establishment of businesses in other countries (Mode 3), which is a focus of advanced-industrialized states with established services industries seeking to expand abroad into other markets. Mode 4—labor mobility—was seen as a potentially important area for developing countries; but the (fairly limited) liberalization that actually took place under Mode 4 was slanted toward the interests of the developed countries. The inclusion of Mode 4 liberalization in the GATS was promoted by service industries in the US and other advanced-industrialized states. Influential lobby groups in those countries, in particular the US Coalition of Service Industries (CIS), persuaded their trade officials to tackle barriers that inhibited the mobility of business visitors or intracorporate transferees within their multinational firms (Jurje and Lavenex 2014). The commitments ultimately made in the Uruguay Round refer almost exclusively to highly skilled intracorporate transferees or contractual service suppliers linked to commercial presence (Mode 3). Other categories of service suppliers, with significance especially for developing countries, while potentially falling under the scope of GATS, were not liberalized (Jurje and Lavenex 2014).

Mode 4 is an area where developing countries stand to potentially make massive gains, dwarfing the goods aspects of WTO negotiations, although it is also the area where the trading system has seen the least liberalization (Winters et al. 2003). Lower wages give developing countries and their workers a competitive advantage in providing many services. The temporary movement of labor has become a significant aspect of the new globalized economy, whether Mexican farm workers harvesting fruit in Canada, Philippine nurses providing healthcare in Europe, Bangladeshi construction workers building skyscrapers and football stadiums in the Gulf states, or Indian software engineers providing services at client sites in the US. The resulting remittances have become a substantial source of income and foreign exchange for many developing countries. The developing world as a whole now receives more than $400 billion annually in remittances (World Bank 2012). India is the world's top recipient of remittances, valued at nearly $70 billion per year (World Bank 2012). Remittances constitute almost 4 percent of India's GDP and represent an important source of external finance for the country. The largest portion of its remittances comes from the US, driven by its high-skilled software and other IT workers (RBI 2010).

Embracing the commodifying logic of global neoliberalism, many developing countries are increasingly viewing labor "exports" as a means to boost their economic growth and development. Given their abundant supply of cheap labor, this is an area of global trade where states in the Global South believe they could gain much from liberalization. Estimates suggest that liberalization by destination countries of 3 percent of their workforce would create over $150 billion per year in additional economic welfare, or roughly four times the current level of development assistance provided to developing countries (Martin 2006: 9; Winters et al. 2003: 1138). Fully realized, the principle of free markets would demand open borders for all factors of production, including capital and labor. Yet such an outcome is viewed as completely untenable by the countries of the Global North. The US and other Western powers are fiercely resistant to efforts to subordinate their own immigration policies to WTO trade rules. Mode 4 is therefore one of the most contentious issues not only in the services negotiations but in the entire Doha Round.

Driven by the desire to protect and extend its exports, services constitute India's prime area of offensive interest in the Doha negotiations (Chanda and Sasidaran 2007; Jha et al. 2006). As one of India's negotiators explained, "We're not major exporters in agriculture. In manufacturing, the markets have already been overwhelmingly captured by China. For us, services are where the big gains are to be made."[20] Two aspects of the services negotiations are particularly important to India: Mode 1 (outsourcing) and Mode 4 (temporary movement of workers). According to an Indian negotiator, "These are the areas where we think our firms can benefit most from further liberalization, and they would be hugely beneficial for India's economic development."[21] India adopted an aggressive position in seeking liberalization commitments on Mode 1 and Mode 4 from the US and other advanced-industrialized states. Although Indian companies are expanding their operations abroad, India has not been a major *demandeur* on Mode 3, or commercial presence. Instead, India elected to trade off potential gains in Mode 3 for better market access for its professionals under Mode 4 and liberal commitments under Mode 1 (Jurje and Lavenex 2014). India still has areas of protection in its own services markets, just as others do. But it has shown willingness to

trade concessions in the Doha negotiations, including binding the unilateral liberalization it has undertaken (for example, courier service) and further opening
its markets (such as telecommunications, finance) (*Bridges Weekly* 2008; *International Trade Reporter* 2008).[22] Beyond the WTO, India is continuing to undertake
major liberalization unilaterally (such as in its previously highly protected retail
sector), and it has also pursued services liberalization in many of its bilateral and
regional agreements (Alejandro et al. 2010: 18–19).

India is eager to secure its access to foreign markets to counter the very real
prospect of rising protectionism. The US is the largest market for India's IT-BPO
services, accounting for 60 to 70 percent of its exports (NASSCOM 2010). But
services exports are a highly politicized issue in the US and other developed
countries, where there is considerable popular concern over outsourcing and
its impact on domestic unemployment. The movement of people across borders to supply services, Mode 4, is perhaps even more controversial, generating
substantial political resistance in many high-income countries because of its
association with migration (Hoekman and Mattoo 2007). As one Indian services
industry representative stated:

> We are very concerned about rising protectionist sentiment in the US. Our industry is the
> favored whipping boy for unemployment in the US. That is our biggest challenge. We are
> very concerned that some shotgun legislation could go through at any point. And we think
> we are seeing indirect protectionism even now, with visas being denied, raids on outsourc-
> ing places, etc.[23]

The industry has identified the prospect of a rise in protectionism in its major
markets as one of the greatest potential threats to its future health and expansion (NASSCOM 2010).

In the case of Mode 1, cross-border supply, markets to date have been relatively open. This may be due, in part, to the fact that offshoring of services is
such a recent phenomenon, exploding extremely rapidly in less than a decade,
based on the emergence of new technologies that make it possible to deliver
such services from abroad in ways that were largely unforeseen and unanticipated by trade policy. This novelty means that relatively few barriers exist yet.
Efforts to construct protectionist policies are only now beginning to catch up.
According to the World Bank (2004: 23):

> Cross-border supply faces few explicit restrictions. But the dramatic expansion of Indian
> exports and the perceived exodus of white-collar jobs from importing countries is begin-

ning to provoke protection. Measures proposed so far have sought only to prevent governments from procuring Indian services. But as the pain of adjustment grows, so will the temptation to introduce barriers in larger non-government markets.

Such barriers may take varied forms, including outright bans, conditions imposed on outsourcing contracts that inhibit trade, or other policy measures that produce the same effect. Legislation has been introduced in the US Congress, for example, that would ban companies that outsource overseas from access to federal grants and loans, while providing tax incentives to firms that return offshore activities to the US.[24] Several states in the US have introduced outsourcing bans with respect to government contracts. There are also many more subtle measures that are being introduced to create barriers to cross-border services trade. The EU, for example, recently introduced changes to European labor regulations, known as TUPE (Transfer of Undertakings and Protection of Employees), to protect European workers from outsourcing, as well as new privacy requirements related to electronic commerce, along with a refusal to recognize data security in India—all of which threaten to impede trade in services. Under existing WTO rules, there is little to protect India from these barriers.

In the Doha Round services negotiations, India has therefore sought to lock in its existing access to foreign markets with legally binding commitments at the WTO to pre-empt potential protectionism. India has pressed for binding commitments from the US, EU, and other key markets in more than fifty sectors/subsectors that have the most potential for offshoring (India 2007). As one of its negotiator's stated, "This is an issue of protection, insurance—providing us with stability and security in our markets."[25] India's objective is to guard against and prevent the threat of any future market closure and thereby protect the stability of its market access.

In contrast to Mode 1, Mode 4—a form of trade that blurs into the arena of immigration and labor market policy—is an area where significant barriers have always been present (Jha et al. 2006). The movement of persons to supply services in foreign markets is highly restricted by a wide range of barriers, including visa requirements; stringent quotas; wage-parity conditions; the use of Economic Needs Tests (ENT), Local Markets Tests, and Management Needs Tests to restrict entry; discriminatory taxes and standards; licensing requirements; and nonrecognition of professional qualifications (Chakraborty and Khan 2008: 139; World Bank 2004: 23).

For India, trade in Modes 1 and 4 can be intertwined, such that access under

Mode 4 is necessary for Mode 1 exports. In the software sector, for example, an offshore project for supplying software services (Mode 1) may require some software professionals to be present onsite (Mode 4). Being able to place some of its employees with clients in the US or other foreign markets on a temporary basis is thus important to the outsourcing business model in IT. But this temporary movement of workers is currently subject to significant restrictions and constraints. Mode 4 (for example, an Indian software firm sending employees to the US to work on-site for its clients) is therefore particularly important for India because 30 percent of the work of its outsourcing firms takes place on-site (in the US or other foreign markets).[26]

Significant numbers of Indian nationals immigrate to the US on a temporary basis to supply services (Alejandro et al. 2010). Indian workers accounted for the largest portion of admissions under "H1B" visas (a temporary, nonimmigrant visa that allows hiring foreign workers for skilled occupations) in recent years, with 38 percent (154,726) of total H1B admissions in 2008 (Monger and Barr 2008). India-based companies were the top sponsors of H1B visas in 2008: Infosys and Wipro received approval for 4,559 and 2,678 visas, respectively, while US-based Microsoft received approval for 1,018 visas (Herbst 2009). US-registered units of Indian companies apply for the visas and then often locate the recipient at a client's company to support the software they are supplying.

India would like not only to maintain but expand the number of its workers that firms can bring to the US, as well as other markets. However, as with Mode 1, there has been increasing protectionism in this area as well. Legislation adopted by the US in August 2010 introduced new rules that steeply raised the fees that companies must pay for H1B visas, disproportionately harming Indian firms and works, given that they make up the bulk of these visa users. This policy change—comparable to a tax or tariff on Indian workers in the US—is estimated to have added as much as $200 million to the annual costs of Indian outsourcing firms (*Financial Times* 2010; *Washington Post* 2010). Although the Indian government and NASSCOM immediately lodged strong objections to the new policy, they were unable to alter it. Further changes to H1B visas were proposed in 2013, under the umbrella of US immigration reform, which would increase the costs fivefold for some companies to $10,000 per worker and bar some companies from placing holders of the visa with clients in the US. Such regulations would seriously damage the business model of many of India's outsourcing firms and could sap as much as $8 billion from India's economy annually (Bloomberg 2013). India thus faces threats even to its existing level of access to the US market.

Consequently, obtaining commitments at the WTO that would not only secure but also expand its access for Mode 4 trade to the US and other foreign markets is one of India's key priorities in the Doha negotiations. As one of its negotiators stated, "GATS Mode 4 is India's strongest offensive interest in trade negotiations."[27] Another Indian negotiator explained further: "Our exports are predominantly in professional skilled workers. This is the area where barriers are highest (in terms of certification and professional requirements). We think if these can be reduced, our exports will shoot up."[28] At the same time, both the Indian government and the services export industry recognize the sensitivities surrounding their services exports and the need to "tread carefully and deftly," as one industry representative put it, in negotiating these issues.[29] Not unlike China, India too is concerned with the need to prevent a large-scale backlash that could threaten to shut down its effort to further liberalize global markets. India has thus been careful to frame its market access demands in terms of high-skilled, temporary migration, involving seemingly obscure technical changes to visa and other regulations that are largely unintelligible to the wider public, yet would have a significant impact on its exports.

From the start of the Doha negotiations, India has been the key *demandeur* on labor mobility: it provided the most comprehensive request on Mode 4 of all states (Winters et al. 2003), and subsequently led a plurilateral initiative representing fifteen states seeking Mode 4 liberalization from the US and other developed countries.[30] This was the only plurilateral services liberalization request sponsored by a group consisting entirely of developing countries (*Bridges Weekly* 2011). Beyond this specific plurilateral initiative, India has gained broad support from the developing world for championing the cause of liberalizing the temporary movement of workers. Like Brazil on agriculture subsidies, India established itself as a leading voice of developing countries on Mode 4 and mobilized a group of countries behind it to push for liberalization. Mode 4 has been heavily sold by India as a major interest of developing countries in the international trading system. India's chief negotiator, Rahul Khullar, described Mode 4 as "the most important market access area for *all* developing countries" (cited in Kanth 2008, emphasis added).

India is not alone in promoting Mode 4 but is joined by a range of actors including the World Bank, the WTO Secretariat, and various research centers and NGOs (such as the International Center for Trade and Sustainable Development [ICTSD], Oxfam International, and the Overseas Development Institute). Over the past decade, Mode 4 has arguably become the second most celebrated cause of developing countries, after agriculture subsidies, within the global community of trade experts and analysts, generating a vast amount of attention and discourse. Labor exports are being touted as a prime instance of how developing countries can use their comparative advantage in low-wage labor to benefit from international trade liberalization and further integration into global markets. Oxfam, for example, heralds Mode 4 as presenting a "great opportunity," potentially "giving developing countries an opportunity to exploit labor as an abundant resource" (Oxfam 2008). Countless workshops, briefings, and strategy sessions have been held in Geneva and around the world to discuss the economic benefits of such trade, how it could be operationalized in trade agreements, and how to overcome resistance to Mode 4 commitments from receiving countries.[31]

India has played an important role in fostering this discourse. Yet, although India has framed its efforts on Mode 4 liberalization as representing a shared interest of the developing world as a whole (see, for example, India 2007), the specific agenda that it has actually pursued in the Doha Round is one from which it stands to be the primary beneficiary. While most developing countries could potentially gain from increased mobility of non- or semiskilled labor, which they have in abundant supply, India's objectives in the Doha Round are concentrated on Mode 4 liberalization for high-skilled workers. Liberalization of low-skilled workers under Doha is considered politically infeasible, given the intense opposition of developed states and the difficulties involved in trying to operationalize and regulate this trade; in the words of an Indian negotiator, "Realistically I think it would be very difficult to go after Mode 4 for low-skilled workers, because it's so difficult to track those workers in a country and ensure their return, as opposed to high-skilled."[32] India, along with a handful of other advanced developing countries, stands to reap the vast majority of gains from Mode 4 liberalization for high-skilled workers, and that is where it has concentrated its efforts. There are also suggestions that India has its own concerns about low-skilled workers from its less prosperous neighbors seeking to enter its market (Jurje and Lavenex 2014). Thus, like Brazil, while pursuing its own fairly narrow trade interests, India has gained force for its cause by construing those interests as shared by the rest of the developing world and part of a larger North-South struggle.

While agriculture, manufacturing, and services constitute the three core market access pillars of the Doha Round, the negotiations on services have lagged behind the other areas of the negotiations. This was due in part to the decision to begin the negotiations by focusing first on trade in goods—agriculture and NAMA—and once modalities were agreed on in these areas, then to turn more focused attention to services (Hoekman and Mattoo 2011). However, when negotiations became bogged down by stalemate in agriculture and NAMA, services wound up, in the words of one of India's negotiators, being "held hostage to other areas of negotiations."[33] The initial offers of liberalization tabled by states at the start of negotiations were paltry and, with the conflict on agriculture and NAMA holding them up, the services negotiations made little progress for much of the round.

At the July 2008 Ministerial, however, a "signaling conference" was convened to give countries an opportunity to signal where they would be willing to undertake further liberalization commitments in the services negotiations. Many countries indicated that they were willing to substantially improve their offers, conditional on a deal on agriculture and NAMA modalities, which negotiators at the time thought could be close to fruition (Hoekman and Mattoo 2011). India, in particular, was highly satisfied with the movement indicated at the signaling conference. The US and EU indicated they were willing to improve their existing offers in cross-border supply of services in a range of sectors; most notably, they both indicated that they were prepared to make concessions allowing more services professionals from India and other developing countries to work temporarily in their markets (Mode 4). This was remarkable given that the US and other developed countries had previously opposed any negotiations on Mode 4 at all, as the US Congress is highly resistant to including immigration-related provisions in trade agreements (*International Trade Reporter* 2008). The new concessions from the US and EU would, however, be limited to skilled professionals rather than low-skilled workers. The US, for example, indicated it would be willing to increase the number of H1B visas for foreign professionals, while the EU said it would eliminate the cumbersome economic needs tests for foreign workers when issuing temporary visas (Bridges Weekly 2008). These concessions were favorably received by India's commerce minister, Kamal Nath, who stated: "The signals are constructive. There was good movement by the United States and the EU" (*International Trade Reporter* 2008).

Yet Indian negotiators and its services export industry report that while these concessions by the US and EU were significant, especially in light of their earlier fierce resistance, overall progress was still underwhelming. Indeed, Indian negotiators see the concessions made by the US and EU as far less than what India has been willing to do in terms of liberalizing its own market. As one stated:

On services, almost all service sectors (except one or two like multi-brand retail) have been completely opened up, though in some cases, we don't allow up to 100 percent foreign ownership. We're willing to bind that, but in exchange we want to see binding of the present level of cross-border trade and we want to see more Mode 4 contractual and independent services suppliers. But there's been very little movement on that, at least in the USA.[34]

Indian negotiators contend that their position—not only in services but in the Doha Round more broadly—is more liberal than that taken by the US.

Having engaged in significant autonomous liberalization in services, agriculture, and manufactured goods, India's current trade policy in many areas is considerably more liberal than the commitments it was required to make in the Uruguay Round. It has a significant amount of "water" in its tariffs—its bound rates are far higher than those it is actually applying—in agriculture and NAMA, as well as a more liberal services regime than what it is bound to under the existing GATS agreement. This gave India considerable room to maneuver in the Doha Round: it could make significant concessions in the round, with little or no impact on its real, applied tariffs on goods or opening of its services market.

India approached the Doha Round seeking to have the liberalization it undertook on its own initiative recognized and compensated for by reciprocal liberalization from the US and other developed countries.[35] As one former Indian negotiator stated regarding the negotiations on manufactured goods:

We have brought down our industrial tariffs to about 10 percent (from pre-Uruguay Round levels of 150 percent) and much of that we've done autonomously. And we're willing to bind our current levels. We should get paid for this, but no one is willing to. The fact that the US and Obama are making demands for India to further reduce its tariffs [via sectorals] without any talk of reductions from that side is atrocious. We've reduced by about 70 percent from base rates (rates present at the time the Doha Round began) and we're not getting that kind of reduction from the industrialized countries even with the current coefficients. We're not even getting full reciprocity, never mind less than full reciprocity.[36]

Likewise, India has been willing to bind and extend its unilateral liberalization of its service markets, but it has seen only tepid concessions from the US in services in exchange. On agriculture, Indian negotiators argue, the new disciplines on subsidies currently on the table would touch only US bindings but not affect its current levels of subsidies. From India's perspective, if any state has been an irresponsible and illiberal player at the WTO, it is the US.

Protectionism in Agriculture

India's trade policy has thus undergone a significant shift from purely defensive to outwardly oriented and seeking to make offensive gains in foreign markets. As its former chief negotiator stated, "Those days of the Uruguay Round—when everyone thought we were selling off the country—are gone. People now see the positive side of trade agreements—*what we can get*." He continued by adding an important caveat: "The key though is that our defensive interests are taken care of."[37] In interviews, negotiators in Geneva frequently complained that the US acts as though it is the only state with important domestic political constituencies (Congress, various industry groups, its farm lobby, and so forth) that it needs to appease when formulating its trade policy and deciding what it can or cannot agree to at the WTO. US negotiators, they contend, are generally oblivious to the fact that other states are equally compelled to take into account and manage potential political heat from domestic constituencies. But, just like the US, as one Indian negotiator explained, "We have our own political constituencies we have to worry about."[38] And consequently, "We need flexibilities to ensure our sensitive domestic sectors are protected."[39] Thus, not unlike the US, India has sought to balance the interests of its emergent export-oriented sectors with its vulnerable sectors (Efstathopoulos and Kelly 2014; Lilja 2012).

For India, its most sensitive domestic sector by far is agriculture. It has approximately 800 million people who are dependent on agriculture. This large population of peasants and farm workers—many barely on the brink of survival, as evidenced by the human development indicators cited above—are highly vulnerable to liberalization and fiercely oppose any market opening. Their sheer numbers make for a significant political constituency, with important implications for India's negotiating position at the WTO (Gupta and Ganguly 2014; Mahrenbach 2013; Stephen 2012). Given the strength of resistance from peasant farmers, as one of India's senior trade officials responsible for agriculture stated: "Any package will be difficult to sell down here domestically."[40]

Some in Geneva find India's position in the Doha agriculture negotiations—and its insistence on flexibilities such as the special safeguard mechanism (SSM) and special products exemptions (SPs)—incomprehensible. They speculate that because India has so much water in its tariffs, it does not in fact need these flexibilities and could afford to be more pliant and conciliatory on agriculture. Because of India's unilateral liberalization undertaken since the 1990s, the tariffs the country actually applies at its border fell far below the bound rates it committed to in the Uruguay Round. Its applied tariffs are now so much lower than its bound rates that India could afford to commit to large reductions in its tariff bindings in the Doha Round without having to make any real cuts to its applied tariffs. In other words, based on the current formula and flexibilities on the table for agriculture, in terms of the actual extent of India's market opening, there would be no change from the status quo (Gopinath and Laborde 2008). It would simply be making much of India's existing liberalization legally binding at the WTO. In order to make sense of India's insistence on securing flexibilities in the agriculture negotiations, then, it is necessary to understand the position of its agricultural constituency.

As part of India's economic reforms beginning in the 1990s, the state reduced subsidies and brought down import barriers in agriculture. India's peasant farmers found themselves caught between increasing exposure to foreign imports (which reduced prices and markets for their goods), rising input costs (for seeds, pesticides, and the like), and usurious moneylenders. The growing desperation of India's peasants has been evident in an epidemic of farmer suicides, with rates three times the national average (Barry 2014). Its peasant farmers are critical of India's trajectory of economic reform and liberalization; according to the leader of one of India's largest peasant movements, "Things are worse now. The real India is suffering a lot because of this development model and no one wants to see them [the rural poor]."[41] Peasant movements have waged a prolonged and ongoing struggle against India's liberal economic reforms. In the words of the peasant leader above:

We've been continuously fighting against these things. Because agriculture is a way of life for us, not trade. Farmers here have an average of one hectare of land, probably with debt. Sometimes they can't even sell their products in the local market, and if they do, the moneylender takes it first. Our trade policymakers can't understand that that's the difference with the West, with the US and EU. There farmers are only a small percent [of the population] and with huge landholdings—they have subsidies, they have huge farms, they can export. But even they are dependent on the government to survive, even they need subsidies to survive. So how can our government expect us to survive with no subsidies? Our farmers are totally ignored in the decision-making.[42]

It is interesting that the peasant leader highlights the difficulties faced by Indian farmers by referring to the disparities between the state support provided to agriculture in countries like the US and EU and that in India. India's peasant movements are seeking a return of quantitative restrictions, tariff protections, and government subsidies. The farm groups and associated NGOs effectively want state policy to move backward—to reverse the entire trend of India's liberalization and undo the previous decades of liberalization that they view as highly damaging.[43] However, bringing down India's tariff bindings through the Doha Round would have the effect of locking in its existing liberalization, and thus would permanently prevent the policy changes they are seeking. Overall, India's peasant movements are highly critical of the government, which they do not feel adequately represents their interests; as one representative stated, "They don't care about people, only industry."[44]

The Indian state has indicated that it is willing to substantially reduce its tariff bindings in the Doha Round (by an average of at least 36 percent and potentially as much as 50 percent in some areas) (WTO 2008), which would lock in and prevent it from rolling back the autonomous liberalization it has undertaken, but it has sought flexibilities through the SSM and SPs. As one of its officials stated, "The SSM, SPs—if these don't go the right way, it will be very difficult to deal with our constituency here. We need the SSM."[45] In the words of an adviser to the Indian government, regarding its peasant farm lobby: "The positions they take are extremely hardline."[46] During one stakeholder consultation prior to the Hong Kong Ministerial, one farm representative reportedly told negotiators: "You hear a lot about farmer suicides, but never trade negotiator suicides. If you sell us out and don't get us a good deal, don't bother coming home."[47] India has made the SSM and SPs a key part of its negotiating objectives in the Doha Round in order to appease its peasant farm lobby.

Thus while India has keen offensive interests in the round, it also has important defensive interests as well. To quote an Indian trade official: "What's important is balance—we need to push both our offensive and defensive interests."[48] In combining offensive and defensive elements, India's negotiating position is no different from that of the US, EU, or many other states. India has taken an aggressive offensive stance on services, seeking to expand market opportunities for its IT-BPO exporters, as well as on rich country agriculture subsidies, along with a defensive position in seeking to secure a SSM and SPs.

Along with India, China has also been an advocate of flexibilities for developing countries in agriculture, and specifically SPs and the SSM. China is a member of the G33 and backed India during the fight over the SSM in the Green Room at the 2008 Ministerial. Like India, a significant portion of China's population (35 percent) remains employed in agriculture.[49] Poverty is concentrated in rural areas, and China's manufacturing boom, concentrated in cities along the coast, has fueled a significant rise in income inequality between rural and urban areas. The income gap between urban and rural households in China is one of the largest in the world, with average incomes in urban areas more than three times higher than in rural areas (Frazier 2013). Although not subject to democratic politics as is India, the Chinese state is highly concerned about the potential for civil unrest generated by rising urban-rural inequality. Seen as potentially volatile and politically destabilizing, the conditions in rural areas have become a major focus of Chinese policy; since the early 2000s, the Chinese government has made promoting rural development and increasing rural incomes one of its top policy objectives. Yet the Doha Round could undermine these objectives, since—in contrast to India—China's current agricultural tariff levels would be significantly affected by the Doha Round. As described in the last chapter, with its WTO accession, China was required to substantially reduced its tariffs and nontariff barriers; it now has relatively low tariffs in agriculture and very little water in its tariffs (its bound and applied rates are virtually identical), such that cuts in its bound rates under Doha would result in cuts to its applied tariffs. The tariff reduction formula now on the table in the Doha Round and largely agreed to by states would force China to make real tariff cuts. Whereas for India the Doha Round would require little or no additional market opening in agriculture, it would require China to further open its agriculture market. This is why China has supported efforts by India and the G33 to secure flexibilities like SPs and the SSM; in fact, many negotiators contend that these measures are of greater economic significance to China than India.

Some critics contend that the defensive maneuvers of India and China to protect their vulnerable agricultural sectors—their push for an SSM and SPs— represent a departure from the liberal principles of the WTO. These measures have been advanced in the name of food security, livelihood security, and rural development. The SSM, in particular, has been portrayed by the US and other developed country negotiators as a threat to the foundation of the WTO and its project of progressive trade liberalization. The SSM would allow developing countries to raise tariffs in response to an import surge; a key point of contention in the debate over the SSM is whether countries should be allowed to breach their Uruguay Round commitments (that is, to raise tariffs above the maximum level at which they capped them in the last round), which is sought by India, China, and the other members of the G33. Opponents argue that this would provide a way for countries to effectively undo the commitments they made in the Uruguay Round, thus undoing liberalization they have already undertaken. In their view, this would represent a move backward, away from the progress of trade liberalization. US Trade Representative Susan Schwab, for example, described India's and China's efforts to secure a SSM as "unconscionable," accusing them of "blatant protectionism," which, if successful, would have "rolled the global trading system back" by decades (quoted in *BBC News* 2008; *Guardian* 2008).

However, despite the rhetoric of US trade officials, India's and China's efforts to secure the SSM and SPs do not represent a systemic challenge to the multilateral trading system or a break with the fundamental principles of the WTO. The multilateral trading system has always operated by providing for some exceptions to liberalization, seen as necessary to smooth impediments and allow the larger program of liberalization to occur. These measures are in keeping with the WTO's pre-existing tool kit; they do not represent a radical change or the emergence of an alternative policy program. SPs are no different than other exemptions—such as the "sensitive products" (SEs) exemption granted to both developed and developing countries—that have been used to shield certain products from tariff cuts in order to facilitate the broader process of liberalization. Likewise, the SSM is modeled after the Special (Agricultural) Safeguard (SSG) created during the Uruguay Round. Like the SSM, the SSG provides a means for countries to protect themselves against dramatic price fluctuations and import surges; yet the SSG was highly unequal in its application and limited almost exclusively to developed countries. Most developing countries are prevented from using the SSG because they did not "tariffy" (that is, convert their quantitative trade restrictions [such as quotas] into tariffs and then cut) during the Uruguay Round (Wilkinson, Hannah, and Scott 2014).[50]

The SSG thus operated as a form of reverse special and differential treatment privileging the developed countries. In demanding the SSM, India and the G33 are only seeking access to a safeguard provision similar to that provided to the US, EU, and other rich countries. Moreover, if effective, the SSM would, at best, help to protect the existing incomes of peasant farmers in the face of an import surge. It would thus maintain the status quo but it would do nothing to alter present circumstances or improve their incomes in any way. The SSM and SPs merely represent exemptions that would facilitate rather than challenge the WTO's program of liberalization. The measures advanced by India and China would not fundamentally deviate from or alter the existing trading system, nor are they intended to.

As detailed in Chapter 3, the GATT/WTO has always operated as a strange blend of liberalism and mercantilism. India and China are simply behaving as the traditional powers always have—seeking to protect vulnerable parts of their own markets, while pressing other countries to open theirs. As Krasner (1985: 67) wrote decades ago regarding the traditional powers: "Trade barriers have been regarded as unfortunate concessions to interest-group pressure. They do not indicate that the North has abandoned its commitment to liberal rules of the game." Just as the US and Europe have long sought to protect their powerful farm lobby groups, so too are India and China now seeking to protect their large populations of vulnerable—and politically weighty (in the case of democratic India) or potentially politically destabilizing (in the case of authoritarian China)—peasant farmers.

A further instance of India seeking to protect sensitive areas of its own society, particularly agriculture, emerged more recently. In 2013, India passed a new National Food Security Bill intended to provide subsidized food for more than 800 million people. This initiative was widely seen as a political tool by the ruling party at the time, the National Congress Party led by Prime Minister Manmohan Singh, to boost its popular support in advance of the hotly contested 2014 national elections. Although the Congress Party was ultimately defeated, once in power the new Bharatiya Janata Party (BJP) government under Prime Minister Narendra Modi, which had previously opposed the food security program, not only maintained the program but also continued to staunchly defend it at the WTO. Under WTO rules, trade-distorting subsidies to farmers in a developing country cannot exceed 10 percent of the value of its total agricultural production. Since India's food security bill involves providing minimum support prices to farmers, if the associated subsidies (the difference between the support price and the market price) breach the 10 percent limit, India would be in violation of WTO rules and potentially vulnerable to a legal challenge.

While the US, in particular, has decried India's new food security scheme as a violation of the free market principles of the WTO, the reality is that WTO members have used such schemes for many years and consideration was explicitly made for them in the Uruguay Round (Wilkinson, Hannah, and Scott 2014). The fact that India's program risks running afoul of WTO rules while the US and other advanced-industrialized states are able to subsidize their agriculture sectors to a far greater extent is a product of the highly asymmetrical nature of the Uruguay Round Agreement on Agriculture. Ironically, the Uruguay Round was structured such that rich countries like the US, with huge agricultural subsidies, were allowed to maintain their high subsidies provided they agreed to marginally reduce them; meanwhile, most developing countries like India, which did not subsidize agriculture at the time, were left with much stricter limits (*Economist* 2014).

Specifically, developed countries like the US were required to cap and commit to reducing their "Amber Box," or most trade distorting, subsidies by 20 percent over six years (referred to as reducing their "total aggregate measurement of support," or AMS). Based on this commitment, the US is subject to a spending limit of $19.1 billion in Amber Box outlays. However, it is also permitted to exempt from this calculation any subsidies falling within its "de minimis" limits: non-commodity-specific support that is less than 5 percent of the value of total agricultural production (based on US agriculture production of $297 billion in 2007, for example, this would allow it to exempt up to $15 billion in non-product-specific support), as well as commodity-specific support that is below 5 percent of that specific commodity's value of production (for corn, to take one commodity as an example, it could exempt up to nearly $4 billion in product-specific support) (Schnepf 2014). In other words, for developed countries like the US, the cap imposed on their subsidies was set high (Total AMS), and they were allowed considerable exemptions (de minimis). In contrast, because India and most other developing countries had few domestic subsidies at the time of the Uruguay Round, they were required to limit any Amber Box support solely to de minimis levels of 10 percent. To quantify this, the US could be allowed to provide nearly double the amount of highly trade distorting subsidies permitted to India ($49.1 billion versus $24.8 billion).[51]

Under existing WTO rules, rich countries are thus allowed more space to support their farmers. The Uruguay Round essentially worked to codify or lock in existing discrepancies in levels of subsidization between developed and developing countries by imposing differential limits on how much each could subsidize. In addition, many developed countries like the US have engaged in "box shifting," moving the vast majority of their subsidy programs from the Amber Box to the "Green Box"—a category created by the US and EU in the Uruguay Round for measures designated "least trade distorting"—which has the effect of shielding them from any cuts.[52] The current structure of WTO obligations is further biased against India because rich countries are allowed to subsidize their agricultural exports, while India is not (Subramanian 2014). Existing WTO subsidy rules are thus inherently unbalanced, providing considerably more flexibility to developed countries than to developing countries (de Shutter 2011). As a result, rich countries like the US "are still able to protect their own producers from competition, distort world market prices and depress farm revenues in food importing developing countries" (Haberli 2014).

India, however, came to be in danger of breaching its obligations made in the Uruguay Round, since those obligations bound it to a much lower level of agricultural subsidies than those provided by the rich countries. Like many developing countries, lacking the resources to provide big subsidies to its farmers along the lines of the US and EU, India's agricultural policies used to consist of protecting farmers via tariffs. Since the early 1990s, as a result of a combination of unilateral liberalization, IMF-imposed structural adjustment, and the Uruguay agreement, India's tariffs have fallen steadily and dramatically. India's agricultural policies are starting to resemble those of advanced countries as it moves away from tariffs to subsidies as the primary means to protect its agricultural sector (Subramanian 2014). In seeking changes to WTO rules to enable it to operate its new food security program free from the risk of a WTO challenge, India has simply been claiming the right to do what the rich countries have long done, which is subsidize agriculture. It is a sign of India's growing clout that in 2013–14 it was able to overpower fierce opposition from the US and secure an interim agreement that its food security program would indeed be protected from WTO challenges along with the commitment to negotiate a permanent solution.

Conclusion

This chapter has sought to contest the dominant depiction of India put forward by the US and other advanced-industrialized states as a troublesome malcontent intent on disrupting the liberal trade agenda at the WTO. As it has shown, India's economic reform program, grounded in the principles of neoliberal orthodoxy, has driven a fundamental reorientation of its trade policy. Having undertaken substantial unilateral liberalization of its own economy, India has embraced integration into the global economy as essential to its economic development. With the emergence of the world's leading IT-BPO services export sector, it has major offensive trade interests that it has sought to advance through the Doha Round. Yet I have argued that, just like the traditional powers, emerging powers like India must balance a complex mix of trade interests. India's negotiating position at the WTO—combining efforts to promote liberalization in its areas of export interest and protection in its areas of sensitivity—is no more incoherent or contradictory than that of the US or other traditional powers. Moreover, historically, the WTO as an institution and its rules have been specifically designed to meet these needs on the part of the US and other advanced-industrialized states.

Chapter 8

Conclusion

A S the preceding chapters have demonstrated, there has been a significant
shift in power at the WTO. The rise of Brazil, India, and China has brought
an end to the unfettered dominance of the US and its advanced-industrialized
allies, and the corresponding marginalization of developing countries, which
characterized the multilateral trading system for more than half a century.
These three developing countries have joined the inner circle of power and
become central players, exercising considerable influence in both negotiations
and dispute settlement. This concluding chapter returns to the central objective of the book: assessing the impact of these power shifts on multilateralism
and the neoliberal project of the WTO. As I will show, the implications have
been profound, severely disrupting the workings of the institution.

Agendas of the Emerging Powers

Brazil, India, and China have seen their economies transformed by the
emergence of highly competitive export-oriented sectors—in agriculture, services, and manufacturing, respectively. The emerging powers have been among
the primary beneficiaries from the neoliberal turn in the global political economy and the free trade policies adopted by many countries in recent decades,
which have opened markets for their exports and fueled their newfound wealth
and prosperity. Their economic rise has occurred within, and been made possible by, the existing system of open markets and trade. All three countries have
a significant interest in maintaining and strengthening the rules of the multilateral trading system, as well as major offensive trading interests that they
have sought to advance through the Doha Round—whether strengthening the
protection provided by WTO rules against potential trade barriers being raised
against their exports or pursuing (to varying degrees) liberalization in their sectors of export interest. Beyond the negotiations, the new powers have become

major users of the WTO's existing rules and dispute settlement system to advance their interests vis-à-vis the traditional powers and other states; and, as will be discussed below, they are also increasingly going outside the WTO—to bilateral and regional trade agreements, for example—to advance their trade interests, access inputs, and expand markets for their exports.

Rather than rejecting the rules, norms, and principles of the liberal trading system, the new developing country powers have embraced them, seeking to work within the rules and use them to their advantage. In effect, the new powers have turned the WTO system against its originators, focusing attention on the hypocrisy of the US and its industrialized allies and demanding that they undertake further market liberalization. In a major shift in roles, the US—the main proponent of liberalization throughout the history of the GATT/WTO—has been put on the defensive, as its own protectionist policies, particularly in agriculture, became a central issue of contention in the Doha Round. The emerging powers have accepted the basic tenets of the trade regime; their objection is to how the system and its rules have been applied in practice. What the new powers have sought to challenge is their subordination to the traditional powers, and specifically the dominance of the US. As a representative of Indian business stated, "The sentiment in India is not anti-WTO, but anti-WTO that is one-sided."[1] The rising powers are thus seeking to use the WTO to bind and constrain the US and other rich countries, just as they have been bound and constrained by its rules and disciplines.

This dynamic—of developing country powers going on the offensive against the advanced-industrialized states and pushing them to open their markets and reduce trade barriers through the WTO—is new. It represents a major break with their agendas and strategies in earlier decades. Like many developing countries, Brazil, India, and China all once sought to insulate themselves from global capitalism, through domestic policies of import-substitution industrialization and/or state socialist economic planning, and to bring about a sweeping overhaul of the liberal international economic order. Now, however, the recent actions of Brazil, India, and China at the WTO look nothing like their previous radical activism.

Disillusioned with the older ideology of anti-imperialism and projects of national development, the new powers have embraced the global market and trade. From seeking to delink from the global economy, shield themselves from trade, and turn inward to foster economic development, these countries have each shifted to outward-oriented, export-led growth strategies that seek to increase their integration into the global economy. They have bought into the global free trade paradigm—that exports are essential to economic growth, development, and prosperity—and, therefore, that their interests lie in opening foreign markets via the WTO. The new powers are no longer putting forward alternative visions for how the global economy should be structured and organized, or questioning the basic value of global trade liberalization. Rather, they have become staunch supporters of the existing global economic order that has provided markets for their exports and fueled their economic expansion—only now they seek to mobilize it in the service of their own interests. In a marked departure from the past, the emerging powers are pushing for change *within* the GATT/WTO system, and their goals—including subsidy reduction, increased market access, and stronger rules to combat contingent protections—fit well within its norms and principles.

This analysis of the objectives and behavior of the emerging powers at the WTO departs from the interpretation put forward by many Western negotiators, officials and trade analysts, particularly those originating from the US. Such accounts routinely blame the rising powers for the failure of the Doha Round and allege that these states are undermining the principles of the multilateral trading system. Typically pointing to measures such as the SSM, they paint the emerging powers as "antitrade" "protectionist blockers," whom they accuse of "hijacking" the round or "trying to kill the round," and being unwilling to "pull their weight" by granting sufficient concessions.[2] However, as the preceding chapters have illustrated, to suggest that Brazil, India, and China are antitrade is disingenuous, if not ludicrous—trade is the very basis of their economic growth and stability. Furthermore, they have each embarked on major programs of market reform and liberalization in recent decades, centered on embracing global economic integration and including significant unilateral trade liberalization.

Although the new powers have gained considerable power, they are not entirely unconstrained in their ability to pursue their offensive trade interests at the WTO. One such constraint is the risk of backlash, which operates most acutely upon China and has caused it to be less aggressive than expected in seeking market access gains in the Doha Round. China's behavior at the WTO has been heavily shaped by the desire to *avoid* provoking a systemic challenge to the regime of increasingly open markets and liberalized trade that could jeopardize the continued functioning of the system as a whole. Another factor constraining the ability of the rising powers to aggressively pursue liberalization through the WTO is the need to maintain alliances with and the backing of other developing countries. The existence of such constraints should not, however, be taken to mean that Brazil, India, and China lack power. No country has ever had complete free rein or the ability to force the WTO to operate exactly as it liked. Even US power at the height of its hegemony was constrained: it had to grapple with opposition from other states, compromise to secure their participation (even if such compromises tended to be tilted in its favor), and never fully got what it wanted.

To be clear, each of the emerging powers has an active state, engaged in interventionist policies to promote the growth of their exports and foster economic development. Unquestionably, their domestic economic policies depart from the "pure" dictates and standards of neoliberal orthodoxy. But so do those of *all* states, including the US and other advanced-industrialized countries. Moreover, even if the emerging powers have embraced an active role for the state in their own domestic economies (Ban and Blyth 2013), they are still eager to push Washington Consensus–type policies (that is, trade and market liberalization with tight restrictions on state economic intervention) on other states.

Furthermore, while they have substantial export interests, this is not to say that the emerging powers do not also have defensive interests that affect their negotiating position and strategy at the WTO—again, *all* countries do—but that is not equivalent to being antisystemic, as some of their critics have claimed. In areas where their exports have the potential to flourish, the new powers have become eager adherents to the doctrine of free trade—proselytizing the virtues of free markets, preaching the need for strict adherence to the doctrine of laissez-faire, and singing the virtues of liberating international trade to flow freely without state interference. Simultaneously, however, just like the old powers, the emerging powers have also sought to maintain protections in uncompetitive and sensitive areas of their own markets. The motto of the new powers, like the old, could perhaps best be characterized as "free markets . . . for other states" or "let free markets reign . . . in my areas of competitive advantage." Their embrace of free trade has been just as self-serving, selective, and inconsistent as that of the traditional powers.

The expansion of their export sectors has given Brazil, India, and China powerful interests in global trade liberalization, and the thrust of their domestic economic policies over the past several decades has been toward greater liberalization and integration into global markets. At the same time, however, the emerging powers also each have politically volatile sources of opposition to liberalization domestically with which they must grapple. They have therefore sought to maximize policy space within the framework of the multilateral trading system to manage push-back within their own societies. In this, the emerging powers are no different than the old. While China and India, for example, have indeed fought hard to protect their vulnerable agricultural sectors, so too has the US. Although the specifics of their situations and motives may differ— with China seeking to reduce the risk of a rural revolt that could overthrow the state, India to mollify its large constituency of peasants to keep the ruling government of the day in power, and the US to avoid provoking its rich and politically powerful farm and agribusiness lobbies—their agendas are remarkably similar. Domestic tensions are precisely why *no* state is advancing a purely neoliberal agenda at the WTO. Instead, their negotiating positions reflect these contradictory impulses of liberalization and protection.

As I have shown, even the most controversial measures the emerging powers have advanced—such as agricultural protection for developing countries via the SSM and SPs—accord with the framework and principles of the liberal trading system and closely resemble the exemptions that the developed countries have long secured for themselves. The trading regime explicitly adopted a "progressive liberalization" approach to allow states to introduce changes gradually, as a means of ensuring the feasibility of liberalization given inevitable opposition from negatively affected constituencies. The GATT/WTO has always contained exemptions, exceptions, and safeguards for countries, though until now they have largely been designed to benefit the dominant advanced-industrialized states. Such measures are justified as allowing states to manage contentious social forces within their own polities by creating small buffers that would enable the larger project of liberalization to progress without disruption. The multilateral trading system thus embodies a gradualist approach to liberalization, which is exactly what the emerging powers are undertaking through their domestic reform programs. While the new powers have each embarked on a trajectory of market opening and liberalization, they still seek to maximize their autonomy to direct and control their own processes of liberalization, which is directly comparable to the US's own resistance to relinquishing its sovereignty over economic policy to the WTO and other external institutions and actors.

In their behavior at the WTO, the new powers are thus motivated by similar objectives and political pressures as the old. Contrary to the allegations of the US and other traditional powers, the agendas Brazil, India, and China have been pursuing accord with, rather than depart from, the principles of the multilateral trading system and, in fact, mirror the agendas the traditional Western powers have themselves long pursued within the multilateral trading system.

Multilateral Disintegration

The new powers are challenging the hegemony of the US rather than the neoliberal paradigm of the WTO. Yet the result has been a clash between the old and new powers, with each side demanding additional liberalization from the other but refusing to yield itself. This conflict has been the defining feature of the Doha Round and produced its repeated breakdown. As the WTO director-general has acknowledged, at the core of the Doha impasse is a dispute over "the balance in contributions and responsibilities between emerging and advanced economies" (WTO 2011). The emergence of new powers to counterbalance American, and more broadly Northern, dominance has shifted the terms of a prospective WTO agreement. The US and other advanced-industrialized states can no longer impose a highly unbalanced deal upon developing countries as they have in the past. In fact, quite the reverse—because of the important gains and concessions secured by the developing world over the course of the round, the US is now confronted with a prospective Doha agreement that key figures in Congress and its business and farm lobby groups find deeply unsatisfactory. The US, they contend, is being made to significantly cut its tariffs on industrial and agricultural goods and agricultural subsidies, while gaining insufficient new access to foreign markets for its exports. Consequently, as its own trade policies have increasingly come under fire over the course of the Doha Round, the US has responded by progressively ratcheting up its demands for trade concessions from other states, and particularly the large emerging economies. The American stance is set out, for example, in the President's Trade Agenda (US 2011):

In a negotiation in which the United States is being asked to significantly cut tariffs on all industrial and agricultural goods, we are asking these emerging economies to accept responsibility commensurate with their expanded roles in the global economy.... For these talks to remain relevant, they must address the world as it is and as it will be in the coming decades. Our requests of key emerging economies will continue to be based on the reasonable proposition that countries with rapidly expanding degrees of global competitiveness and exporting success should be prepared to contribute meaningfully toward trade liberalization.

Similarly, a European negotiator stated, "For our industry, what is currently on the table is definitely not enough, and for the US even more. We expect a lot from these countries [the emerging economies] because they are the new competitors."[3] As a result, in the latter stages of the round, the US and EU have aggressively pressed for greater market-opening from the large emerging economies for manufactured and agricultural goods, as well as services; with the US in particular, for example, pressuring the major developing countries to participate in specific industrial goods sectorals and commit to not using their agricultural flexibilities in key areas of interest to American exporters.

For their part, however, China, India, and Brazil contend that these demands are out of proportion to the reforms that the US itself is willing to undertake, particularly on agriculture subsidies, and that the US position is rife with double standards. The US is minimalist in making concessions, but maximalist in making demands of others, especially in the area of agriculture, which has been a critical issue in the Doha Round (Bhagwati 2007). Furthermore, the rising powers emphasize that Doha was sold to the developing world as a "Development Round," with the promise that it would deliver real benefits to the Global South (for example, see China 2007). A key aspect of the Doha development mandate is the principle that developing countries, including China, India, and Brazil, would not be required to engage in an equal exchange of concessions with the advanced-industrialized states, but rather that the final bargain would be struck on the basis of "less than full reciprocity" in favor of developing countries. Developing countries envisioned this as crucial to beginning to redress the historical imbalances built into previous multilateral trade agreements. From the perspective of the emerging powers, the US is now trying to change the terms of the deal, and its present demands—which have escalated over the course of the Doha Round in response to the complaints of its domestic lobby groups—are unfair and unjustified. The US, they contend, is seeking not even equal reciprocity but less than full reciprocity in its *own* favor, in clear contravention of the development mandate of the round. For American negotiators, however, the vague development promises attached to the round were primarily a political maneuver to ensure its launch; the US has never intended to fulfill such promises if doing so would require a significant sacrifice of its own commercial interests, especially in favor of its emerging competitors.

Their new power has enabled Brazil, India, and China to resist what they perceive to be unfair demands from the traditional powers. In response, the US has eagerly placed blame for the Doha breakdown on their shoulders. US Trade Representative Michael Froman, for example, attributed the fact that expanding global trade rules has become "increasingly difficult" to "the emergence of emerging economies that have been unwilling to date to assume enhanced responsibilities commensurate with their increased role in the global economy" (cited in *Bridges Weekly* 2014b). Of course, assigning blame is part of the strategy of trade negotiations. As Andrew Hurrell (2010) has written in another context, the question of "responsibility" in international negotiations is one of perspective. Accordingly, determinations of who is responsible for the failure of the Doha Round depend largely on where one sits in the negotiations (Scott 2015). From the perspective of the emerging powers and much of the rest of the developing world, it is the US who is the irresponsible actor. Even European negotiators privately refute the US's vocal assertions that what is currently on the table from the large emerging economies is "useless" and indicate that it still offers significant gains for both the US and EU, only not as much as the traditional powers had expected coming into the round.[4]

The Doha Round impasse centers on the issue of what constitutes a fair exchange. At the heart of this conflict is a distributional struggle over the outcome of the round and where its costs and benefits should fall. But this is a conflict taking place *within* the existing normative and institutional framework of the WTO; in other words, it is a norm-governed rather than norm-contesting conflict (Ruggie 1982). And now that the two sides are relatively evenly matched—insofar as neither has been able to overpower the other and impose its preferences—a stalemate has resulted.

The Doha negotiations have broken down repeatedly in a North-South confrontation centered on the traditional and emerging powers. The collapse of the Cancun Ministerial in 2003 was only the beginning of a series of highly publicized and acrimonious failures that have beset the round. Following another collapse of talks in July 2006, the director-general declared the round "suspended," and it remained so for most of the latter half of that year. The renewed talks broke down again at the June 2007 negotiations between the US, EU, Brazil, and India in Potsdam, Germany, over agriculture subsidies and market access in the North and industrial tariffs in the South. Then negotiations failed yet again at the July 2008 Mini-Ministerial in Geneva, ostensibly as a result of conflict among India, China, and the US over the SSM, although the same deeper issues remained at play. As one journalist wrote in the *Financial Times* (2008): "Following [the Doha Round's] repeated collapses is no longer simply like watching *Groundhog Day*: it now resembles being forced to watch *Groundhog Day* over and over again."[5] Although the Doha Round was originally meant to be concluded by early 2005, that and all subsequent deadlines have been missed.

The Doha Round has remained deadlocked along the same fault line with no significant progress since 2008. With the old and new powers unable to reach agreement, the negotiations were once again officially declared at an impasse at the Geneva Ministerial Meeting in December 2011 (WTO 2011). While member states expressed their commitment to continuing to work toward agreement, they publicly acknowledged that conclusion of the full round was unlikely. In short, the Doha Round has effectively collapsed. At the G20, APEC, and other global summits, world leaders continue to proclaim support for concluding the round, but many believe it is now effectively dead. The persistent failure of the negotiations has led even the director-general to acknowledge that "the WTO is in crisis" (WTO 2006).

This has spurred a desperate effort to rescue the credibility of the WTO, with the institution going into damage control mode. Negotiations shifted to a last-ditch effort to salvage a small number of issues from the round on which states appeared closer to agreement, with the goal of achieving an "early-harvest" at the Bali Ministerial in December 2013. There was a strong sense among the WTO Secretariat and many states and observers that a successful conclusion to the Bali meeting could help counter the WTO's increasing marginalization as a forum for international trade negotiations (Wilkinson, Hannah, and Scott 2014: 1037). At the Ministerial, states reached agreement on the "Bali Package," the centerpiece of which was an agreement on trade facilitation that would streamline customs procedures to expedite trade flows and also included select issues related to agriculture and SDT for LDCs (WTO 2013). In spite of efforts to portray the Bali package as a historic agreement and a victory for the WTO, it was in fact quite limited. Aside from trade facilitation, it included an agreement to allow developing countries a temporary dispensation from existing WTO-mandated subsidy limits to engage in public food stockholding for food security purposes; however, this was highly contentious, and a permanent resolution was put off for future negotiation. The remainder of the deal consisted of various "best-endeavor" (non-legally binding) promises to help LDCs gain greater access to rich-country markets for their exports, but these were limited to political statements without force (many of which were actually made a decade before at the Hong Kong Ministerial and are unlikely ever to be implemented), as well as pledges to engage in future negotiations (Wilkinson, Hannah, and Scott 2014). The micro-deal agreed to in Bali represents only a tiny fraction of the original Doha mandate, and even this limited agreement proved fractious and difficult to achieve (Wilkinson, Hannah, and Scott 2014). In addition, its enactment was nearly derailed in subsequent months by continuing conflict between the US and India over trade facilitation and food stockholding.

Despite the Bali agreement, the future of the Doha Round is bleak. Divisions over the core issues in the round remain deeply entrenched, and it appears highly unlikely that states will be able to conclude the round. For the first time at the GATT/WTO, no one country, or bloc of countries, is dominant or can dictate outcomes. In these new circumstances, in which power is balanced between the traditional and emerging powers, these states have proven unable to reach agreement. Once again, we have what Mortimer (1984: 141), in the context of the NIEO, termed a "politics of stalemate"—the inability to move forward an international agenda because of North-South conflict—only for very different reasons today. Brazil, India, and China are no longer seeking to effect structural change in the international system. On the contrary, the rising powers have become supporters of the existing global order, which has supplied the conditions for their newfound economic success, and they have sought to advance their interests within the liberal trade paradigm of the WTO. However, in turning the tools of the multilateral trading system against the traditional Northern powers, the result has been stalemate.

In a situation of more equitable power relations among states, multilateralism—the ability of states to cooperate to construct international laws, rules, and institutions—has disintegrated. The emergence of competing powers to counterbalance the traditional dominance of the US has brought the Doha Round to a standstill. The current deadlock at the WTO thus starkly reveals how much the successful multilateralism of the past was, in fact, reliant on highly unequal power relations. Agreement among states required the ability of the more powerful to force the less powerful to consent. Now, greater equality among states has caused the multilateral trading system to fail in its central endeavor: states have been unable to cooperate in pursuit of the WTO's agenda of expanding the institutional architecture governing trade.

The Disruption of the Neoliberal Project at the WTO

As described at the start of the book, neoliberal globalization is an institution-building project, and the creation of the WTO represented not the realization of the neoliberal project in the realm of trade but only its beginning. The multilateral trading system is intended to work through successive rounds of negotiations to progressively liberalize trade. Indeed, the necessity of perpetual progress in expanding and deepening liberalization is among its fundamental organizing principles. WTO negotiators and officials frequently draw analogy to a bicycle that must be continuously moving forward lest it topple over (Siles-Brügge 2013; Strange 1985; Wilkinson 2009b). This sentiment is expressed, for example, by James Bacchus (2004), former US legislator, trade negotiator, and chair of the WTO's appellate body: "[L]ike a bicycle, the world trading system must always go forward. For, if it ever stops going forward, it will surely fail." He explains:

[T]he history of trade, and of trade policymaking, teaches us that a failure to move steadily forward toward freer trade condemns the world trading system to topple over and fall due to the accumulating pressures of protectionism.... [W]e must move steadily, gradually, incrementally forward on the bicycle, because, if we do not, the world will be overwhelmed by all the many reactionary forces that would have the nations of the world retreat from trade. If we do not, the world will turn away from growing economic integration, turn away from the mutual prosperity of growing economic interdependence, and turn inward toward all the self-deceiving illusions and the self-defeating delusions of an isolating and enervating economic autarky.... [W]e must keep lowering the barriers to trade or we will risk losing all the many gains from trade.

Thus, whatever the pressures, whatever the economic happenstances, and whatever the political circumstances, we must always keep the bicycle we call the "world trading system" going forward by making ever more progress toward ever freer trade. We must keep pedaling.... [A]bove all, we must never, never stop. (Bacchus 2004)

The bicycle metaphor is linked to a widely held belief that an interruption in multilateral trade liberalization generated an outbreak of protectionism that caused the Great Depression and led, ultimately, to World War II (Wilkinson

2009b). Since its inception in the postwar era, the multilateral trading system has been driven by "the perception that a fundamental crisis might result should trade liberalization be allowed to stall" (Wilkinson 2009b). Fred Bergsten (2005), a prominent trade economist and adviser to the US government, for example, invoked these fears in a caution to trade ministers prior to the Hong Kong Ministerial:

Since history clearly shows that trade policy must move forward continuously or risk sliding backward into protectionism and mercantilism ... the consequences of Doha's failure for international security as well as economic relations around the world could be enormous.

This belief in the necessity of perpetual liberalization is a core tenet of the ideology that motivates the WTO.

The establishment of the WTO in the Uruguay Round provided the forum and the framework for subsequent rounds of negotiations intended to advance its project of liberalizing trade. The Doha Round was intended to be the next step in the liberalization of global markets. After years of deadlock, however, the "promise" of the Doha Round has yet to be realized. Instead, the future of the round is in doubt, with good reason to believe that it may never be concluded. At the WTO, the new balance of power in the global political economy appears to have brought a halt to the construction of new rules to further the process of neoliberal globalization.

Even if negotiators managed to salvage the Doha Round and bring it to a conclusion, it would be a dramatically watered down version of what was originally intended. The extent of liberalization that would occur as a result of Doha is now minuscule compared with what was initially foreseen: estimates of the value of liberalization—its impact on global income—anticipated from the round have shrunk dramatically from when the round began. When Doha was first launched, the World Bank (2001) estimated that an ambitious round could yield as much as $830 billion in global welfare gains; in stark contrast, most current estimates place the value of the core pillars of the round in the range of $40–95 billion (Decreux and Fontagne 2009; Hufbauer et al. 2010; Polaski 2006). The Doha Round is now "a greatly diluted version of what was launched in December 2001" (Dadush 2009: 1), and its potential impact, if concluded, is expected to be "minimalist and inconsequential" (Whalley 2006). An adviser to the Indian government described it as "Doha-lite."[6]

This view is shared even by opponents of liberalization. Many NGOs—who have been among the strongest critics of neoliberalism and the expansion of WTO rules resulting from the Uruguay Round—view the prospective Doha agreement as much less of a threat than it was initially. As an NGO representative stated, "The agenda they are negotiating has changed a lot from where they started. The Doha agreement has gotten much less bad as the pushback from developing countries has gotten stronger in the last few years."[7] Over the course of the round, the extent of liberalization has been progressively whittled away. With the relatively equal status of the old and new powers, no side has been able to force major new liberalization on the other, and each has been able to carve out significant exemptions. The new powers, for example, have been able to push back against the demands of the US and EU and secure concessions (both weaker formulas for tariff reductions and extensive flexibilities) that significantly reduced the extent of liberalization developing countries would be required to undertake in either agriculture or manufactured goods. Seeking to curry favor—and isolate the large emerging economies—the US and EU have extended significant concessions to many other categories of developing countries. In addition, many major areas of intended liberalization have been taken off the agenda and removed from the Doha Round altogether, such as the Singapore Issues.

Moreover, if we look at the current substance of the prospective Doha agreement, there is no new expansion of WTO rule-making and liberalization into new areas as occurred in the Uruguay Round. The effort to continue the expansion of the scope of WTO rules begun in the Uruguay Round by adding the Singapore Issues—investment, competition, and government procurement—failed. Of the "new issues" that were brought into the WTO in the Uruguay Round—such as services and intellectual property—little additional liberalization is expected to occur in these areas as a result of the Doha Round. In services, only relatively moderate new liberalization, beyond what states have already taken unilaterally, is likely to occur through Doha. In intellectual property, the fierce criticism of the TRIPs agreement from developing countries forced the US and EU to relinquish their hopes of pursuing expanded IP protections (TRIPs+) at the WTO and to pursue such provisions elsewhere (such as bilateral and regional agreements). As a result, the Doha Round has now been limited primarily to tariff and subsidy reductions, and most negotiators report that they view the proposed cuts in these areas as relatively small.[8] Tariffs and subsidies in agriculture and manufacturing emerged at the center of the conflict between the old and new powers. Interestingly, tariffs and subsidies are the very issues that constituted the traditional bread and butter of trade agreements under the old embedded liberalism of the GATT. In fact, with a narrow agenda confined to tariffs and subsidies and the inclusion of major flexibilities for most countries, even before its collapse, the Doha Round came to look much more like the embedded liberalism of the GATT than the neoliberalism of the WTO.

What has occurred at the WTO defies the expectations of existing international relations theory. As described in the introductory chapter, liberal institutionalism sees multipolarity as conducive to international cooperation and predicts that new powers will be smoothly integrated into the Western-made liberal world order. Yet, as I have shown, contrary to such expectations, contemporary power shifts have created serious problems for multilateralism at the WTO. Such an outcome is more consistent with the expectations of realism, which foresees power struggles, conflict, and a weakening of multilateralism as the result of the emergence of new powers and the corresponding decline of US hegemony. Realists tend to assume, however, that this conflict will be caused by the emerging powers rejecting the norms and principles of the existing liberal economic order created by the Western powers. Similarly, critical theorists inspired by world-systems and dependency theory and critical Marxism raise the prospect that new powers could challenge the existing international economic order, although they express hope that this could disrupt the current trajectory of neoliberal globalization and usher in a new, more equitable and progressive economic order. Although the emergence of new centers of power has, indeed, disrupted multilateral cooperation and the institutional project of neoliberal globalization at the WTO, this is not for the reasons assumed by either realism or critical approaches. Instead, as I have demonstrated, the cause of multilateral disintegration has been not the rejection of the existing liberal international economic order by the rising powers, but their embrace of that system and demand that it now also serve their interests.

Explaining the Destabilizing Impact of Power Shifts

Although the intentions of Brazil, India, and China are not antisystemic—they are decidedly *not* seeking to fundamentally disrupt or alter the structures of global capitalism—their rise has nonetheless had antisystemic effects. This raises the important question of why a situation of greater equality among states—specifically the emergence of new powers from the developing world capable of countering the dominance of the US and other advanced-industrial states—has undermined the ability of the WTO to fulfill its intended mandate.

The rising powers have embraced the core principles supposedly embodied by the WTO: multilateralism, based on the sovereign equality of states engaged in the reciprocal exchange of concessions, and free trade. Why, then, has this had such a subversive effect on the WTO? The answer, I argue, is that the institution was never genuinely intended to achieve either of these things—at least not as fully realized principles, applied equally by and to all parties. In reality, both the purported multilateralism and free trade of the WTO were highly asymmetrical, shaped by unequal power relations among states. As Hurrell (2010: 8) aptly writes, "Multilateralism worked for much of the post-1945 period in part because it was not very multilateral." In the case of the multilateral trading system, it worked for more than half a century because it was neither very multilateral *nor* genuinely about free trade.

The purported equality and universalism of the multilateral trading system was a myth that veiled the exercise of US power and obscured the role of the GATT/WTO as an instrument of American hegemony. Its liberal principles have never been equally or universally applied, but only partially and selectively, to the benefit of the American hegemon and other dominant states. The contradictions and asymmetries of the multilateral trading system reached their height in the Uruguay Round, which launched the neoliberal project at the WTO as a strategy aimed at reinforcing and enhancing US power by expanding markets for its goods and capital. The US deployed the rhetoric of liberalism, and subsequently neoliberalism, as a means to advance its economic and political interests—but, crucially, this does not mean it had any intention of subjecting itself to the same doctrines and practices it sought to impose on other states.

The organized hypocrisy underlying the WTO worked very effectively during the era of overwhelming US dominance, when it served to mask, legitimate, and therefore make more efficient its exercise of power. In the context of contemporary power shifts, however, the inherent hypocrisy of the liberal international economic order created vulnerability, not only in the authority of the US as hegemon, but also in the ability of the system itself to function. When pressure was brought to bear on this weak point of the system, it fractured.

Part of the reason the challenge posed by the emerging powers at the

WTO has been so powerful is that they are able to challenge the US *on its own terms*. Had the emerging powers advocated a more radical agenda, such as a new version of the NIEO, I suggest that their challenge to the US would have been far less effective. Brazil, India, and China have gained considerable force precisely because they are not calling for an overthrow of the existing liberal economic order, but only for the realization of the very norms upon which that order is ostensibly based and designed to promote. In the end, this challenge "from within" has turned out to be far more threatening to the power of the US and destabilizing for the multilateral trading system than any external critique could have been.

The emerging powers have taken the liberal principles of the WTO at face value and demanded their more universal fulfillment. They have pressed the WTO to live up to its claims of multilateralism and free trade, which would require that the US no longer be treated as an exceptional state, beyond the bounds of the rules and principles of the multilateral trading system, but instead be equally subject to its disciplines.[9] The emerging powers have claimed the right to make demands for meaningful liberalization concessions from the US—even in areas where it faces strong domestic resistance to liberalization, such as agriculture—as well as the right to refuse to agree to demands from the US that they perceived as inequitable. While the GATT/WTO long served as a tool for the US to intervene and force policy changes on weaker states, emerging challengers are now seeking to use the WTO to intervene and compel policy changes in the US. In seeking to use the WTO to discipline US trade policy, Brazil, India, and China are effectively pressing for a greater equalization of sovereignty; they are demanding to be treated as genuinely free and equal states and now have the power to back that up.

The US, however, is fiercely resistant to relinquishing the privileges of its hegemony. The changes sought by the emerging powers are highly unpalatable to the US Congress and domestic interest groups, which are not interested in a more balanced agreement based on an equitable exchange of concessions but want to replicate the kind of highly unbalanced deals the US has secured in the past. Unless a clear case can be made that the US is winning more than it is giving up, many such actors have no interest in a Doha agreement. Furthermore, in a context of rising economic competition from countries like China, India, and Brazil, there is a strong sense of economic insecurity, of a country threatened and under siege, in the US. Consequently, the US is unwilling to take any steps that could further diminish its economic power and is intent instead on securing a deal that will contain rising challengers and lock in what competitive advantages it retains. Pressed to make concessions in its own market—particularly in the politically sensitive area of agriculture subsidies—the US has responded by lashing back at the emerging powers and demanding large new concessions in their markets, as it tries to re-engineer a deal that would tilt the balance in its favor. But the ground has shifted at the WTO. The US and other Western powers can no longer rely on their overwhelming power to get their way; instead, they are now faced with countervailing powers from the Global South with their own agendas and interests and therefore forced to truly negotiate with these states in a way they never have had to before. It is precisely this new reality—the US and other traditionally dominant powers being forced to negotiate on terms of greater equality—that has caused the system to fall apart.

In essence, what the emerging powers have pushed for is a small move toward reconciling the disjuncture between the rhetoric and practice of both the American hegemon and the multilateral trading system it created. The failure of the Doha Round indicates that this has proven impossible. Instead, their effort to move the reality closer to the rhetoric caused the primary function of the WTO—the negotiation of international trade agreements to push forward the liberalization of trade—to collapse. The rise of new powers, precisely because it overloaded a key stress point in the liberal international economic order—the tension between universalism and exclusion in the application of its rules and principles—created a rupture in that order.

The underlying pretense of the multilateral trading system—of equally sovereign states coming together for the purpose of freeing trade for the mutual benefit of all—was critical to enabling the system to function. Combined with varying degrees of coercion, backed by the reality of raw American economic and military power, as well as some compromise and concessions, it is what enabled states to achieve international cooperation. Consent for the multilateral trading system rested on convincing others that the system would also benefit them—that they too would be able to have a say in decision-making, shape outcomes, and make gains from the opening of markets. As Steven Bernstein (2012: 10) contends, the legitimacy of the liberal international order was "a function of the degree to which multilateral institutions were perceived as mutually binding and as allowing at least some reciprocal influence on actual policies." The rise of new powers at the WTO put exactly these core claims of the multilateral trading system—reciprocal influence and mutually binding rules—to the test. The result, however, was that the system failed.

The collapse of the Doha Round represents the breakdown of a central institution in the US-led project of neoliberal globalization. It is an important signal of the weakening ability of the US to impose its will globally. The fate of the round makes it clear that the US and other Western powers can no longer control the process of globalization and the governance of the global economy to the same degree they once did. The WTO has spun beyond the control of the US—or, for that matter, any other single state or group of states.

Alternative Explanations for the Failure of the Doha Round

The primary purpose of this book has been to understand the effect of contemporary power shifts on the evolution of global neoliberalism. To this end, I have put forward the WTO as an illuminating case to understand how and why changes in the distribution of power among states are disrupting its existing governing institutions. Over the past several years, as the impasse in the Doha Round hardened and the crisis faced by the WTO became increasingly apparent, there has been a great deal of hand-wringing within the community of trade scholars and other experts surrounding the WTO (where the lines between the academic and policy worlds are often blurred), and much ink has been spilled trying to explain the breakdown of the round and prognosticate about the future of the multilateral trading system (Gantz 2013; Jones 2010; Martin and Mattoo 2011; Steger 2010; Warwick Commission 2008; Wilkinson and Scott 2013). Yet such analysis has been driven by a very different set of objectives and commitments, primarily concerned with understanding what can be done to rescue or salvage the Doha Round or, if it is destined to go down in flames, at least to save the WTO and its mandate from the wreckage. In contrast, my goal here has not been to explain the breakdown of the Doha Round per se; instead, my interest has stemmed from the belief that the failure of the Doha Round can offer important insights into the contemporary dynamics of global capitalism. The argument I have made is that current power shifts have disrupted the expansion of the institutional project of neoliberal globalization, which is manifest in the collapse of the Doha Round at the WTO. Given the centrality of the Doha Round to the analysis presented here, however, it is useful to consider the alternative explanations that have been put forward to explain its breakdown.

Some attribute the round's failure to the complexity of the negotiations, based on the large number of countries and issues involved (Jones 2010). The problem with this explanation, however, is that the preceding Uruguay Round was equally complex—with a similarly expansive agenda, the inclusion of many new issues that had never been subject to negotiation before (such as services, investment, intellectual property, and agriculture), and a comparably large number of participants (123 states versus 161 today)—and still successfully concluded.

Others have attributed the breakdown to the institutional design of the WTO, arguing that institutional features such as the single undertaking and consensus-based decision-making ultimately made agreement impossible (Gantz 2013; Hufbauer and Suominen 2012; Jones 2010; Lanoszka 2007; Warwick Commission 2008). Yet, while the institutional design of the WTO has undoubtedly played a role, it cannot be the principal cause of the breakdown of the Doha Round, as the very same institutional features were operating during the Uruguay Round but did not prevent agreement then. Both of these institutional features were advanced by the American hegemon—decision-making by consensus as a means to boost the legitimacy of the institution while maintaining its dominance and the single-undertaking as a tactic to force developing countries to sign on to the new issues in the Uruguay Round. Only recently have these institutional features come to work against the interests of US power and impede conclusion of a trade round. First, while the system of consensus-based decision-making operated smoothly for much of the history of the GATT/WTO under conditions of American hegemony, in the last decade it has made the WTO far more sensitive and responsive to rising powers than the fixed weighted-voting systems of the IMF and World Bank, which have more firmly locked-in global power relations circa 1945, including the dominance of the US and other Western powers. At the WTO, consensus-based decision-making helped to empower emerging challengers and accelerate and intensify contemporary power shifts. Second, the principle of the single undertaking—which requires all states to sign on to all elements of the final package—worked effectively in a context of overwhelming US power, but now, with the rising powers acting as a countervailing force, has become an obstacle to concluding the round. It has meant that objections from states to one part of the agreement have been able to hold up the entire round, making assembling a final package considerably harder. While these institutional features in the design of the

WTO have unquestionably contributed to the current breakdown, they alone are not responsible; instead, they are moderating factors (affecting the strength of the relationship between cause and effect) rather than causal factors themselves. The root cause of the collapse of the round lies in contemporary power shifts, which specific institutional factors have intensified.

Other observers have sought to locate the Doha failure in the inclusion of agriculture in the round, positing that there is something unique about agriculture that makes it unusually resistant to liberalization. Many see agriculture as a "sacred cow"—particularly in the US and EU—that cannot be touched, which is why multilateral trade disciplines and liberalization in agriculture have lagged behind manufacturing (Katz 2005; Sauvé and Subramanian 2004). Agriculture was a major sticking point when first brought into the international trading system in the Uruguay Round and liberalization was largely left for future rounds. The Doha Round was consequently saddled with tackling the "landmine" of agriculture (Grady and Macmillan 1999), which is what, some contend, ultimately broke the round. Agriculture is indeed loaded with substantial political and economic sensitivities in many countries, both developed and developing. Moreover, with the G20-T's offensive against rich country subsidies, agriculture became a pivotal issue in the Doha Round and one that fundamentally transformed its dynamics. However, over the course of the round, the US and other Western powers showed that they were willing to trade concessions on agriculture subsidies for gains in other areas (especially improved market access for their agricultural and manufactured exports). The EU agreed to relinquish export subsidies, a cornerstone of its agriculture programs, and both the US and EU signaled their willingness to accept substantial reductions in domestic support, provided they made (what they deemed to be) adequate compensatory gains of their own. This indicates that there was nothing specifically sacred about agriculture that rendered it untouchable. Rather, it was the inability of the old and new powers to agree on the specific terms of what constituted a fair deal—in agriculture and beyond—that caused the stalemate.

Still others have suggested that the Doha Round was derailed by changing economic conditions that outpaced the round and rendered it irrelevant (Mattoo and Subramanian 2009). The most common tenet of this argument is that rising commodity prices meant that at least the agriculture component of the round—which was formulated in a context of low prices—and specific issues under negotiation within it were no longer relevant (the increase in agricultural prices, for example, caused the most trade-distorting form of subsidies—countercyclical direct payments to producers—to decline, while unanticipated issues such as export restrictions came to the fore during the 2007–8 food crisis). Yet this fails to explain why states were unable to reach agreement even before commodity prices spiked in 2007–8. In addition, the economic history of the last century suggests that the recent increase in agricultural prices is far more likely to be a transitory phenomenon than a long-term structural change. Furthermore, if it was in fact the case that the issues under negotiation, such as subsidies and market access, were no longer as important to states, this should have made it *easier* for them to reach agreement. But instead, even at the 2008 Ministerial—at the height of the food crisis—it was precisely these issues that remained highly contested and a central factor in the impasse. Clearly, states continue to view the "traditional" agricultural trade issues as significant. Moreover, the Doha negotiating mandate extended well beyond agriculture to include issues such as services, one of the fastest growing and most lucrative areas of the global economy with major commercial significance to both old and new powers; yet the negotiations on services never truly got off the ground because of the impasse in agriculture and manufactured goods.

Finally, some contend that a lack of "political will" is responsible for the failure of the round (Gantz 2013). One suggestion often made, for example, is that the US simply lost interest in the Doha negotiations and the WTO, possibly as a result of declining domestic support for trade liberalization. Related is the notion that, given its continued preponderance of political and economic power, if the US had really wanted a Doha agreement, the deal would have been done. However, the US continues to pursue trade liberalization through the ongoing negotiation of bilateral and regional free trade agreements. Even more important, such explanations erroneously treat "political will"—a state's desire to conclude a trade round—as something independent of and external to trade negotiations, when the reality is just the opposite. "Political will" is not exogenous but endogenous to the negotiations; that is, it is a direct function of a state's perception of whether the negotiations are going in its favor and its calculation of what gains and losses it will incur. The US would be delighted to conclude the Doha Round *if* it could do so on its terms, as it was largely able to achieve in previous rounds. But the rise of competing powers has limited the ability of the US to engineer an agreement in its favor. If the US desire to conclude the Doha Round has waned, it is no coincidence but directly related to its dissatisfaction with the substance and terms of the prospective agreement on the table.

Ultimately, any explanation that seeks to explain the failure of the Doha Round without attention to power relations among states is unsatisfying. The account I have developed here locates the collapse of the Doha Round in contemporary power shifts that, I contend, have precipitated the WTO's current crisis by exacerbating the contradictions contained in its foundational myths of multilateralism and free trade.

A Moment of Historical Disjuncture

Drawing on the case of the WTO, I have shown that the inherent contradictions of global neoliberalism have created a crisis in one of its governing institutions. The term "crisis" has appeared with some frequency in recent years—in the context of the global finance crisis, the food crisis, the Euro zone crisis, the US budget sequestration crisis, and the looming climate change crisis, to name only a few. Moreover, the discourse of crisis at the GATT/WTO is not a new phenomenon but has been invoked at various moments in its history as a strategy to build momentum for the liberalization process (Wilkinson 2009b). As the impasse in the Doha Round became undeniable, many observers and participants began to worry publicly that this time the WTO really *was* in crisis. Others were just as quick to deny the existence of a crisis and assert that the multilateral trading system would survive the collapse of the round. It is therefore important to specify exactly what I mean in stating that the WTO is in crisis and to clarify both what I am and am *not* claiming.

The crisis to which I refer is a crisis in the international architecture that has played a central role in driving and facilitating the spread of neoliberal globalization to date. This should not be taken, however, to mean the death or collapse of neoliberalism. For one, the existing rules and institutional structures that have been created to date remain in place. Despite the apparent collapse of the Doha Round, for example, the WTO continues to exist and function as an institution. Its existing rules (created by the Uruguay Round and earlier agreements under the GATT) remain in force and binding upon states, and its dispute settlement mechanism continues to actively arbitrate disputes originating from those rules. However, it is the WTO's larger project of continual liberalization that is in crisis. While its existing architecture remains, the intended *expansion* of WTO trade rules and its neoliberal agenda—which is central to its raison d'etre—has been brought to a halt by contemporary power conflicts among states. It is as though the architects set out to construct a skyscraper stretching infinitely into the sky and never got past the first eight floors (composed of the GATT/WTO trade rounds successfully concluded to date). The edifice is only partially built and prematurely truncated. The collapse of the Doha Round has not yet proven a terminal crisis for the WTO, though it could become one: as bilateral and regional trade and investment agreements proliferate (and include their own mechanisms for settling disputes), even existing WTO rules and its dispute settlement system could be superseded and become irrelevant (Baldwin 2011; Bhagwati 2008).

The crisis within the WTO does not necessarily presage a collapse of international trade or an outbreak of protectionism and a return to the 1930s. As just stated, the existing rules and institutional structures of the GATT/WTO remain in place and—as long as they maintain authority and continue to be respected—act to constrain states. Bilateral and regional agreements are also in place to lock in trade and investment liberalization. The structural transformation of the global economy that has occurred over the last three decades has produced an unprecedented degree of interdependence and created powerful vested interests in maintaining the market opening that has occurred. This, combined with the current power of the neoliberal ideology of free markets and free trade, may make a widespread move toward market closure less likely. Despite concerns among trade experts and officials that the financial crisis could trigger an upsurge in protectionism, for example, no such change has yet occurred.

Finally, although it is my contention that recent developments at the WTO signal a crisis in the global institutional arrangements that have shepherded the process of neoliberal globalization to date, this does not imply that the process of neoliberal globalization has been brought to a halt. Rather, my argument is that the means by which neoliberal globalization has been advanced until now—through multilateral institutions and propelled by US power—have been disrupted by power shifts and may now be blocked. But global capitalism is remarkably fluid and dynamic and has proven highly adaptable at evolving through a recurrent pattern of crisis and adjustment. If existing multilateral institutions like the WTO are no longer able to play their previous role in facilitating the expansion of global capitalism, then new and alternative institutional arrangements may be created instead. Like the changing course of a river, if the existing institutional channel becomes blocked, neoliberal globalization will likely find others, though it may be transformed in the process.

In the realm of trade, for example, as the capacity of the WTO to expand the rules and institutional architecture of global trade has broken down, states and business actors have sought other institutional means by which to advance trade liberalization. At the same time that trade liberalization has withered and potentially ground to a halt at the WTO, there has simultaneously been a proliferation of bilateral and regional free trade and investment agreements. As Uri Dadush (2009: 3) states: "During the fifteen years of the WTO's existence, trade liberalization has occurred everywhere *except* Geneva." This process initially began with the traditional powers: when the rise of opposition led by the emerging powers began to impede the US and EU from securing their objectives at the WTO, they started more aggressively pursuing bilateral and regional free trade agreements (FTAs), particularly as a means to advance their most neoliberal objectives (such as TRIPS+ rules on IP protection that were stricter than the WTO's, investment protections, and extensive services liberalization). The traditional powers have greater leverage in bilateral negotiations, enabling them to extract more than they could in the WTO context, and they sought to use the threat of turning from the WTO to FTAs as a means of pressuring other countries to capitulate to their demands in the Doha Round (Whalley 2006). After Cancun, the US indicated that it was going to intensify its strategy of "competitive liberalization" that had begun under the Bush administration in 2000. In an op-ed in the *Financial Times,* US Trade Representative Bob Zoellick (2003) lashed out at Brazil and India—blaming them for the breakdown at Cancun—and made it clear that the US was going to reward cooperative countries and punish uncooperative ones by pursuing alternate trade deals:

The key division at Cancun was between the can-do and the won't-do. For over two years, the US has pushed to open markets globally, in our hemisphere, and with sub-regions or individual countries. As WTO members ponder the future, the US will not wait. We will move towards free trade with can-do countries.

Zoellick elsewhere acknowledged: "The ability to be able to say, 'We'll do bilaterals' is very important when you're trying to negotiate a WTO agreement. . . . [I] understand how to use national power. Bilaterals have been a very useful means of exerting influence" (quoted in Blustein 2009: 178). Unfortunately for the US, this strategy proved unsuccessful as a pressure tactic in the Doha Round, since the rising powers in particular refused to be cowed.

Moreover, the US move to FTAs prompted other countries to start initiating their own. There has since been an explosion of FTAs involving one or more developing countries, with the emerging powers especially active in negotiating such deals. By the time the US-Colombia FTA was signed and waiting to be ratified by the US Congress, for example, thirty-five other states were negotiating FTAs with Colombia (Schwab 2009). The US currently has sixteen FTAs in force or under negotiation. By comparison, China and India now, respectively, each have twenty-nine and thirty-seven FTAs proposed, under negotiation or in effect, and Brazil has seventeen FTAs signed or in force.[10] As one representative of Indian industry stated, for example, "Now when we're looking for market access, it's in FTAs" rather than the WTO.[11] It is thus not only the traditional powers that are turning away from the multilateral system to pursue bilateral and regional agreements, but all of the major economies. Nearly 400 FTAs are currently under negotiation or in force.[12] The result has been what two prominent trade economists have termed an "epidemic" of FTAs (Bhagwati and Garnaut 2003). Until this point, most such agreements have been of limited economic significance compared with the GATT/WTO (Mattoo and Subramanian 2012), but that may be changing, particularly if new mega-regional deals such as the Trans-Pacific Partnership (TPP), the US-EU Transatlantic Trade and Investment Partnership (TTIP), and the India-EU FTA are successfully concluded.

In trade, the action has shifted away from the WTO. Many states have pulled their most skilled and experienced negotiators and officials away from the WTO to the bilateral and regional agreements that they are now prioritizing.[13] In addition to FTAs, some states are engaged in significant unilateral liberalization; India's recent efforts to open its large retail sector to foreign capital provide one prominent example. There is also the prospect of a growing turn toward "minilateral" or "plurilateral" agreements, encompassing only smaller subsets of states, whether outside the WTO (such as negotiations for the proposed Trade in Service Agreement [TiSA] initiated by the US, launched in 2013, and which to date the emerging powers have refused to join) or within its auspices (such as an expanded Information Technology Agreement [ITA] and the Environmental Goods Agreement [EGA]). States may continue to attempt to carve off and seek agreements on small pieces of the Doha agenda, in contrast to the comprehensive agreement originally intended, though the struggles over the Bali package suggest that even this may be very difficult to achieve.

All of these new developments raise the prospect of a tangled web of hundreds, or even thousands, of different mini-institutions governing transnational flows of trade, capital, and labor, each with different rules, provisions, and dispute resolution mechanisms. Since such agreements draw the states involved closer together, while concurrently displacing and repelling others, they create new lines of unity and division among states. This kind of fragmentation in the governance architecture of the international trading system represents something qualitatively distinct from the effort since the end of World War II to create a single, centralized "one world" system of rules and institutions to govern the capitalist global economy, with the US its political, economic, and ideological epicenter (Ikenberry 2010). There have also been signs of more novel institutional experiments and arrangements emerging that represent an even further departure from the ideal of a unified, liberal global trading system, ranging from the aid-for-resources deals China has signed with several African states to global "land grabs" (Margulis, McKeon, and Borras 2013).

Some have suggested that interstate conflict is lessening in the contemporary capitalist era and that the most significant political fault lines of global capitalism are now running within rather than between states. Panich and Gindin (2012), for example, contend that "the conflicts that have emerged today in the wake of the greatest capitalist crisis since the 1930s are taking shape ... less as conflicts *between* capitalist states and their ruling classes than as conflicts *within* capitalist states." However, analysis of developments at the WTO over the last decade suggests just the opposite: the fierce and protracted battles waged over the outcome of the Doha Round indicate that competition and conflict among states remain intense. Were conflict among states less salient, a Doha Round agreement would likely have been reached long ago. Instead, the traditional and emerging powers are engaged in a hard-fought struggle to eke out an advantage by tilting the rules of the global economy in their favor, while resisting the efforts of their rivals to do the same.

All of these states are engaged in what is essentially a mercantilist struggle. They are trying to engineer improved trade balances, boost their exports at the expense of other states, give their producers a competitive edge in global markets, while shielding their industries from imports and foreign competition, and only selectively open their markets, while convincing or compelling other states to open theirs more fully. Yet both the old and new powers nonetheless wrap their mercantilist impulses in a discourse of free trade and neoliberalism.

The new world of multipolarity we are entering appears to be one of competing states (and their business actors) engaged in mercantilist struggles. It may be that agreements involving select groups of states (such as bilateral and regional FTAs) are more conducive to such a world than multilateral institutions like the WTO, specifically because they are designed to enable participating states to boost their competitiveness and exports at the expense of states that are excluded and not party to the agreement. In contrast to the multilateralism of the WTO, where the most-favored-nation principle extends the benefits of trade agreements to be shared by all member states, bilateral and regional FTAs are explicitly intended to benefit some states at the expense of others. This is, for example, a key reason why the US is pursuing the TPP as part of its China containment strategy—to give the US a competitive advantage compared with China in its trade and economic relations with states in the Asian region. Part of the reason that FTAs have become so appealing in the current historical moment may be that they are implicated in the heightened struggles taking place among multiple, competing poles of global power.

Arrighi and Silver (1999: 22) argue that periods of hegemonic transition generate "a fundamental reorganization of the system and a change in its properties." The case of the WTO suggests that we may indeed be in the midst of a period of such systemic change. Many scholars in both the realist and critical traditions have posited that the decline of US hegemony could usher in a period of escalating systemic chaos (Arrighi 1994; Arrighi and Silver 1999; Kagan 2012; Mearsheimer 2005; Patrick 2010). Arrighi and Silver (1999: 33) define such systemic chaos as:

a situation of severe and seemingly irremediable systemic disorganization. As competition and conflicts escalate beyond the regulatory capacity of existing structures, new structures emerge interstitially and destabilize further the dominant configuration of power. Disorder tends to be self-reinforcing, threatening to provoke or actually provoking a complete breakdown in the system's organization.

The systemic disorganization they describe, I contend, bears a striking resemblance to what is currently occurring in the governance of international trade.

Competitive struggles among states appear to be producing increasing fragmentation in the regulation of the international economy, in contrast to the comparatively centralized political-economic structures established under American hegemony. As Efstathopoulos and Kelly (2014: 1069) describe, prior to 1945 there was a "near absence of effective international regulations governing capitalism." The integrated system of institutions created to govern the global economy in the postwar era—the IMF, World Bank, and GATT/WTO—was a distinct and defining feature of the era of US hegemony. These institutions provided the gravitational center of global economic governance for the entire latter half of the twentieth century. Currently, however, with the emergence of multiple centers of global economic power, governance may be becoming more diffuse and dispersed, with the locus of action shifting away from the traditional multilateral institutions centered on and dominated by the waning American hegemon and other Western states—which, in the case of the WTO, has ceased to function effectively to advance the process of economic globalization—and instead toward a proliferation of alternative governance structures and mechanisms. It would appear that the centripetal tendencies of hegemony are being replaced by centrifugal forces of multipolarity. From an era of (relative) centralization, we may now be entering an era of greater fragmentation and decentralization, in which governance, at least, is far more chaotic.

The analysis presented here suggests that we are in the midst of an important transformation in the institutional structures of global capitalism. The shift in global power relations is changing the nature of the neoliberal globalization project, including how and where it is being advanced, and by which actors. The institutional architecture that has governed the global economy for the last half-century and fueled the process of neoliberal globalization is no longer working as intended; as a result, states and business actors have disengaged from the multilateral trading system and turned instead to constructing alternative arrangements. While it is impossible to predict the future direction global capitalism will take or what form its enabling institutional arrangements will assume, we do appear to be at an important moment of disjuncture, in which the old status quo is beginning to break down, though it is far from clear what will emerge in its place.

Beyond the WTO

The rise of Brazil, India, and China has produced a crisis in one of the core governing institutions constituted under US hegemony. While the present study has been limited to the WTO, there is reason to believe that similar disruptions may be occurring elsewhere in global governance. Closely mirroring the conflict at the WTO that has blocked conclusion of the Doha Round, the negotiations on a new international climate change agreement, for instance, have been severely hampered by a dispute between the existing and emerging powers—centered particularly on the US and China—over whether and to what extent the large developing countries should be required to cap and reduce their carbon emissions (Roberts 2011). As at the WTO, the battle line has been drawn between the old and new powers, caught in a distributional struggle over the balance of their respective contributions, with each side highly resistant to making concessions that could yield an economic advantage for the other. While the US and China reached a tentative agreement on carbon emissions in 2014, it is generally regarded as extremely limited and insufficient to adequately address the real threat of climate change (Stanway 2014). Likewise, despite the initial enthusiasm spurred by its creation, the G20 Leaders Summit has been increasingly criticized as ineffectual and failing to produce sufficient meaningful action in responding to the aftermath of the 2008 financial crisis or reforming the international financial architecture (Vestergaard and Wade 2012). The intractability of divisions within the G20 have resembled those within the WTO—and with a similar result: as a recent article in the *Financial Times* (2011) stated, "[T]he G20's bickering and brinkmanship bear an uncanny and unfortunate resemblance to the stalled Doha trade talks." Power shifts thus appear to be impeding multilateral cooperation and the construction of new and expanded global rules—not only at the WTO but across multiple arenas of governance as well.

There are also signs that, like the WTO, the Bretton Woods institutions are increasingly being bypassed and their primacy undermined. In the case of the IMF, since their bitter experiences of its loan conditionalities in the 1980s and 90s, many emerging economies have sought to self-insure against financial crises by building their own arsenals of foreign exchange reserves, specifically in order to avoid being forced to turn to the IMF and subject themselves to its disciplines (Allen et al. 2013; Goldstein 2009; Subramanian and Kessler 2013). In the case of the World Bank, it has now been surpassed by China as a source of lending to developing countries (Dyer and Anderlini 2011; Gallagher, Irwin, and Koleski 2012). Furthermore, amid growing frustration among the emerging powers that the governance structures of the international financial institutions are not being reformed to reflect changes in the global distribution of power, the BRICS have begun going outside these institutions to create their own alternatives (Reisen 2015; Woods 2010). In response to the perceived failure of the World Bank to meet the needs of developing countries, particularly for infrastructure financing, the BRICS have established their own New Development Bank (NDB) (Chin 2014; Hochstetler 2014b). With only limited voting reforms at the World Bank and agreed reforms of the IMF's quota system blocked until recently by the US Congress, China has also led the creation of the new Asian Infrastructure Investment Bank (AIIB) (Reisen 2015; Vestergaard and Wade 2015). These developments threaten to displace the old triumvirate—the IMF, World Bank, and WTO—from their central position in global economic governance and circumscribe their reach and authority. And similar patterns of fragmentation are evident in other areas of global governance. Even in the case of the international climate change negotiations, for example, the ineffectual nature of multilateral climate governance has led to experimentation with myriad alternative initiatives, often at the national and subnational levels or undertaken by nonstate actors (Hoffmann 2011). Multipolarity may thus be breeding more complex, diffuse, and fragmented forms of global economic governance in a range of different areas.

Ironically, growing multipolarity appears to be causing the multilateral system of global governance to come under severe stress. While the US still maintains a preponderance of power in the international system, contemporary power shifts may be profoundly disrupting the governing institutions of the global economy constructed under American hegemony.

Implications for the Rest of the Developing World

I will conclude by turning to the important issue of the impact the growing power of Brazil, India, and China is having on the rest of the developing world. Are developing countries as a whole being empowered by the rise of new powers from the Global South? Certainly, as this book has shown, the rising powers portray themselves as advancing a common developing country cause, and their ability to marshal the broader support of the developing world has played a pivotal role in driving power shifts at the WTO. Yet the case of the WTO highlights the complexity of the relationship between the new powers and the rest of the developing world.

Contemporary developing world alliances centered on the emerging powers have undoubtedly strengthened the bargaining power of developing countries in relation to the traditional powers, and the significance of this should not be underestimated. The contribution of the G20-T was particularly striking in this regard: by enabling developing countries to assume the role of aggressors and drawing attention to the protectionism and hypocrisy of the US and EU, the G20-T strengthened the negotiating position not only of its own members but also of all developing countries at the WTO. The success of the G20-T fundamentally altered the balance of power between developed and developing countries and reduced the vulnerability of the latter. As a result, the change in the Doha Round—compared especially with the Uruguay Round—has been profound: developing countries have demonstrated a new and unprecedented ability to resist the demands of the traditional powers while securing meaningful demands of their own. Developing world solidarity—in the G20-T, G33, and beyond—has thus served as an important tool enabling developing countries to enhance their bargaining position and lessen the historical imbalance between North and South that has long characterized the multilateral trading system.

But the emerging powers' emphasis on developing country solidarity and North-South struggle is far from purely altruistic. Their claim to be acting in behalf of the developing world has served as a powerful tool to advance their own particular commercial interests, while simultaneously obscuring the issue of whose interests are truly being served by their actions at the WTO. Even within their alliances relations among developing countries are themselves shaped by power asymmetries, and in formulating and expressing the collective interests of the developing world, the interests of the most powerful have predominated. The degree to which most developing countries would benefit from the substantive agenda being pursued by the emerging powers—which has been heavily shaped by the protrade orientation of the emerging powers and their competitive export sectors—is highly questionable. Despite Brazil's rhetoric regarding the objectives of the G20-T, for example, it is far from clear that reducing rich country agriculture subsidies will in fact generate development, enable developing countries to "trade their way out of poverty," or ultimately serve the interests of the majority of developing countries. Instead, it is Brazil—and specifically its agribusiness exporters—that stands to capture the greatest gains from the reduction of rich country subsidies and the liberalization of global agriculture markets. The same holds true for India and China with regard to liberalization in services and manufactured goods.

By lining up behind Brazil, India, and China, developing countries gained a degree of leverage at the WTO, but there are nonetheless major questions about how well the agenda being advanced by the emerging powers truly corresponds to the interests of most developing countries. The emerging powers frequently make generalizations for the developing world based on their own experiences and interests; all three present themselves as a development model for other developing countries to follow in order to expand their exports and foster economic growth. At times, the emerging powers sound remarkably like the original advocates of the Washington Consensus in their rhetoric propounding the virtues of freer trade and presenting increasing global economic integration as the solution to underdevelopment. It is not clear, however, that this is true for most developing countries, nor that the opening of global markets being sought by Brazil, India, and China at the WTO will in fact bring benefits to the rest of the Global South. Indeed, because of the nature of competition in global markets, the economic gains made by one developing country often come at the expense of another (such that the success of China's textile and clothing sector, for instance, came at the cost of other developing countries, such as Mexico, and is now, in turn, increasingly threatened by competition from Bangladesh and Vietnam). The interests of the emerging powers are thus not necessarily congruent with those of other developing countries, beyond their shared opposition to the dominance of the Global North. As a trade adviser to the Indian government stated, "We are in a bit of an identity crisis situation, midway between the developing countries and the developed countries."[14] Their rising levels of development, as well as economic and political power, increasingly set Brazil, India, and China apart from other developing countries. Yet the emerging powers each present themselves and their interests as aligned with the developing world for the purpose of strengthening their negotiating position and enhancing their power at the WTO.

At present, the emerging powers and the rest of the developing world have broadly aligned together to counter the dominance of the US and EU. Yet there are inherent tensions between the economic interests of the emerging powers and those of many other developing countries that may grow stronger in future and test the bounds of Southern solidarity. Despite the gains made by Brazil, India, and China, developing countries as a whole remain highly disadvantaged within the international trading system and the changing structure of power in the global political economy.

Appendix: Data and Methods

The analysis presented in this book draws on fifteen months of field research conducted at the WTO in Geneva, as well as in Beijing, New Delhi, Brasilia, Sao Paulo, and Washington between June 2007 and June 2010. This research involved in-depth interviews, ethnographic fieldwork, and analysis of a variety of documentary sources. I interviewed 157 WTO member-state delegates (ambassadors and trade negotiators) and other senior government officials, secretariat officials, and representatives of business lobby groups, nongovernmental organizations, media, research institutes, and think tanks. Interviews varied in length from forty-five minutes to three hours. Given the politically sensitive nature of the material disclosed and the small diplomatic community from which interview respondents were drawn, respondents were guaranteed that their identities would be confidential and protected. Interview respondents are therefore not identified by name, and every effort has been made to remove identifying information. For some officials, this has required omitting their state affiliation in cases where revealing such information could make it possible for others to identify them.

In addition to interviews, I conducted more than three hundred hours of ethnographic observation. While it is not possible to observe WTO meetings (which take place behind closed doors, attended only by select member-state delegates and secretariat officials), there are a large number of peripheral events frequently held in Geneva for WTO policy-makers and related actors. These include the annual WTO Public Forum, speeches, briefings, policy workshops, meetings, panel presentations, and conferences. Such events are organized and hosted by a variety of actors, including the WTO Secretariat, states, UN agencies, NGOs, research institutes, and think tanks. In addition to these events, I also had the opportunity for observation at more informal gatherings, such as receptions and dinners, key sites of professional networking within the Geneva diplomatic community.

My ability to undertake this research was enhanced by my previous professional experience as a trade official for a WTO member-state. This conferred a degree of "insider" status that brought both advantages and disadvantages. On the one hand, it provided a strong initial network of contacts and facilitated access to trade officials. It was particularly useful for gaining access to trade officials in more informal settings—such as joining a small group of negotiators for dinner in a restaurant in Geneva, or chatting with a negotiator over drinks after work—which provided valuable sources of information. My professional background also helped to establish trust and rapport and likely encouraged trade officials to be more open and frank in sharing their views, when they may have been more on guard with a perceived "outsider" and engaged in greater self-censorship. On the other hand, while the level of access I was granted enabled me to gather a considerable amount of information outside of official interview settings, there were ethical limitations on how I could use this information. Although they were aware that I was an academic engaged in gathering data for research, trade officials were often remarkably candid in informal settings. In order to ensure that I did not violate their trust in the use of this data, I made it clear to those I engaged with in these settings that I would treat any information communicated as "deep background" (a journalistic practice familiar to officials). I have therefore not quoted any of the information gathered in informal settings, but instead used this as background information to inform the argument presented here. Information gleaned in informal settings was verified and substantiated through formal interviews, and all quotations used in the book were taken from formal interviews.

Interview and ethnographic data were supplemented with an analysis of a wide range of written materials and documents. I examined official WTO documents (such as reports of the director-general and negotiation chairs, ministerial declarations, draft texts, member-state negotiating proposals, and dispute settlement panel reports); member-state speeches, press releases, and media statements; WTO Secretariat documents (such as annual reports, world trade reports, speeches of the director-general, press releases, policy papers, and public information documents); and news reportage. I also analyzed materials produced by other actors, such as industry lobbyists and NGOs, related to the WTO, including press releases, policy and position papers, websites, emails to supporters, and other communications. I triangulated among these three sources of data—interviews, observation, and documentary analysis—to ensure the validity of the findings presented here.

Notes

Chapter 1

1. IMF Data, measured at purchasing power parity (PPP) rates, 2014.

2. China is the world's second largest economy measured at market exchange rates and the world's largest when measured at PPP rates.

3. China was not yet a member of the GATT/WTO.

4. In the context of the WTO, there are two primary indicators of a state's power. The first is a seat at the high-table of decision-making within the institution, which can be considered a necessary but not sufficient condition of power. The second is demonstrated influence in decision-making, or the ability to shape the negotiating agenda and outcomes, which can take two forms: (1) the ability of a state to get others to accede to its demands, and (2) the ability to block the demands of others.

5. While quota reforms of the IMF agreed in 2008 became effective in March 2011, further reforms agreed in 2010 were blocked by the US Congress until 2015.

6. Although Russia is frequently grouped together with these countries as one of the "BRICs" (Brazil, Russia, India, China), a term originally coined in a 2001 Goldman Sachs investment report, it did not become a member of the WTO until 2012 and therefore did not play a role in the power shift analyzed in this study.

7. A note regarding my use of the term "protectionism" is in order. I am *not* ascribing to this terms the normative judgments with which it is typically invested in the dominant neoliberal trade discourse (where it is essentially taken for granted that protectionism is akin to an economic sin). Instead, I am using the term merely to describe economic policies that depart from the principles of free trade. Throughout the book, my purpose in discussing the protectionist policies of the US is not to condemn those policies per se, but to evaluate the US's practices by the standards of its own free market discourse and the policy prescriptions it has pressed on other states.

8. The only progress since 2008 has been the "Bali Package" agreed upon in December 2013, which consists primarily of a trade facilitation agreement intended to streamline customs procedures. While of limited consequence, even this agreement proved highly factious and difficult to achieve, and only narrowly averted collapse in subsequent months.

9. I use the term "multilateral" as it is used in the realm of trade, to refer to the sys-

tem at the global level operated by the WTO, in contrast to actions taken bilaterally, regionally, or by other smaller groups of countries.

10. The previous eight multilateral trade rounds were conducted and successfully concluded under the auspices of the WTO's predecessor, the GATT.

Chapter 2

1. Of course, the internal history of the United States was a vast process of territorial seizure and occupation; the absence of colonial occupation of territories "abroad" was founded on unprecedented territorial expansion "at home" (Stedman Jones 1972). The "removal" of native populations cleared the way for a massive influx of immigrants and created a territory enormous in size and rich in natural resources that enabled the US to become the world's largest domestic market and a sponge for foreign labor, goods, and capital, fueling its growth and development.

Chapter 3

1. Trade rounds are often named after the location at which they were launched, such as the Doha Round and the Uruguay Round.

2. The WTO Secretariat is composed of approximately 600 staff. By comparison, the World Bank employs more than 10,000 staff, the IMF 2,500, and the UN 60,000.

3. The term "Green Room" originated from the color of the wallpaper in the small conference room next to the director-general's office, where such meetings frequently take place (Moore 2003: 128–31). Although the wallpaper was long ago replaced, the name and institution of informal, elite, small-group meetings remain central to the governance of the WTO.

4. Article XIX of the GATT 1947 and subsequently the Uruguay Agreement on Safeguards (AGS).

5. Interviews with negotiators, Geneva, September 2008 to June 2009.

6. As James Bacchus (2004), a former member of the appellate body, has written, the WTO works by a "reverse consensus" rule, whereby a ruling in WTO dispute settlement is adopted automatically unless *all* of the members agree that it should *not*. Such a situation would effectively never occur, as it would mean that the winning party in a trade dispute would have to agree to set aside its own victorious judgment. Under the GATT, by comparison, countries were not required to submit to dispute settlement and could be sued in a particular dispute only if they agreed. In addition, there was no assurance that rulings in dispute settlement would be binding. A losing party in a dispute could single-handedly block the consensus needed to adopt a ruling. With such a weak enforcement system, the GATT was sometimes derided as the "General Agreement to Talk and Talk."

7. The prime instance of SDT, for example, was the creation of an exemption to GATT rules in the 1970s for the Generalized System of Preferences (GSP). Established under the auspices of the UN rather than the GATT, and one of the sole victories of the developing country activism described later in the chapter, the GSP is a system allowing advanced-industrialized countries to grant preferential tariff rates to imports from devel-

oping countries. The role of the GATT was limited to merely providing an exemption—to its most-favored nation (MFN) principle (which requires members to treat imports from GATT member countries equally)—to allow the GSP to operate. The GSP programs ultimately put in place by countries like the US have been extensively criticized. Such preference schemes are created by individual states on a voluntary basis and are therefore dependent on their willingness to grant trade concessions to poor countries (which is often truncated by the competing economic interests of their own protectionist lobbies), and because they lie outside the purview of the binding GATT legal system, they can be unilaterally modified or canceled at any time. Their intentionally narrow product coverage excludes many of the products in which developing countries have the greatest comparative advantage, such as textiles and clothing (Ray 1987; UNCTAD 1999; WTO 2000); countries impose binding export ceilings on GSP product eligibility (Finger and Winters 1998; MacPhee and Rosenbaum 1989); and complex rules of origin requirements restrict the use of preferences (UNCTAD 1999). As a result, the GSP was severely disappointing, with limited impact on the trade performance of developing countries (Ozden, Caglar, and Reinhardt 2005).

8. Several decades later, in a reversal that typifies the ideological sea change that took place among developing countries, Cardoso went on to become the architect of Brazil's liberalization program as its finance minister and then president.

9. Indicating the contemporary ideological affinity between the two entities, the current secretary-general of UNCTAD, Supachai Panitchpakdi, assumed that post after serving as director-general of the WTO.

10. During the 1980s, as Robert Wolfe (1998) has chronicled, a "Farm War" broke out between the US and EU. Over the course of the twentieth century, agricultural prices had been on a long-term trajectory of decline. Tensions over farm policy had been brewing for some time—with US exporters resenting restrictions on their access to the European market—but intensified from the late-1970s. Subsidies provided under the EU's Common Agriculture Policy (CAP) began to generate huge production surpluses, which it disposed of through exports to foreign markets. Heavily subsidized exports from the EU undercut US access to those third country markets; as a result, the EU's share of world agricultural exports increased in the 1980s, while the US's share declined. This prompted the US to retaliate by increasing its own subsidies. A war of competitive subsidization broke out between the US and EU for global market share. The battleground was developing world markets, which constituted the primary destination for their exports (more than half of cereal exports from the US were going to the developing world, for example, and only about 5 percent to Europe). The proliferation of subsidies had the effect of further driving down agriculture prices, exacerbating the underlying problem, and producing huge fiscal burdens with the skyrocketing budgetary costs of farm support.

This trade war prompted the US to play a leading role in the move to bring agriculture under the disciplines of the international trading system by including it in the Uruguay Round. The levels of subsidization provided in the US remained much lower than those in the EU. In the period from 1986 to 1988, for example, at the start of the Uruguay Round, the Producer Support Estimate (PSE)—a measure of subsidies as a percentage of total farm receipts—was 22 percent for the US, compared with 39 percent for the EU. The US's position in the negotiations was complicated, however, by the fact that it also had its own subsidies and tariff barriers in agriculture, as well as powerful interest groups seeking to maintain them.

Agriculture proved highly complex and contentious in the Uruguay Round. It became a key sticking point between the US and EU, which threatened to block the agreement and was only resolved through a complex bilateral deal between the two parties.

11.   Overall levels of support in agriculture changed little as a result of the Uruguay Round, but theoretically shifted to less trade distorting modes of support to be compatible with WTO rules (Swinnen, Olper, and Vandemoortele 2012). The AoA created a system of "traffic light" boxes to categorize subsidies with an Amber Box for measures that were most trade distorting, to be reduced over time, and a Green Box for measures deemed least trade distorting. It also created a Blue Box as an exemption to the Amber Box (Article 6) that allows policies that should be considered trade distorting (and therefore part of the calculation of the aggregate measure of support (AMS) and subject to a cap and reduction) to be excluded from the calculation of AMS. Under the peace clause included in the AoA, Blue Box payments are exempt from challenge as long as they do not exceed 1992 levels (the peace clause expired in 2003 and its proposed extension has been the subject of contentious debate in the Doha Round). As Robert Wolfe (1998) states, "The Blue Box was clearly created because of the power of the two largest traders." To avoid reducing their agricultural subsidies, the US and EU have engaged in extensive "box switching"—restructuring their support programs to ensure they are classified in a different box, exempt from cuts, without reducing overall levels. Moreover, "Besides providing a host of exceptions to reduction commitments, such as the Blue Box and the Green Box, URAA provisions can be evaded in a myriad of ways, such as manipulation and inflation of base rates from which tariff levels and reduction commitments are deduced" (Bukovansky 2010).

12.   Interview, Brasilia, May 2010.

13.   Interview, Brasilia, May 2010.

14.   Interviews with developing country negotiators, Geneva, September 2008 to June 2009; see also Page 2003.

15.   Interview, Geneva, March 2009.

16.   Interviews with developing country negotiators, Geneva, September 2008 to June 2009, and with Indian officials, New Delhi, March 2010, and Brazilian officials, Brasilia, May 2010.

17.   Interview with G20-T member, Geneva, May 2009.

18.   Interview with WTO Secretariat official, Geneva, March 2009.

19.   Interview, Brasilia, May 2010.

20.   Interview, New Delhi, March 2010.

21.   Interview, New Delhi, March 2010.

22.   Interview with industry representative, Geneva, January 2009.

23. Interview with business representative, Geneva, January 2009.

24. Quoted in Agence-France Presse, accessed January 25, 2012, available at www.wto.org/trade_resources/quotes/new_round/new_round.htm.

25. See, for example, remarks of former US Trade Representative Charlene Barshefsky, in "Managing Globalization: Interview with Charlene Barshefsky on Doha," *International Herald Tribune,* January 31, 2007.

26. Nonreciprocal preferences arrangements, such as those the EU grants to the ACP countries, are considered in violation of WTO rules unless a waiver is obtained from the other WTO members. The ACP countries would therefore likely have lost these preferences had the waiver not been obtained.

27. For comparison, "WTO" appears thirty-eight times and "trade" sixty-five.

28. Statement to Agence-France Presse, accessed January 25, 2012, available at www.wto.org/trade_resources/quotes/new_round/new_round.htm.

29. Interview, Geneva, March 2009.

Chapter 4

Note: This chapter is derived, in part, from an article published in *Review of International Political Economy* on June 16, 2015, available at www.tandfonline.com/10.1080/0969 2290.2014.927387.

1. IMF and WTO data, 2012. Economic growth rates are an average of the previous fifteen years.

2. I use the term "veto" in the informal, practical sense of having the power to block an initiative or agreement; no state has formal, legal veto power at the WTO.

3. The composition of this inner circle has taken different forms, with various peripheral members at times included or excluded, but since 2004, the US, EU, Brazil, and India have been the core states and their participation has been a constant. In 2004, for example, the FIPS, or "Five Interested Parties"—the US, EU, Brazil, India, and Australia (representing the Cairns Group of agricultural exporting countries)—emerged as the core negotiating group (ultimately negotiating the 2004 "July Framework" that formed the basis for all future negotiations in this round). By 2005/6, Japan was brought back in and the core negotiating group became known as the G-6. By the summer of 2007, the "extras" were dropped and the core players—the US, EU, India, and Brazil (the "G-4")—met among themselves in Ministerial-level meetings in Potsdam, Germany, in an effort to break the impasse in the negotiations (an effort that ultimately failed in a storm of media coverage and recriminations thrown back and forth from both sides). After the spectacular breakdown at Potsdam, and the apparent inability of the majors to break the deadlock among themselves, they sought to bring other players in to try to change the dynamic in the Green Room and get some movement in the negotiations. At the Ministerial meeting held in Geneva in July 2008, the group was expanded to include China, Japan, and Australia (a group that came to be known as the "G-7"); ultimately, however, this effort also resulted in breakdown, based on differences between the US, India, and China.

4. Interview with WTO Secretariat official, Geneva, March 2009.

5. Interview with negotiator, Geneva, May 2009.

6. Interview, New Delhi, March 2010.

7. I refer to the coalition of developing countries at the WTO as the G20-Trade (G20-T) to avoid confusion with the G20 Leaders Summit.

8. The Cairns Group consists of nineteen members: Argentina, Australia, Bolivia, Brazil, Canada, Chile, Colombia, Costa Rica, Guatemala, Indonesia, Malaysia, New Zealand, Pakistan, Paraguay, Peru, Philippines, South Africa, Thailand, and Uruguay.

9. Quotation from interview with WTO Secretariat official, Geneva, May 2009.

10. The members of the G20-T currently include Argentina, Brazil, Bolivia, Chile, China, Cuba, Egypt, India, Indonesia, Mexico, Nigeria, Pakistan, Paraguay, Peru, Philippines, South Africa, Thailand, Tanzania, Uruguay, Venezuela, and Zimbabwe.

11. The proximate cause of the collapse was opposition from many developing countries to the inclusion of the so-called Singapore Issues (investment, competition, government procurement, and trade facilitation) before the agriculture texts could even be discussed, but agriculture was widely viewed as equally, if not more, contentious (Clapp 2007), and the US made it clear that it blamed Brazil and India for the breakdown (see Zoellick 2003).

12. Interview, Geneva, May 2009.

13. Interview, Geneva, March 2009.

14. Relative to Brazil and India, Japan's economy was about seven times larger, and Canada's 50 percent larger. Among developing countries, Mexico and Korea each had economies bigger than that of Brazil and almost identical to India's. Moreover, China's economy was more than twice as big as India's and almost three times bigger than Brazil's. In addition, these countries are all far bigger traders than either Brazil or India. Although Brazil is emerging as a significant agricultural exporter, it is not a major trader overall—Brazil accounts for only about 1 percent of world trade. India's share of world trade is only slightly greater.

15. Interview, secretariat official, Geneva, March 2009.

16. OECD and USDA Economic Research Service Data.

17. USDA Economic Research Service Data.

18. Direct export subsidies are used primarily by the EU, while the US relies instead on export credits and food aid to fulfill a similar purpose, in addition to regular subsidies.

19. Interview with WTO negotiator, Geneva, May 2009.

20. The agenda-setting process that takes place between the launch and conclusion of a round is critical to determining its final outcome and the time when powerful countries flex their muscles (Steinberg 2002). While some issues remain subject to considerable dispute, states have agreed on much of what would constitute the final deal. Trade negotiations occur not in one fell swoop, but as a series of smaller steps toward a final agreement. Over the course of the Doha Round negotiations, areas of agreement among states have been progressively expanded and areas of disagreement whittled down. We can chart the progress of the negotiations in what has been agreed upon so far (known as the "acquis" and consisting of the 2004 July Framework Agreement and 2005 Hong Kong

Ministerial Declaration), as well as in the evolution of the draft modalities (draft agreements for each area of the negotiations that are currently on the table and effectively constitute the blueprints for the final deal) and negotiating chairs' reports (indicating the issues in the negotiations that have been agreed to among states and those that continue to be subject to disagreement).

21. Interview, Geneva, May 2009.

22. Interview, Geneva, May 2009.

23. Interview, Geneva, May 2009.

24. Interview, Geneva, May 2009.

25. Interview, Geneva, June 2009.

26. Interview, Geneva, May 2009.

27. Interview, Geneva, May 2009.

28. Interview, Geneva, May 2009.

29. Interview, Geneva, May 2009.

30. Interview, New Delhi, March 2010.

31. Interview, Geneva, February 2009.

32. Interviews with Indian negotiators, Geneva, September 2008 to June 2009.

33. The members of the G33 are Antigua and Barbuda, Barbados, Belize, Benin, Bolivia, Botswana, Côte d'Ivoire, China, Congo, Cuba, Dominica, Dominican Republic, El Salvador, Grenada, Guatemala, Guyana, Haiti, Honduras, India, Indonesia, Jamaica, Kenya, Korea, Madagascar, Mauritius, Mongolia, Mozambique, Nicaragua, Nigeria, Pakistan, Panama, Peru, Philippines, Saint Kitts and Nevis, Saint Lucia, Saint Vincent and the Grenadines, Senegal, Sri Lanka, Suriname, Tanzania, Trinidad and Tobago, Turkey, Uganda, Venezuela, Zambia, and Zimbabwe.

34. The fourth issue introduced at the Singapore Ministerial—trade facilitation—is considered by some to be in the interests of developing countries; it has remained part of the Doha Round negotiations, with an "early harvest" agreement on the issue reached at the 2013 Bali Ministerial.

35. The NAMA-11 consists of Argentina, Brazil, Egypt, India, Indonesia, Namibia, Philippines, South Africa, Tunisia, and Venezuela.

36. Interview with negotiator, Geneva, June 2009.

37. Interview with WTO delegate, Geneva, December 2008.

38. Interview, New Delhi, March 2010.

39. Interview with negotiator, Geneva, March 2009.

40. Interview, Geneva, April 2009.

41. Interview, Geneva, May 2009.

42. Interviews with Chinese negotiators, Geneva, March and May 2009.

43. Interview, Geneva, May 2009.

44. Interview, Geneva, May 2009.

45. Multiple interviews, Geneva, September 2008 to June 2009.

46. Interview, Beijing, July 2009.

47. Interview, Geneva, May 2009.

48. Interview, Geneva, May 2009.

49. Interview with negotiator, Geneva, May 2009.

50. Interview with WTO Secretariat official, Geneva, March 2009.

51. Interview, Geneva, April 2009.

52. Interview, Geneva, May 2009.

53. Interview with WTO Secretariat official, Geneva, March 2009.

54. A "Mini"-Ministerial because it was a meeting of only a select group of thirty-five trade ministers, rather than of ministers from all member states of the WTO. The meeting is therefore described by the WTO Secretariat as an "informal" meeting, although it was chaired by the WTO director-general, organized by the secretariat and took place at the WTO.

55. In the years since Cancun, Australia (as leader of the Cairns Group) and Japan had been included off and on in such meetings, but they were considered only peripheral players compared with the core of the US, EU, Brazil, and India, which have been the central figures in *every* such meeting. Indeed, according to negotiators, at the 2008 Ministerial, the Japanese trade minister was actually left sitting outside in the hallway for much of the meeting, his presence not deemed necessary by the key players.

56. Interview with secretariat official, Geneva, March 2009.

57. Interview, Geneva, May 2009.

58. Interview, Geneva, May 2009.

59. Interview with WTO Secretariat official, Geneva, March 2009.

60. Interview with negotiator, Geneva, April 2009.

61. Interviews with negotiators, Geneva, September 2008 to June 2009.

62. Interview, Geneva, January 2009.

63. Interviews with negotiators, Geneva, September 2008 to June 2009.

64. Interview, New Delhi, March 2010.

65. WTO DS 408, *European Union and a Member State—Seizure of Generic Drugs in Transit.* Brazil, a major recipient country, launched a concurrent challenge, WTO DS 409.

66. As of May 2014. Source: WTO Dispute Settlement Database.

Chapter 5

Note: This chapter is derived, in part, from an article published in *New Political Economy* on August 6, 2013, available at www.tandfonline.com/10.1080/13563467.2013.736957.

1. Ministério da Agricultura, Pesca e Abastecimento and USDA, 2009.

2. Calculated using data from EIU 2010b.

3. Information available at www.jbs.com.br.

4. Information available at www.brf-br.com.

5. Interview, Geneva, May 2009.

6. With poverty defined as living on less than $2 per day. World Bank data, available at http://databank.worldbank.org.

7. Ministério do Desenvolvimento, Indústria e Comércio Exterior do Brasil (MDIC), available at www.desenvolvimento.gov.br.

8. Interviews with Brazilian officials, September 2008 to June 2009 and May 2010.

9. Interview with Brazilian negotiator, Geneva, June 2009.

10. *EC—Export Subsidies on Sugar,* WT/DS266; and *United States—Subsidies on Upland Cotton,* WT/DS267.

11. Unlike other international organizations such as the UN, the WTO system is based on hard law enforced by a binding dispute settlement system. If a country's policies are found to be in violation of its WTO commitments, it is required to bring its policies into compliance, provide compensation to the complainant country, or face retaliation in the form of trade sanctions.

12. The IDEAS Centre was created in 2002 by a former GATT director-general and a former Swiss trade negotiator, with the mission of "helping developing countries to integrate into the world trading system."

13. Interview, Brasilia, May 2010.

14. Interviews with WTO negotiators, Geneva, September 2008 to June 2009.

15. ICONE's funding is supplied by the major Brazilian agribusiness associations, including: ABIOVE (Brazilian Association of Vegetable Oil Industries), ABIPECS (Brazilian Pork Industry and Exporter Association), ABIEC (Brazilian Meat Industry and Exporter Association), ABEF (Brazilian Poultry Industry and Exporters Association), UNICA (Brazilian Sugar Cane Industry Union), ABAG (Brazilian Agribusiness Association), FIESP (Federation of Industries of the State of Sao Paulo), and IRGA (Rice Institute of Rio Grande do Sul). While American and other foreign multinationals operate in Brazil's agriculture sector, ICONE has not shied away from taking stances in direct opposition to the interests of ADM, Cargill, and the other major foreign multinationals, such as in challenging US food aid, a form of export subsidy that generates significant revenues for the large US trading companies.

16. Interview with ICONE representative, Sao Paulo, May 2010.

17. Interview with Brazilian officials, Brasilia, May 2010.

18. Interview with Brazilian officials, Brasilia, May 2010.

19. Interviews conducted with Brazilian officials in Geneva, September 2008 to June 2009, and Brasilia, May 2010.

20. Interviews conducted with Brazilian officials in Geneva, September 2008 to June 2009, and Brasilia, May 2010.

21. As the Doha negotiations evolved and grew increasingly focused on determining specific provisions of the future agreement, internal divisions within the Brazilian state—between the Ministry of Agriculture (MAPA, dedicated to promoting the commercial agribusiness sector) and the Ministry of Rural Development (MDA, promoting small farmers and agricultural workers)—crystallized primarily in heated debate in the working group over the issues of the special safeguard mechanism (SSM) and special products (SP). Agribusiness sought to restrict the use of the SSM and SP as much as possible, to maximize its access to developing country markets, while small farmers sought maximum flexibility in the SSM and SP. Ultimately, however, Brazil decided that it would not have to take a firm position either way on the issues. Taking a hard stance to restrict the SSM and SP would alienate its allies and be untenable within the G20-T. Instead, Brazil

realized that it could sit back and let the US and other developed countries push aggressively to restrict the SSM and SP and take the associated political heat. For its part, MDA was left unsatisfied that Brazil had not pushed harder to expand the SSM and SP; while agribusiness was largely satisfied that Brazil had not pushed harder to limit the SSM and SP, viewing this as a necessary and pragmatic approach.

22. When word of the working group ultimately spread, it generated some criticism. According to interviews, a senator, for example, complained to the agriculture minister about the government working so closely with a research institute advocating on behalf of agribusiness and against the interests of small farmers.

23. For example, the G20-T's push for product-specific caps on subsidies and the criteria it put forward for how they should be determined was driven largely by ICONE (G20 2005b; G20 2007; ICONE 2006; ICONE 2007b). Similarly, the G20-T's position on the tariff reduction formula in market access—its rejection of the US-EU proposal for a blended formula and its own proposal for a tiered formula (G20 2004; G20 2005a)—came from ICONE's research and analysis. (Information obtained in interviews with G20-T negotiators, Geneva, September 2008 to June 2009, and Brazilian officials and ICONE representatives, June 2010, and confirmed through review of private ICONE documents prepared for and presented to the G20-T and subsequent G20-T proposals.)

24. Interviews conducted with Brazilian officials in Geneva, September 2008 to June 2009, and Brasilia, May 2010.

25. Interview, Geneva, June 2009.

26. Interview, Brasilia, May 2010.

27. Interview, Geneva, June 2009.

28. Interview, Geneva, June 2009.

29. Interviews with G20-T members and other delegations, Geneva, September 2008 to June 2009.

30. Interview, Brasilia, May 2010.

31. It also pursued reductions of tariffs in rich countries, but its position on this issue was much weaker and less aggressive, given that many of its members had their own very high tariff levels that they sought to protect. On the issue of improving access to developing country markets, there was no consensus within the group—with its offensively and defensively interested members taking opposing positions—and the issue was put aside with no joint position ever reached.

32. The argument is not that the G20-T was the first to link agriculture subsidies to development or to the concerns of developing countries, but that it was because of the G20-T that this became the dominant framing of the issue.

33. This was in sharp contrast to many of the pre-existing conceptions of development, in which it was equated with industrialization and agriculture was seen as the antithesis of development.

34. Interview with NGO representative, Geneva, May 2009.

35. Interview with NGO representative, Geneva, April 2009.

36. Interview with Brazilian delegate, Geneva, March 2009.

37. Interviews with NGO representatives, Geneva, September 2008 to June 2009. Brazil also tried to use NGOs to convince the C-4 countries to join the cotton case against the US as third parties.

38. Interviews conducted with Brazilian officials in Geneva, September 2008 to June 2009, and Brasilia, May 2010.

39. Interview, Geneva, June 2009.

40. Interview, Geneva, May 2009.

41. OECD PSE Data, 2010 to 2012 average.

42. Developing country agricultural subsidies are largely exempt from the Doha Round negotiations.

Chapter 6

1. See "Members' Contributions to the WTO Budget and the Budget of the Appellate Body for the Year 2013," available at www.wto.org/english/thewto_e/secre_e/contrib13_e. htm.

2. IMF Data.

3. World Bank Data, 2013.

4. Stated poverty rate based on poverty headcount ratio at $2 per day (PPP) and extreme poverty at $1.25 per day (PPP). World Bank Data, 2009.

5. Figure for China's GINI in the early 1980s taken from World Bank Data.

6. Interviews with Chinese officials, Beijing, July to August 2009. In fact, the Chinese government is actively working to cultivate greater private sector input into its process of trade policy formulation.

7. World Bank Data.

8. Interview with negotiator, Geneva, April 2009.

9. The RAMs include Albania, Armenia, Cabo Verde, China, Chinese Taipei, Ecuador, Former Yugoslav Republic of Macedonia, Georgia, Jordan, Kyrgyz Republic, Moldova, Mongolia, Oman, Panama, Russian Federation, Saudi Arabia, Kingdom of, Tajikistan, Tonga, Ukraine, Vietnam.

10. Interview, Geneva, April, 2009.

11. These figures refer to total goods exports, not solely those of manufactured goods, but more than 95 percent of China's goods exports consist of manufactured goods. Data from UN Comtrade and IMF.

12. These include the EU's Everything But Arms (EBA) initiative and the US's African Growth and Opportunities Act (AGOA), Caribbean Basin (CBERA), and Andean Trade Preferences (ATPDEA) arrangements.

13. See WTO Data, "Anti-dumping Initiations: By Exporting Country 01/01/1995–31/12/2013," available at www.wto.org/english/tratop_e/adp_e/adp_e.htm.

14. WTO Data, "Anti-dumping Initiations: By Exporting Country 01/01/1995–31/12/2013," available at www.wto.org/english/tratop_e/adp_e/adp_e.htm.

15. WTO Data, "Anti-dumping Initiations: By Exporting Country 01/01/1995–31/12/2013," available at www.wto.org/english/tratop_e/adp_e/adp_e.htm.

16. WTO Data, "Anti-dumping Initiations: By Exporting Country 01/01/1995–31/12/2013," available at www.wto.org/english/tratop_e/adp_e/adp_e.htm.

17. As Zeng and Liang (2010: 575) detail, the argument for this designation was that as China is undergoing a transition from a planned to market economy, its domestic prices may not reflect market demand and supply. Consequently, instead of comparing the price of a good imported from China with the price of the same good marketed in either the Chinese or a third country market, foreign authorities engaged in an antidumping investigation against China may use either "the constructed cost of producing the same good in a third country where the prices of factor inputs are determined by the market or the 'normal value' of the cost of production in a surrogate country as a benchmark for determining whether a product from China is being dumped in the US market." These methodologies for antidumping determination are disadvantageous to Chinese producers for several reasons. Most notably, foreign authorities are allowed discretion in choosing surrogate countries to be used to estimate the costs of Chinese firms and "countries that are selected as surrogate countries or whose prices are used in the constructed value approach often have much higher labor costs than those in China. This increases the possibility that the US Department of Commerce will rule positively in an antidumping case when in fact the price exceeds the cost of production in China. This practice effectively undermines China's comparative advantage in labor-intensive goods over its competitors."

18. Interview, Geneva, April 2009.

19. Countries agreed in the industrial goods negotiations to apply a formula to determine the average level of tariff cuts each country would be required to undertake, with different coefficients (which determine the depth of the cuts) for developed countries (a lower coefficient resulting in higher cuts) and developing countries (a higher coefficient resulting in lower cuts).

20. Interview, WTO Secretariat official, Geneva, March 2009.

21. Interview, Geneva, April 2009.

22. Interview, Geneva, April 2009.

23. Interview, New Delhi, March 2010.

24. Interview with negotiator, Geneva, May 2009.

25. Interview with negotiator, Geneva, March 2009.

26. Both negotiators and secretariat officials indicated that the emphasis placed on fish subsidies in the Doha Round was motivated in part by a desire to improve the WTO's environmental image, which has long been the subject of criticism and protest from environmental groups.

27. Interview with negotiator, Geneva, March 2009.

28. Interview with negotiator, Geneva, April 2009.

29. Interview, Geneva, April 2009.

30. Interview, Geneva, April 2009.

31. Interview, Geneva, January 2009.

32. Interview, Geneva, April 2009.

33. Interview with negotiator, Geneva, May 2009.

34. When Chinese officials spoke in interviews about the challenges China faces in the trading system, antidumping was always one of the first things they mentioned, and they spoke of it almost exclusively in terms of the US.

35. Interviews with trade officials, Brasilia, May 2010.

36. Interviews, Geneva, May 2009.

37. Interview, New Delhi, March 2010.

38. Interview, Geneva, April 2009.

Chapter 7

1. Interview, Geneva, January 2009.

2. As discussed later in the chapter, India often refers to its high rates of farmer suicides to explain the vulnerabilities of its agricultural sector and justify its need for agricultural protections. The "suicidal farmers" quotation appeared in multiple interviews with Western negotiators, Geneva, September 2008 to June 2009.

3. World Bank data.

4. Interview, Geneva, May 2009.

5. Data from NASSCOM.

6. Information accessed at www.ge.com/news/company-information/india.

7. Information obtained from publicly available information on corporate websites: www.wipro.com/, www.infosys.com/, www.tcs.com/about/corp_facts/Pages/default.aspx.

8. The Indian government made several policy changes to facilitate the internationalization of Indian firms. Starting in 2000, Indian companies were allowed to invest 100 percent of the proceeds from issuing shares (a common method of financing outward FDI) to acquire foreign companies. In 2002 the limit on Indian investment in foreign joint ventures and wholly owned subsidiaries was increased from $50 million to $100 million per financial year. In 2004, Indian firms were allowed to borrow in foreign exchange for direct investments in foreign joint ventures and subsidiaries. In 2007, the limit on overseas investment by Indian companies was raised to 400 percent of the investing firm's net worth. In 2008 the limit on overseas investment by India-based mutual funds was increased to $7 billion (Alejandro et al. 2010).

9. Interviews with Indian services industry representatives and government officials, New Delhi, March 2010.

10. Interview, Geneva, May 2009.

11. Interviews, New Delhi, March 2010.

12. GDP measured at PPP rates.

13. Unless otherwise indicated, all data is from the World Bank. Poverty data is from 2010.

14. World Bank data. Vulnerable employment is defined as unpaid family workers and own-account workers. According to the ILO, they are more likely to lack decent working conditions, adequate social security, and "voice" through effective representation by trade unions and similar organizations. Vulnerable employment is often characterized by

inadequate earnings, low productivity, and difficult conditions of work that undermine workers' fundamental rights (ILO 2010).

15. India's Tenth Five Year Plan (2002–7), Volume I—Volume and Dimensions, pp. 97–98.

16. India's Tenth Five Year Plan (2002–7), Volume I—Volume and Dimensions, pp. 119–21.

17. Interviews with Indian negotiators, Geneva, September 2008 to June 2009.

18. Interview, Geneva, May 2009.

19. Interview, former Indian negotiator, New Delhi, March 2010.

20. Interview, Geneva, May 2014.

21. Interview, Geneva, May 2014.

22. "Unilateral" liberalization refers to measures undertaken autonomously (that is, not mandated by any multilateral or bilateral trade agreement). New market access commitments included increasing its foreign equity cap in the telecommunications sector from 50 to 74 percent and allowing 51 percent foreign ownership in its previously closed asset management sector.

23. Interview, New Delhi, March 2010.

24. US Call Center and Consumer Protection Act of 2013.

25. Interview, Geneva, May 2009.

26. Interview with Indian services industry representative, New Delhi, March 2010.

27. Cited in Jurje and Lavenex 2014: 1.

28. Interview, Geneva, May 4, 2009.

29. Interview, New Delhi, March 2010.

30. The fifteen states participating in the plurilateral request were Argentina, Brazil, Chile, China, Colombia, Dominican Republic, Egypt, Guatemala, India, Mexico, Morocco, Pakistan, Peru, Thailand, and Uruguay.

31. The WTO Secretariat, for example, organized a symposium on Mode 4 in 2008. For further information, see www.wto.org/english/tratop_e/serv_e/mouvement_persons_e/sym_sept08_e/sym_sept08_e.htm.

32. Interview, Geneva, May 4, 2009.

33. Interview, Geneva, May 4, 2009.

34. Interview, former Indian negotiator, New Delhi, March 2010.

35. Interviews with Indian negotiators and officials, Geneva, September 2008 to June 2009, and New Delhi, March 2010.

36. Interview, New Delhi, March 2010.

37. Interview, New Delhi, March 2010.

38. Interview, Geneva, April 2009.

39. Interview, Geneva, April 2009.

40. Interview, New Delhi, March 2010.

41. Interview, New Delhi, March 2010.

42. Interview, New Delhi, March 2010.

43. Interviews with peasant movements and NGOs, New Delhi, March 2010.

44. Interviews with peasant movements and NGOs, New Delhi, March 2010.

45. Interview, New Delhi, March 2010.

46. Interview, New Delhi, March 2010.

47. Interview, trade adviser to Indian government, New Delhi, March 2010.

48. Interview, New Delhi, March 2010.

49. OECD Data.

50. Thirty-nine WTO members are eligible to use the SSG. These include Australia, Barbados, Botswana, Bulgaria, Canada, Colombia, Costa Rica, Czech Republic, Ecuador, El Salvador, the EU, Guatemala, Hungary, Iceland, Indonesia, Israel, Japan, Korea, Malaysia, Mexico, Morocco, Namibia, New Zealand, Nicaragua, Norway, Panama, Philippines, Poland, Romania, Slovak Republic, South Africa, Swaziland, Switzerland-Liechtenstein, Chinese Taipei, Thailand, Tunisia, USA, Uruguay, and Venezuela.

51. India's Amber Box subsidies are not allowed to exceed $12.4 billion in product-specific support and a total of $12.4 billion in non-product-specific support (10 percent of total agricultural production), while the US is allowed to provide up to $19.1 billion in Amber Box support, along with up to $15 billion in non-product-specific exemptions as well as $15 billion in product-specific exemptions, totaling as much as $49.1 billion in allowable Amber Box subsidies permitted under existing WTO rules. Calculation of India's de minimis ceiling is based on 2007 to 2008 total agricultural production, as provided in Gopinath and Laborde 2008. US de minimis calculations are based on USDA total agricultural production figures for 2007.

52. It is widely recognized that many measures classified as least trade distorting actually do have significant impacts on production and trade.

Chapter 8

1. Interview, New Delhi, March 2010.

2. Interviews, negotiators, and officials, Geneva, September 2008 to June 2009. Similar sentiments are expressed in Western media accounts; see sources such as Blustein 2009; *Economist* 2014; *Wall Street Journal* 2014.

3. Interview, Geneva, April 2009.

4. Interview, Geneva, April 2009.

5. The allusion to *Groundhog Day* refers to a Hollywood film about a man who finds himself in a time loop, repeating the same day over and over again.

6. Interview, New Delhi, March 2010.

7. Comment by NGO representative at civil society conference in Geneva, November 2008.

8. Interviews with negotiators and officials, Geneva, September 2008 to June 2009.

9. It is true that in signing on to the creation of the WTO, the US subjected itself—like other states—to its dispute settlement mechanism (DSM). This is frequently pointed to as evidence of the US relinquishing a degree of its sovereignty and submitting itself to the supranational authority of the WTO (Chorev 2008). Yet two points here should be noted. One, the DSM has authority only where the US has breached commitments it has

willingly made under existing WTO agreements. The authority of the WTO over the US is thus limited to what the US itself has agreed to via prior WTO negotiations. Two, this greatly increases the weight and consequence of WTO negotiations for the US (or any other state), because whatever it agrees to can potentially be enforced under the DSM.

10. See WTO (www.wto.org/english/tratop_e/region_e/region_e.htm); USTR (www.ustr.gov/trade-agreements/free-trade-agreements); ADB (http://aric.adb.org/fta-country); and OAS (www.sice.oas.org/ctyindex/BRZ/BRZAgreements_e.asp).

11.   Interview, New Delhi, 2010.

12.   As of June 15, 2014, the WTO has been notified of some 585 regional and bilateral trade agreements, of which 379 were in force. See WTO data, accessed at www.wto.org/english/tratop_e/region_e/region_e.htm.

13.   Interviews with negotiators and government officials, Geneva, September 2008 to June 2009.

14.   Interview, New Delhi, March 2010.

References

A. T. Kearney. 2009. *The Shifting Geography of Offshoring: The 2009 A. T. Kearney Global Services Location Index*. Chicago: A. T. Kearney.

Adams, Nassau A. 1993. *Worlds Apart: The North-South Divide and the International System*. London: Zed Books.

Alejandro, Lisa, Eric Forden, Allison Gosney, Erland Herfindahl, Dennis Luther, Erick Oh, Joann Peterson, Matthew Reisman, and Isaac Wohl. 2010. "An Overview and Examination of the Indian Services Sector." US International Trade Commission, Working Paper, August.

Allen, F., E. Carletti, J. Qian, and P. Valenzuela. 2013. "Does Finance Accelerate or Retard Growth? Theory and Evidence." In *Towards a Better Global Economy Project*. Global Citizen Foundation. Available at www.gcf.ch/?page_id=1272 (accessed November 23, 2014).

Altman, Daniel. 2007. "Managing Globalization: Interview with Charlene Barshefsky on Doha." *International Herald Tribune*, January 31.

American Enterprise Institute. 2005. "Time to End Agricultural Subsidies: Can WTO Raise the Poor from Poverty?" Washington, DC.

Amiti, Mary, and Caroline Freund. 2007. "China's Export Boom." *Finance and Development* 44(3). International Monetary Fund, September.

Amorim, Celso. 2003. "The Real Cancun." *Wall Street Journal,* September 25, P. A18.

Anderson, Carol. 2003. *Eyes Off the Prize: The United Nations and the African American Struggle for Human Rights.* Cambridge: Cambridge University Press.

Anderson, Perry. 2013. "Imperium." *New Left Review* 83:5–111.

Andreas, J. 2008. "Changing Colors in China." *New Left Review* 54(November/December):123–42.

Apeldoorn, Bastiaan van, and Nana de Graaff. 2012. "Beyond Neoliberal Imperialism? The Crisis of American Empire." Pp. 207–28 in *Neoliberalism in Crisis*, edited by Henk Overbeek and Bastiaan van Apeldoorn. New York: Palgrave Macmillan.

Arrighi, Giovanni. 1994. *The Long Twentieth Century: Money, Power, and the Origins of Our Times.* London: Verso.

———. 2007. *Adam Smith in Beijing: Lineages of the Twenty-First Century.* New York: Verso.

Arrighi, Giovanni, and Beverly J. Silver. 1999. *Chaos and Governance in the Modern World System*. Minneapolis: University of Minnesota Press.

Arrighi, Giovanni, and Lu Zhang. 2011. "Beyond the Washington Consensus: A New Bandung?" Pp. 25–57 in *Globalization and Beyond: New Examinations of Global Power and Its Alternatives*, edited by Jon Shefner and Patricia Fernandez-Kelly. University Park: Pennsylvania State University Press.

Babb, Sarah. 2005. "The Social Consequences of Structural Adjustment: Recent Evidence and Current Debates." *Annual Review of Sociology* 31(1):199–222.

———. 2009. *Behind the Development Banks: Washington Politics, World Poverty, and the Wealth of Nations*. Chicago: University of Chicago Press.

Babones, Salvatore. 2011. "The Middling Kingdom: The Hype and the Reality of China's Rise." *Foreign Affairs* 90(5):79.

———. 2015. "American Hegemony Is Here to Stay." *National Interest* (July/August).

Bacchetta, Marc, and Bijit Bora. 2003. "Industrial Tariff Liberalization and the Doha Development Agenda." WTO Discussion Paper. Available at www.wto.org/english/res_e/booksp_e/discussion_papers_e.pdf.

Bacchus, James. 2004. *Trade and Freedom*. London: Cameron May.

Bailin, Alison. 2005. *From Traditional to Group Hegemony: The G7, the Liberal Economic Order and the Core-Periphery Gap*. Burlington, VT: Ashgate.

Bair, Jennifer. 2009. "Taking Aim at the New International Economic Order." In *The Road from Mt. Pelèrin: The Making of the Neoliberal Thought Collective*, edited by Phil Mirowski and Dieter Plehwe. Cambridge: Harvard University Press.

Baker, Dean. 2010. *Taking Economics Seriously*. Cambridge, MA: MIT Press.

Baldwin, Richard. 2011. "Twenty-first Century Regionalism, Doha, and the Future of the WTO." German Marshall Fund of the United States, Economic Policy Program, April 7.

Baldwin, Robert E. 1987. "The New Protectionism: A Response to Shifts in National Economic Power." National Bureau of Economic Research Working Paper No. 1823, November.

———. 2006. "Failure of the WTO Ministerial Conference at Cancun: Reasons and Remedies." *World Economy* 29(6):677–96.

Ban, Cornel, and Mark Blyth. 2013. "The BRICs and the Washington Consensus: An introduction." *Review of International Political Economy* 20(2):241–55.

Barry, Ellen. 2014. "After Farmers Commit Suicide, Debts Fall on Families in India." *New York Times,* February 22.

Bayliss, K., B. Fine, and E. van Waeyenberge. 2011. *The Political Economy of Development: World Bank, Neoliberalism, and Development Research*. London: Pluto Press.

BBC News. 2008. "World Trade Talks End in Collapse." Available at http://news.bbc.co.uk/2/hi/business/7531099.stm (accessed July 29, 2008).

Beeson, Mark. 2009. "Trading Places? China, the United States, and the Evolution of the International Political Economy." *Review of International Political Economy* 16(4):729–41.

Beeson, Mark, and S. Bell. 2009. "The G-20 and International Economic Governance: Hegemony, Collectivism, or Both." *Global Governance* 15:67.

Berger, Brett, and Robert F. Martin. 2011. "The Growth of Chinese Exports: An Examination of the Detailed Trade Data." Board of Governors of the U.S. Federal Reserve System, International Finance Discussion Paper, No. 1033, November.

Bergsten, C. Fred. 2005. "Rescuing the Doha Round." *Foreign Affairs* 84(7).

———. 2008. "A Partnership of Equals: How Washington Should Respond to China's Economic Challenge." *Foreign Affairs* 87(4):57–69.

Bernstein, Steven. 2012. "Grand Compromises in Global Governance." *Government and Opposition* 47(3):368–94.

Bhagwati, Jagdish. 2004. "Don't Cry for Cancun." *Foreign Affairs* 83(1):52.

———. 2005. "Reshaping the WTO." *Far Eastern Economic Review* 168(2):25–30.

———. 2007. "Bhagwati: US Must Rethink Doha Demands (Interview)." Council on Foreign Relations. Available at www.cfr.org/india/bhagwati-us-must-rethink-doha-demands/p12592 (accessed Febrary 9, 2007).

———. 2008. *Termites in the Trading System: How Preferential Agreements Undermine Free Trade.* New York: Oxford University Press.

Bhagwati, Jagdish, and Ross Garnaut. 2003. "Say No to This Free Trade Deal." *Australian,* July 11.

Birdsall, Nancy, Dani Rodrik, and Arvind Subramanian. 2005. "How to Help Poor Countries." *Foreign Affairs* 84(4):136–52.

Blackhurst, R., B. Lyakurwa, and A. Oyejide. 2000. "Options for Improving Africa's Participation in the WTO." *World Economy* 23(4):491-510.

Block, Fred, and Peter Evans. 1994. "The State and the Economy." Pp. 505–26 in *The Handbook of Economic Sociology*, edited by Neil J. Smelser and Richard Swedberg. Princeton: Princeton University Press.

Blomeyer, Roland, Ian Goulding, Daniel Pauly, Antonio Sanz, and Kim Stobberup. 2012. *The Role of China in World Fisheries.* Study produced for the EU Parliament. Available at www.europarl.europa.eu/meetdocs/2009_2014/documents/pech/dv/chi/china.pdf.

Bloomberg. 2007. "China's Power Erodes Free-Trade Support in Developing Nations." April 2.

———. 2013. "Outsourcing Made by India Seen Hit by Immigration Law." Available at www.bloomberg.com/news/2013-07-23/outsourcing-made-by-india-seen-hit-by-immigration-law.html (accessed July 24, 2013).

Blustein, Paul. 2009. *Misadventures of the Most Favored Nations: Clashing Egos, Inflated Ambitions, and the Great Shambles of the World Trade System.* New York: Perseus Books.

Blyth, Mark. 2002. *Great Transformations: Economic Ideas and Institutional Change in the Twentieth Century.* Cambridge: Cambridge University Press.

Bourdieu, Pierre. 2000. *Pascalian Meditations.* Oxford: Polity Press.

Bown, Chad P. 2010. "China's WTO Entry: Antidumping, Safeguards, and Dispute settlement." Pp. 281–337 in *China's Growing Role in World Trade*, edited by Robert C. Feenstra and Shang-Jin Wei. Chicago: University of Chicago Press.

———. 2011. "Taking Stock of Antidumping, Safeguards and Countervailing Duties, 1990–2009." *World Economy* 34(12):1955–98.

Braithwaite, John. 2008. *Regulatory Capitalism: How It Works, Ideas for Making It Work Better.* Northampton, MA: Edward Elgar.

Braithwaite, John, and Peter Drahos. 2000. *Global Business Regulation.* New York: Cambridge University Press.

Branford, Sue, and Jan Rocha. 2002. *Cutting the Wire: The Story of the Landless Movement in Brazil.* London: Latin America Bureau.

Bremmer, I., and N. Roubini. 2011. "A G-Zero World: The New Economic Club Will Produce Conflict, Not Cooperation." *Foreign Affairs* 90(2):2.

Brenner, Neil, Jamie Peck, and Nik Theodore. 2010. "Variegated Neoliberalization: Geographies, Modalities, Pathways." *Global Networks* 10(2):182–222.

Brenner, Neil, and Nik Theodore. 2002. "Cities and the Geographies of 'Actually Existing Neoliberalism.'" *Antipode* 34(3):349–79.

Breslin, Shaun. 2010. "China's Emerging Global Role: Dissatisfied Responsible Great Power." *Politics* 30:52–62.

Bridges Weekly. 2004 (September 1). "ACP Countries Concerned as Brazil Celebrates Favourable Sugar Ruling." *Bridges Weekly Trade News Digest* 8(28).

———. 2008 (August 7). "Strong Signals Sent on Services." *Bridges Weekly Trade News Digest* 12(27).

———. 2009 (December 9). "WTO Ministerial Lifts Hopes for Doha, but Scepticism Lingers." *Bridges Weekly Trade News Digest* 13(42).

———. 2010a (May 12). "All Eyes on US Ahead of High-level Doha Meeting." *Bridges Weekly Trade News Digest* 14(17).

———. 2010b (December 22). "EU, India Resolve Spat over Generic Drug Shipments, But FTA to Wait until 2011." *Bridges Weekly Trade News Digest* 14(44).

———. 2011 (March 2). "Summary: Council for Services Trade Report." *Bridges Weekly Trade News Digest* 15(15).

———. 2013 (December 5). "Food Stock Subsidies to 'Make or Break' Bali Trade Talks." Bridges Daily Update, WTO Ninth Ministerial Conference (No. 3).

———. 2014a (October 2). "US, Brazil Clinch Deal Resolving Cotton Trade Row." *Bridges Weekly Trade News Digest* 18(32).

———. 2014b (September 25). "WTO Chief Warns of Potential 'Freezing Effect' as TFA, Food Stockholding Deadlock Persists." *Bridges Weekly Trade News Digest* 18(31).

Bukovansky, Mlada. 2010. "Institutionalized Hypocrisy and the Politics of Agricultural Trade." In *Constructing the International Economy*, edited by Rawi Abdelal, Mark Blyth, and Craig Parsons. Ithaca, NY: Cornell University Press.

Burges, Sean W. 2013. "Brazil as a Bridge between Old and New Powers?" *International Affairs* 89(3):577–94.

Bussiere, M., and A. Mehl. 2008. "China's and India's Roles in Global Trade and Finance: Twin Titans for the New Millennium?" *European Central Bank Occassional Paper Series* No. 80 (January).

Cason, Jeffrey W., and Timothy J. Power. 2009. "Presidentialization, Pluralization, and the

Rollback of Itamaraty: Explaining Change in Brazilian Foreign Policy Making in the Cardoso-Lula Era." *International Political Science Review* 30(2):117–40.

Castañeda, Jorge G. 2010. "Not Ready for Prime Time—Why Including Emerging Powers at the Helm Would Hurt Global Governance." *Foreign Affairs* 89:109.

Centeno, Miguel A., and Joseph N. Cohen. 2012. "The Arc of Neoliberalism." *American Review of Sociology* 38:317–40.

Chadee, Doren, Revti Raman, and Snejina Michailova. 2011. "Sources of Competitiveness of Offshore IT Service Providers in India: Towards a Conceptual Framework." *Competition and Change* 15(3):196–220.

Chakraborty, Debashis, and Amir Ullah Khan. 2008. *The WTO Deadlocked: Understanding the Dynamics of International Trade*: SAGE.

Chanda, Rupa, and G. Sasidaran. 2007. "GATS and Developments in India's Service Sector." Pp. 169–212 in *India's Liberalization Experience: Hostage to the WTO?*, edited by Suparna Karmakar, Rajiv Kumar, and Bibek Debroy. New Delhi: ICRIER and SAGE.

Chang, Ha-Joon. 2002. *Kicking away the Ladder: Development Strategy in Historical Perspective*. London: Anthem Press.

Chin, Gregory T. 2014. "The BRICS-led Development Bank: Purpose and Politics beyond the G20." *Global Policy* 5(3):366–73.

China. 2007. "Statement by H. E. Ambassador Sun Zhenyu at the Informal Trade Negotiations Committee Meeting." April 20. Available at wto2.mofcom.gov.cn/article/aboutus/mission/200804/20080405485964.shtml.

Chorev, Nitsan. 2005. "The Institutional Project of Neo-liberal Globalism: The Case of the WTO." *Theory and Society* 34:317–55.

———. 2008. *Remaking U.S. Trade Policy: From Protectionism to Globalization*. Ithaca, NY: Cornell University Press.

———. 2012. "Restructuring Neoliberalism at the World Health Organization." *Review of International Political Economy* 20(4):627–66.

Chorev, Nitsan, and Sarah Babb. 2009. "The Crisis of Neoliberalism and the Future of International Institutions: A Comparison of the IMF and the WTO." *Theory and Society* 38(5):459–84.

Choudhury, Prithwiraj, and Tarun Khanna. 2014. "Charting Dynamic Trajectories: Multinational Enterprises in India." *Business History Review* 88(01):133–69.

Clapp, Jennifer. 2007. "WTO Agriculture Negotiations and the Global South." Pp. 37–55 in *The WTO after Hong Kong: Progress in, and Prospects for, the Doha Development Agenda*, edited by Donna Lee and Rorden Wilkinson. New York: Routledge.

Congressional Research Service (CRS). 2006. "Potential Challenges to U.S. Farm Subsidies in the WTO." Washington, DC.

Conti, Joseph A. 2011. *Between Law and Diplomacy: The Social Contexts of Disputing at the World Trade Organization*. Stanford: Stanford University Press.

Cooper, Andrew, and Daniel Schwanen. 2009. *CIGI Special G20 Report: Flashpoints for the Pittsburgh Summit*. Waterloo, ON: Centre for International Governance Innovation.

Cornelius, Wayne A. 2001. "Death at the Border: Efficacy and Unintended Consequences of US Immigration Control Policy." *Population and Development Review* 27(4):661–85.

Cox, Michael. 2012. "Power Shifts, Economic Change and the Decline of the West?" *International Relations* 26(4):369–88.

Cox, Robert W. 1983. "Gramsci, Hegemony, and International Relations: An Essay on Method." *Millennium: Journal of International Studies* 12(2):162–75.

———. 1992. "Multilateralism and World Order." *Review of International Studies* 18(2):161–80.

———. 1996. *Approaches to World Order*. Cambridge: Cambridge University Press.

Cox, Robert W., and Harold K. Jacobson. 1973. *The Anatomy of Influence: Decision-making in International Organization*. New Haven: Yale University Press.

Cox, Ronald W. 2008. "Transnational Capital, the US State and Latin American Trade Agreements." *Third World Quarterly* 29(8):1527–44.

Curzon, Gerard, and Victoria Curzon. 1973. "GATT: Traders' Club." Pp. 298–333 in *The Anatomy of Influence: Decision-making in International Organization*, edited by Robert W. Cox and Harold K. Jacobson. New Haven: Yale University Press.

Dadush, Uri. 2009. "WTO Reform: The Time to Start Is Now." Washington, DC: Carnegie Endowment for International Peace.

Damico, Flavio Soares, and Andre Meloni Nassar. 2007. "Agricultural Expansion and Policies in Brazil." Pp. 75–96 in *U.S. Agricultural Policy and the 2007 Farm Bill*, edited by Kaush Arha, Tim Josling, Daniel A. Sumner, and Barton H. Thompson. Stanford: Woods Institute for the Environment, Stanford University.

Dawson, Laura Ritchie. 2013. "Labour Mobility and the WTO: The Limits of GATS Mode 4." *International Migration* 51(1).

Dayaratna-Banda, O. G., and John Whalley. 2007. "After the Multifibre Arrangement, the China Containment Agreements." *Asia-Pacific Trade and Investment Review* 3(1):29–54.

De Bièvre, Dirk. 2006. "Legislative and Judicial Decision Making in the World Trade Organization." In *New Modes of Governance in the Global System: Exploring Publicness, Delegation, and Inclusiveness*, edited by M. Koenig-Archibugi and M. Zürn. New York: Palgrave MacMillan.

de Holanda Barbosa, Fernando. 1999. "Economic Development: The Brazilian Experience." Pp. 69–87 in *Development Strategies in East Asia and Latin America*, edited by Akio Hosono and Neantro Saavedra-Rivano. Basingstoke, UK: Palgrave Macmillan.

de Lima, Maria Regina Soares, and Monica Hirst. 2006. "Brazil as an Intermediate State and Regional Power: Action, Choice and Responsibilities." *International Affairs* 82(1):21–40.

de Shutter, Olivier. 2011. "The World Trade Organization and the Post-Global Food Crisis Agenda: Putting Food Security First in the International Trade System." UN Special Rapporteur on the Human Right to Food, Briefing Note 4, November. Available at www.wto.org/english/news_e/news11_e/deschutter_2011_e.pdf.

Deardorff, Alan V., and Robert M. Stern. 2003. "Enhancing the Benefits for Developing Countries in the Doha Development Agenda Negotiations." Research Seminar in International Economics, University of Michigan, Discussion Paper No. 495. Available at fordschool.umich.edu/rsie/workingpapers/Papers476-500/r498.pdf.

Decreux, Yves, and Lionel Fontagne. 2009. "Economic Impact of Potential Outcome of the DDA." CEPII Working Paper, May.

Downes, Gerard. 2009. "China and India—The New Powerhouses of the Semi-Periphery?" Pp. 102–19 in *Globalization and the "New" Semi-Peripheries*, edited by Owen Worth and Phoebe Moore. New York: Palgrave Macmillan.

Drache, Daniel. 2004. "Global Trade Politics and the Cycle of Dissent Post-Cancún." *Policy and Society* 24(3):17–44.

Drezner, Daniel W. 2007. "The New New World Order." *Foreign Affairs* 86(2).

Dyer, Geoff, and Jamil Anderlini. 2011. "China's Lending Hits New Heights." *Financial Times,* January 17.

Eagleton-Pierce, Matthew. 2012. *Symbolic Power in the World Trade Organization.* Oxford: Oxford University Press.

Easterly, William. 2001. "The Lost Decades: Developing Countries' Stagnation in Spite of Policy Reform, 1980–1998." *Journal of Economic Growth* 6:135–57.

Economic Times. 2013 (May 3). "2.97 Million Professionals Employed in IT-ITES Sector in FY13: Government."

Economist. 2008 (August 13). "The dragon in the backyard: Latin American geopolitics."

———. 2010a (September 30). "Business in India: A Bumpier but Freer Road."

———. 2010b (September 23). "Child Malnutrition in India: Putting the Smallest First."

———. 2013 (July 27). "When Giants Slow Down.".

———. 2014a (August 9). "Bailing out from Bali."

———. 2014b (September 25). "Time to Make in India?"

Efstathopoulos, Charalampos, and Dominic Kelly. 2014. "India, Developmental Multilateralism and the Doha Ministerial Conference." *Third World Quarterly* 35(6):1066–81.

EIU. 2008. "Country Profile: India." London: Economist Intelligence Unit (EIU).

———. 2010a. "Country Report: India." London: Economist Intelligence Unit (EIU).

———. 2010b. "The Global Power of Brazilian Agribusiness." Economist Intelligence Unit (EIU).

Emmott, Bill. 2008. *Rivals: How the Power Struggle between China, India and Japan Will Shape Our Next Decade.* New York: Harcourt.

EU. 2007. "Report on US Barriers to Trade and Investment." European Commission. Available at trade.ec.europa.eu/doclib/docs/2008/april/tradoc_138559.pdf.

Evans, Peter. 1979. *Dependent Development: The Alliance of Multinational, State, and Local Capital in Brazil.* Princeton: Princeton University Press.

———. 2008. "Is an Alternative Globalization Possible?" *Politics and Society* 36(2):271–305.

Evenett, Simon. 2007. "EU Commercial Policy in a Multipolar Trading System." Centre for International Governance Innovation (CIGI) Working Paper No. 23.

FAO. 2008. *Trade Reforms and Food Security: Conceptualizing the Linkages.* Rome: UN Food and Agriculture Organization (FAO).

Feng, Hui. 2006. *The Politics of China's Accession to the World Trade Organization: The Dragon Goes Global.* New York: Routledge.

Financial Times. 1999 (November 17). "Hopes for Accord on Farm Talks Agenda."

———. 2005 (July 18). "Waning Expectations: Agreement on Trade Remains Remote as Time."

———. 2008 (August 4). "A Campaign Manual Penned in Vain."

———. 2010 (August 11). "New Delhi Attacks US over 'Discriminatory' Visa Fee Increase."

———. 2011 (April 15). "Slow-running G20 Train Is Worth Keeping on the Tracks."

Finger, J. Michael, Ulrich Reincke, and Adriana Castro. 1999. *Market Access Bargaining in the Uruguay Round: Rigid or Relaxed Reciprocity?* World Bank Paper No. 2258. Washington, DC: World Bank.

Finger, J. Michael, and Philip Schuler. 2000. "Implementation of Uruguay Round Commitments: The Development Challenge." *World Economy* 23(4).

Finger, J. Michael, and L. Alan Winters. 1998. "What Can the WTO Do for Developing Countries?" Pp. 365–92 in *The WTO as an International Organization,* edited by Anne O. Krueger. Chicago: University of Chicago Press.

Fligstein, Neil. 2005. "The Political and Economic Sociology of International Economic Arrangements." Pp. 183–204 in *The Handbook of Economic Sociology,* edited by Neil J. Smelser and Richard Swedberg. Princeton: Princeton University Press.

Fraser, Nancy. 1992. "Rethinking the Public Sphere: A Contribution to the Critique of Actually Existing Democracy." Pp. 109-42 in *Habermas and the Public Sphere,* edited by C. Calhoun. Cambridge: MIT.

Frazier, Mark W. 2013. "Narrowing the Gap: Rural-urban Inequality in China." *World Politics Review,* September 24.

Friedman, Thomas. 2004. *The World Is Flat: A Brief History of the Twenty-First Century.* New York: Farrar, Straus and Giroux.

Furtado, João. 2008. "Muito além da especialização regressiva e da doença holandesa." *Novos Estudos—CEBRAP* 81:33–46.

G20. 2004. "Communication from the G20: The Blended Formula: A Fundamentally Flawed Approach to Agricultural Market Access."

———. 2005a. "G20 Proposal on Market Access."

———. 2005b. "G20 Statement: Blue Box."

———. 2007. "G20 Proposal for the Establishment of Product-specific Caps in AMS."

Gallagher, Kevin P. 2008. "Understanding Developing Country Resistance to the Doha Round." *Review of International Political Economy* 15(1):62–85.

Gallagher, Kevin P., Amos Irwin, and Katherine Koleski. 2012. "The New Banks in Town: Chinese Finance in Latin America." Inter-American Dialogue Report, March. Available at ase.tufts.edu/gdae/Pubs/rp/GallagherChineseFinanceLatinAmericaBrief.pdf.

Gantz, David A. 2013. *Liberalizing International Trade after Doha.* Cambridge: Cambridge University Press.

Gill, Stephen. 1995. "Globalisation, Market Civilisation and Disciplinary Neoliberalism." *Millennium: Journal of International Studies* 24:399–423.

————. 2002. "Constitutionalizing Inequality and the Clash of Globalizations." *International Studies Review* 4(2):47–65.

————. 2003. *Power and Resistance in the New World Order.* New York: Palgrave Macmillan.

Gills, Barry K. 2010. "Going South: Capitalist Crisis, Systemic Crisis, Civilisational Crisis." *Third World Quarterly* 31(2):169–84.

Gilpin, Robert. 1975. *U.S. Power and the Multinational Corporations: The Political Economy of Foreign Direct Investment.* New York: Basic Books.

————. 1981. *War and Change in World Politics.* New York: Cambridge University Press.

————. 1987. *The Political Economy of International Relations.* Princeton: Princeton University Press.

Globerman, Steven, and Daniel Shapiro. 2008. "Economic and strategic considerations surrounding Chinese FDI in the United States." *Asia Pacific Journal of Management* 26(1):163–83.

Go, Julian. 2008. "Global Fields and Imperial Forms: Field Theory and the British and American Empires." *Sociological Theory* 26(3):201–29.

Goldin, I., O. Knudsen, and D. van der Mensbrugghe. 1993. *Trade Liberalization: Global Economic Implications.* Washington, DC: World Bank.

Goldman Sachs. 2006. "Will China Grow Old before Getting Rich?" Goldman Sachs Global Economics Paper No. 138.

Goldsmith, Peter, and Rodolfo Hirsch. 2006. "The Brazilian Soybean Complex." *Choices: The Magazine of Food, Farm, and Resource Issues* 21(3):97–103.

Goldstein, M. 2009. "A Grand Bargain for the London G20 Summit: Insurance and Obeying the Rules." VoxEU. Available at www.voxeu.org/article/grand-bargain-london-g20-summit (accessed November 23, 2014).

Golub, Philip. 2004. "Imperial Politics, Imperial Will and the Crisis of US Hegemony." *Review of International Political Economy* 11(4):763–86.

Golub, S. S. 2003. "Measures of Restrictions on Inward Foreign Direct Investment for OECD Countries." Working Paper No. 357, OECD Economics Department.

Gopinath, Munisamy, and David Laborde. 2008. "Implications for India of the May 2008 Draft Agricultural Modalities." International Centre for Trade and Sustainable Development (ICTSD), Geneva, June.

Gordon, James, and Poonam Gupta. 2004. "Understanding India's Services Revolution." IMF Working Paper 04/171, September.

Grady, P., and K. Macmillan. 1999. *Seattle and Beyond: The WTO Millennium Round.* Ottawa: Global Economics.

Grant, W. 2005. "Agricultural Trade." In *The Politics of International Trade in the Twenty-first Century*, edited by D. Kelly and W. Grant. New York: Palgrave Macmillan.

Gray, K., and C. N. Murphy (eds.). 2015. *Introduction: Rising Powers and the Future of Global Governance.* New York: Routledge.

Guardian. 2008 (July 30). "WTO Talks Collapse after India and China Clash with America over Farm Products."

Guerrero, Dorothy Grace. 2014. "China Rising: A New World Order or an Old Order Renewed?" Transnational Insititute Working Paper, Shifting Power: Critical Perspectives on Emerging Powers Series. Available at www.tni.org/category/series/shifting-power-critical-perspectives-emerging-economies.

Guo, Kai, and Papa N'Diaye. 2009. "Is China's Export-oriented Growth Sustainable?" Washington, DC: IMF Working Paper.

Gupta, Surupa, and Sumit Ganguly. 2014. "Modi Bets the Farm: Why Indian Agricultural Policy Might Unravel the WTO." *Foreign Affairs,* August 12.

Haass, Richard N. 2008. "The Age of Nonpolarity." *Foreign Affairs* 87(3).

Haberli, Christian. 2014. "After Bali: WTO Rules Applying to Public Food Reserves." UN Food and Agriculture Organization (FAO), Commodity and Trade Policy Research Working Paper No. 46, Rome.

Hampson, Fen Osler, and Paul Heinbecker. 2011. "The 'New' Multilateralism of the Twenty-first Century." *Global Governance: A Review of Multilateralism and International Organizations* 17(3):299–310.

Harrison, Glenn W., Thomas F. Rutherford, and David G. Tarr. 1996. "Quantifying the Uruguay Round." Pp. 216–52 in *The Uruguay Round and the Developing Countries,* edited by Will Martin and L. Alan Winters. Washington, DC: World Bank.

Harvey, David. 2005. *A Brief History of Neoliberalism.* Oxford: Oxford University Press.

Hayashi, Michiko. 2007. "Trade in Textiles and Clothing: Assuring Development Gains in a Rapidly Changing Environment." Geneva: United Nations Conference on Trade and Development (UNCTAD).

Helleiner, Gerald K. 2001. "Markets, Politics, and Globalization: Can the Global Economy Be Civilized?" *Global Governance* 7(3):243–63.

Henson, Spencer, and Rupert Loader. 2001. "Barriers to Agricultural Exports from Developing Countries: The Role of Sanitary and Phytosanitary Requirements." *World Development* 29(1):85–102.

Herbst, Moira. 2009. "Indian Firms, Microsoft Top H-1B List." *BusinessWeek,* February 24.

Hochstetler, Kathryn. 2014a. "The Brazilian National Development Bank Goes International: Innovations and Limitations of BNDES' Internationalization." *Global Policy* 5(3):360–65.

———. 2014b. "Infrastructure and Sustainable Development Goals in the BRICS-Led New Development Bank." Centre for International Governance Innovation (CIGI) Policy Brief No. 46.

Hochstetler, Kathryn, and Alfred P. Montero. 2013. "The Renewed Developmental State: The National Development Bank and the Brazil Model." *Journal of Development Studies* 49(11):1484–99.

Hoekman, Bernard. 1995. "Assessing the General Agreement on Trade in Services." Pp. 326–64 in *The Uruguay Round and the Developing Countries,* edited by Will Martin and L. Alan Winters. Washington, DC: World Bank.

Hoekman, Bernard, Ng Francis, and Marcelo Olarreaga. 2002. "Eliminating Excessive Tariffs on Exports of Least Developed Countries." Policy Research Working Paper. World Bank.

Hoekman, Bernard, and Aaditya Mattoo. 2007. "Services, Economic Development and the

Doha Round: Exploiting the Comparative Advantage of the WTO." Pp. 169–85 in *The WTO after Hong Kong: Progress in, and Prospects for, the Doha Development Agenda*, edited by Donna Lee and Rorden Wilkinson. New York: Routledge.

———. 2011. "Services Trade Liberalization and Regulatory Reform: Re-invigorating International Cooperation." World Bank Policy Research Working Paper 5517.

Hoffmann, Matthew J. 2011. *Climate Governance at the Crossroads: Experimenting with a Global Response after Kyoto*. Oxford: Oxford University Press.

Hopewell, Kristen. 2009. "The Technocratization of Protest: Transnational Advocacy Organizations and the WTO." Pp. 161–79 in *Engaging Social Justice: Critical Studies of 21st Century Social Transformation*, edited by David Fasenfest. Leiden: Brill.

———. 2014. "The Transformation of State-business Relations in an Emerging Economy: The Case of Brazilian Agribusiness." *Critical Perspectives on International Business* 10(4).

———. 2015a. "Different Paths to Power: The Rise of Brazil, India and China at the WTO." *Review of International Political Economy* 22(2):311–38.

———. 2015b. "Multilateral Trade Governance as Social Field: Global Civil Society and the WTO." *Review of International Political Economy* 22(6):1128–58.

Hufbauer, Gary, Jeffrey J. Schott, Matthew Adler, Claire Brunel, and Woan Foong Wong. 2010. "Figuring out the Doha Round." Policy Analysis in International Economics 91, Peterson Institute for International Economics, Washington, DC.

Hufbauer, Gary, and Kati Suominen. 2012. "The United States: Trade Policy Sleeping— Short Nap or Long Slumber?" In *The Ashgate Research Companion to International Trade Policy*, edited by Kenneth Heydon and Stephen Woolcock. Burlington, VT: Ashgate.

Hung, Ho-Fung (ed.). 2009. *China and the Transformation of Global Capitalism*. Baltimore, MD: Johns Hopkins University Press.

Hurrell, Andrew. 2006. "Hegemony, Liberalism and World Order: What Space for Would-be Great Powers?" *International Affairs* 82(1):1–19.

———. 2010. "Brazil and the New Global Order." *Current History* 109(724):60–68.

Hurrell, Andrew, and Amrita Narlikar. 2006. "A New Politics of Confrontation: Brazil and India in Multilateral Trade Negotiations." *Global Society* 20(4):415–33.

ICONE. 2006. *Devising a Comprehensive IBSA Strategy on WTO Agriculture Negotiations: The Case of Brazil*. Sao Paulo: Instituto de Estudos do Comércio e Negociações Internacionais (ICONE).

———. 2007a. *Report of Activities: March 2003 through March 2007*. Sao Paulo: Instituto de Estudos do Comércio e Negociações Internacionais (ICONE).

———. 2007b. *Trade-Distorting Domestic Support: Alternatives for Product-Specific Disciplines*. Sao Paulo: Instituto de Estudos do Comércio e Negociações Internacionais (ICONE).

ICTSD. 2007. "Impact of Origin Rules for Textiles and Clothing on Developing Countries." International Centre for Trade and Sustainable Development, Issue Paper No. 3, December.

Ignatieff, Michael (Ed.). 2005. *American Exceptionalism and Human Rights*. Princeton, NJ: Princeton University Press.

Ikenberry, G. John. 1992. "A World Economy Restored: Expert Consensus and the Anglo-American Postwar Settlement." *International Organization* 46(1):289–321.

———. 2001. *After Victory: Institutions, Strategic Restraint, and the Rebuilding of Order after Major Wars*. Princeton: Princeton University Press.

———. 2008. "The Rise of China and the Future of the West: Can the Liberal System Survive?" *Foreign Affairs*, January/February, Pp. 23–37.

———. 2009. "Liberal Internationalism 3.0: America and the Dilemmas of Liberal World Order." *Perspectives on Politics* 7(1):71–87.

———. 2010. "A Crisis of Global Governance?" *Current History,* November, Pp. 315–21.

———. 2011. *Liberal Leviathan: The Origins, Crisis, and Transformation of the American World Order*. Princeton: Princeton University Press.

———. 2014. "The Logic of Order: Westphalia, Liberalism, and the Evolution of International Order in the Modern Era." In *Power, Order, and Change in World Politics*, edited by G. John Ikenberry. Cambridge: Cambridge University Press.

ILO. 2010. "Vulnerable Employment and Poverty on the Rise." Interview with ILO chief of Employment Trends Unit. Available at www.ilo.org/global/about-the-ilo/newsroom/features/WCMS_120470/lang--de/index.htm.

India. 2007. "Plurilateral Request on Cross-Border Supply." Presentation by Dr. Krishna Gupta, Counsellor, Permanent Mission of India to the WTO, Training on Trade in Information and Communication Services, World Bank-COMESA-WTO, Geneva, April 23–27. Available at http://siteresources.worldbank.org.

Ingco, Merlinda D. 1995. "Agricultural Trade Liberalization in the Uruguay Round: One Step Forward, One Step Back?" Policy Research Working Paper. Washington, DC: World Bank.

International Trade Reporter. 2008 (July 31). "U.S., EU Cite Moves in 'Signaling' Talks on Services: India Likes 'Mode 4' Openings."

Irwin, Douglas A. 2005. "The Rise of US Anti-dumping Activity in Historical Perspective." *World Economy* 28(5):651–68.

Jacques, Martin. 2009. *When China Rules the World: The Rise of the Middle Kingdom and the End of the Western World*. London: Allen Lane.

Janow, Merit, Victoria Donaldson, and Alan Yanovich. 2008. *The WTO: Governance, Dispute Settlement and Developing Countries*. Huntington, NY: Juris.

Javalgi, Rajshekhar G., Andrew C. Gross, W. Benoy Joseph, and Elad Granot. 2011. "Assessing Competitive Advantage of Emerging Markets in Knowledge Intensive Business Services." *Journal of Business and Industrial Marketing* 26(3):171–80.

Jawara, F., and A. Kwa. 2003. *Behind the Scenes at the WTO: The Real World of International Trade Negotiations*. New York: Zed Books.

Jenkins, Rhys, and Alexandre de Freitas Barbosa. 2012. "Fear for Manufacturing? China and the Future of Industry in Brazil and Latin America." *China Quarterly* 209:59–81.

Jenkins, Rhys, Enrique Dussel Peters, and Mauricio Mesquita Moreira. 2008. "The Impact of China on Latin America and the Caribbean." *World Development* 36(2):235–53.

Jha, Veena, James Nedumpara, Abhijit Das, Kailas Karthikeyan, and Shailaja Thakur. 2006. "Services Liberalisation: Challenges and Opportunities for India." In *India and the Doha Work Programme: Opportunities and Challenges*, edited by Veena Jha. New Delhi: Macmillan India, UNCTAD, Ministry of Commerce of India, DFID.

Jiang, Yang. 2012. "China's Trade Policymaking: Domestic Interests and Post-WTO Contestations." Pp. 503–17 in *The Ashgate Research Companion to International Trade Policy*, edited by Kenneth Heydon and Stephen Woolcock. Burlington, VT: Ashgate.

Jones, K. 2010. *The Doha Blues: Institutional Crisis and Reform in the WTO*. Oxford: Oxford University Press.

Jurje, Flavia, and Sandra Lavenex. 2014. "Rising Powers' Venue-shopping on International Mobility." NCCR Trade Working Paper No 2014/3.

Kagan, Robert. 2010. "The Perils of Wishful Thinking." *National Interest* 5(3):14–16.

———. 2012. *The World America Made*. New York: Knopf.

Kanth, Ravi D. 2008. "Revised Text Needed for Doha Round Success: India." *Business Standard,* May 8.

Kapoor, Ilan. 2006. "Deliberative Democracy and the WTO." *Review of International Political Economy* 11(3):522–41.

Kapur, Devesh, and Ravi Ramamurti. 2001. "India's Emerging Competitive Advantage in Services." *Academy of Management Executive* 15(2):20–33.

Karriem, Abdurazack. 2009. "The Brazilian Landless Movement: Mobilization for Transformative Politics." Pp. xiv, 290 in *Hegemonic Transitions, the State and Crisis in Neoliberal Capitalism*, edited by Yıldız Atasoy. New York: Routledge.

Katz, Sherman E. 2005. *Trade Policy Challenges in 2005*. A Report of the CSIS-Economist Trade Seminar Series, February.

Kelly, Dominic, and Wyn Grant. 2005. "Introduction: Trade Politics in Context." In *The Politics of International Trade in the Twenty-first Century*, edited by Dominic Kelly and Wyn Grant. New York: Palgrave Macmillan.

Kennedy, D. 1995. "The International Style in Postwar Law and Policy: John Jackson and the Field of International Economy Law." *American University Journal of International Law and Policy* 10:671–716.

Keohane, Robert. 1980. "The Theory of Hegemonic Stability and Changes in International Economic Regimes, 1967–1977." Pp. 131–62 in *Change in the International System*, edited by Ole R. Holsti, Randolph M. Silverson, and Alexander L. George. Boulder, CO: Westview Press.

———. 1984. *After Hegemony: Cooperation and Discord in the World Political Economy*. Princeton: Princeton University Press.

Kindleberger, Charles P. 1973. *The World in Depression, 1929–39*. Berkeley: University of California Press.

Kong, Qingjiang. 2000. "China's WTO Accession: Commitments and Implications." *Journal of International Economic Law* 3(4):655–90.

Krasner, Stephen D. 1976. "State Power and the Structure of International Trade." *World Politics* 28:317–47.

————. 1985. *Structural Conflict: The Third World against Global Liberalism*. Berkeley: University of California Press.

————. 1999. *Sovereignty: Organized Hypocrisy*. Princeton: Princeton University Press.

Krueger, Anne O. 1998. "Introduction." In *The WTO as an International Organization*, edited by Anne O. Krueger. Chicago: University of Chicago Press.

Kupchan, Charles A. 2014. "The Normative Foundations of Hegemony and the Coming Challenge to Pax Americana." *Security Studies* 23(2):219–57.

Lake, David. 2009. *Hierarchy in International Relations*. Ithaca, NY: Cornell University Press.

Lanoszka, Anna. 2007. "The Promises of Multilateralism and the Hazards of Single Undertaking: The Breakdown of Decision Making within the WTO." *Michigan State Journal of International Law* (16):655.

Lardy, Nicholas R. 1993. *Foreign Trade and Economic Reform in China*. Cambridge: Cambridge University Press.

————. 2012. *Sustaining China's Economic Growth after the Global Financial Crisis*. Washington, DC: Peterson Institute for International Economics.

Layne, Christopher. 2009. "The Waning of U.S. Hegemony—Myth or Reality? A Review Essay." *International Security* 34(1):147–72.

Leahy, Joe. 2011. "Tale of Two Classes in Brazil as Millions Climb out of Poverty." *Financial Times*, July 21, P. 6.

Leitner, Kara, and Simon Lester. 2015. "WTO Dispute Settlement 1995–2014—A Statistical Analysis." *Journal of International Economic Law* 18(1):203–14.

Levi-Faur, David. 2005. "The Global Diffusion of Regulatory Capitalism." *Annals of the American Academy of Political and Social Science* 598(1):12–32.

————. 2006. "Regulatory Capitalism: The Dynamics of Change beyond Telecoms and Electricity." *Governance* 19(3):497–525.

Li, Chunding, and John Whalley. 2010. "Chinese Firm and Industry Reactions to Antidumping Initiations and Measures." National Bureau of Economic Research, Working Paper No. 16446. Available at www.nber.org/papers/w16446.pdf.

Li, Minqi. 2009. "Capitalism, Climate Change and the Transition to Sustainability: Alternative Scenarios for the US, China and the World." *Development and Change* 40(6):1039–61.

Lilja, Jannie. 2012. "Domestic-level Factors and Negotiation (In)Flexibility in the WTO." *International Negotiation* 17(1):115–38.

Lima, Maria Regina Soares de, and Monica Hirst. 2006. "Brazil as an Intermediate State and Regional Power: Action, Choice and Responsibilities." *International Affairs* 82(1):21–40.

MacPhee, C. R., and D. I. Rosenbaum. 1989. "The Asymmetric Effects of Reversible Tariff Changes under the United States GSP." *Southern Economic Journal* 56:105–25.

Mahrenbach, Laura Carsten. 2013. *The Trade Policy of Emerging Powers: Strategic Choices of Brazil and India*. New York: Palgrave.

Mann, Michael. 2001. "Globalization Is (among Other Things) Transnational, Inter-national and American." *Science and Society* 65(4):464.

Margulis, Matias E. 2010. "Whistling to the Same Tune? The Contest over Future WTO Agricultural Subsidies." Pp. 34–44 in *Agriculture Subsidies and the WTO*, edited by A. Govinda Reddy. Hyderabad: Amicus Books.

———. 2013. "The Regime Complex for Food Security: Implications for the Global Hunger Challenge." *Global Governance* 19(1):53–67.

———. 2014. "The World Trade Organization and Food Security after the Global Food Crises." Pp. 236–58 in *Linking Global Trade and Human Rights: New Policy Space in Hard Economic Times*, edited by Daniel Drache and Lesley A. Jacobs. Cambridge: Cambridge University Press.

Margulis, Matias E., Nora McKeon, and Saturnino M. Borras. 2013. "Land Grabbing and Global Governance: Critical Perspectives." *Globalizations* 10(1):1–23.

Martha, G. B., E. Contini, and A. Alves. 2013. "Embrapa: Its Origins and Changes." In *The Regional Impact of National Policies: The Case of Brazil*, edited by Werner Baer. Northampton: Edward Elgar.

Martin, L. 2006. "GATS, Migration, and Labor Standards." International Institute for Labour Studies, Discussion Paper 165, ILO, Geneva.

Martin, Will, and Aaditya Mattoo. 2011. *Unfinished Business? The WTO's Doha Agenda.* World Bank and Centre for Economic Policy Research. Washington, DC.

Mastanduno, Michael. 2014. "Order and Change in World Politics: The Financial Crisis and the Breakdown of the US-China Grand Bargain." In *Power, Order, and Change in World Politics*, edited by G. John Ikenberry. Cambridge: Cambridge University Press.

Mattoo, Aaditya, and Arvind Subramanian. 2009. "From Doha to the Next Bretton Woods: A New Multilateral Trade Agenda." *Foreign Affairs* 88(1):15–26.

———. 2012. "China and the World Trading System." *World Economy* 35(12):1733–71.

McIver, R. M. 1932. *The Modern State*. London: Oxford University Press.

McMichael, Phillip. 2004. *Development and Social Change: A Global Perspective*. Thousand Oaks, CA: Pine Forge Press.

———. 2012. *Development and Social Change: A Global Perspective*. Thousand Oaks, CA: Pine Forge Press.

McMillan, Margaret, Alix Zwane, and Nava Ashraf. 2006. "My Policies or Yours: How Do Trade-distorting Agricultural Policies Used by Rich Countries Affect Poverty in Developing Countries?" In *Globalization and Poverty*, edited by Ann Harrison. Chicago: University of Chicago Press for the NBER.

Mearsheimer, John J. 2005. "China's Unpeaceful Rise." *Current History* 105(690):160–62.

Messerlin, Patrick, and Stephen Woolcock. 2012. "Commercial Instruments." In *The Ashgate Research Companion to International Trade Policy*, edited by Kenneth Heydon and Stephen Woolcock. Burlington, VT: Ashgate.

Milligan, Katie. 2004. "Brazil's WTO Cotton Case: Negotiation through Litigation." Harvard Business School Case Study N9–905–405.

Mitoma, Glenn. 2013. *Human Rights and the Negotiation of American Power*. Philadelphia: University of Pennsylvania Press.

Monger, Randall, and Macreadie Barr. 2009. "Nonimmigrant Admissions to the United States: 2008." Office of Immigration Statistics, Department of Homeland Security,

April. Available at www.dhs.gov/xlibrary/assets/statistics/publications/ois_ni_fr_2008.pdf.

Moore, Mike. 2003. *A World without Walls: Freedom, Development, Free Trade and Global Governance.* Cambridge: Cambridge University Press.

Mortensen, Jens L. 2006. "The WTO and the Governance of Globalization: Dismantling the Compromise of Embedded Liberalism?" Pp. 170–82 in *Political Economy and the Changing Global Order*, edited by Richard Stubbs and Geoffrey Underhill. Don Mills: Oxford University Press.

Mortimer, Robert. 1984. *The Third World Coalition in International Politics.* Boulder, CO: Westview Press.

Morton, A. D. 2003. "Social Forces in the Struggle over Hegemony: Neo-Gramscian Perspectives in International Political Economy." *Rethinking Marxism* 15(2):153–79.

MST. 2009. "Nossa proposta de Reforma Agraria Popular." Movimento dos Trabalhadores Sem Terra (MST). Available at www.mst.org.br/.

Mukherjee, Arpita. 2013. "Services Sector in India: Trends, Issues and Way Forward." Indian Council for Research on International Economic Relations (ICRIER) Working Paper.

Mukherjee, Rohan, and David M. Malone. 2011. "From High Ground to High Table: The Evolution of Indian Multilateralism." *Global Governance: A Review of Multilateralism and International Organizations* 17(3):311–29.

Murphy, Gillian H. 2004. "The Seattle WTO Protests: Building a Global Movement." In *Creating a Better World: Interpreting Global Civil Society,* edited by Rupert Taylor. Bloomfield, CT: Kumarian Press.

NAM. 2008. "NAMA Sectorals Essential for Balanced Outcomes." National Association of Manufacturers (NAM) Press Release, July 28.

Narlikar, Amrita. 2003. *International Trade and Developing Countries: Bargaining Coalitions in the GATT & WTO.* London: Routledge.

———. 2010. *New Powers: How to Become One and How to Manage Them.* New York: Columbia University Press.

———. 2013. "India Rising: Responsible to Whom?" *International Affairs* 89(3):595–614.

Narlikar, Amrita, and Diana Tussie. 2004. "The G20 at the Cancun Ministerial: Developing Countries and Their Evolving Coalitions in the WTO." *World Economy* 27(7).

NASSCOM. 2009. "Indian IT-BPO Industry 2009." New Delhi: National Assocation of Software and Service Companies (NASSCOM).

———. 2010. "IT-BPO Sector in India: Strategic Review." New Delhi: National Association of Software and Service Companies (NASSCOM).

Nayyar, Deepak. 2008. "The Internationalization of Firms from India: Investment, Mergers and Acquisitions." *Oxford Development Studies* 36(1):111–31.

Negandhi, Anant R., and Aspy P. Palia. 1987. "The Changing Multinational Corporation—A Nation State's Relationship: The Case of IBM in India." Bureau of Economic and Business Research, University of Illinois, Urbana-Champaign, Working Paper No. 1332, February.

Ngai, Pun, Chris King Chi Chan, and Jenny Chan. 2009. "The Role of the State, Labour Policy and Migrant Workers' Struggles in Globalized China." *Global Labour Journal* 1(1):8.

Norloff, Carla. 2012. *America's Global Advantage: US Hegemony and International Coopera-tion*. Cambridge: Cambridge University Press.

Nye, Joseph. 2015. *Is the American Century Over?* Cambridge: Polity.

O'Brien, Robert, and Marc Williams. 2004. *Global Political Economy: Evolution and Dynam-ics*. New York: Palgrave Macmillan.

Obama, Barack. 2007. "Remarks of Senator Barack Obama to the Chicago Council on Global Affairs." Available at www.cfr.org/elections/remarks-senator-barack-obama-chicago-council-global-affairs/p13172 (accessed April 23, 2007).

ODI. 1995. "Developing Countries in the WTO." Overseas Development Institute (ODI), Briefing Paper No. 3.

OECD. 2009. *Agriculture Policies in Emerging Economies*. Paris: Organisation for Economic Cooperation and Development (OECD).

Ostry, Sylvia. 2000. "The Uruguay Round North-South Grand Bargain." Paper presented at the University of Minnesota, September. Available at: sites.utoronto.ca/cis/ostry/docs_pdf/Minnesota.pdf.

————. 2007. "Trade, Development, and the Doha Development Agenda." Pp. 248–61 in *The WTO after Hong Kong: Progress in, and Prospects for, the Doha Development Agenda*, edited by Donna Lee and Rorden Wilkinson. New York: Routledge.

Oxfam. 2002. "Rigged Rules and Double Standards: Trade, Globalization and the Fight against Poverty." Make Trade Fair Campaign.

————. 2008. "Economic Implications of Mode 4 Trade." Presentation at WTO Sympo-sium on Mode 4, September.

Ozden, Caglar, and Eric Reinhardt. 2005. "The Perversity of Preferences: GSP and Develop-ing Country Trade Policies, 1976–2000." *Journal of Development Economics* 78(1):1–21.

Page, Sheila. 2003. "Developing Countries—Victims or Participants: Their Changing Role in International Negotiations." London: Overseas Development Institute (ODI).

Panagariya, Arvind. 2005. "Agricultural Liberalisation and the Least Developed Countries: Six Fallacies." *World Economy* 28(9):1277–99.

Panich, Leo, and Sam Gindin. 2012. *The Making of Global Capitalism: The Political Economy of American Empire*. New York: Verso.

Patibandla, Murali, and Bent Petersen. 2002. "Role of Transnational Corporations in the Evolution of a High-Tech Industry: The Case of India's Software Industry." *World De-velopment* 30(9):1561–77.

Patrick, S. 2010. "Irresponsible Stakeholders? The Difficulty of Integrating Rising Powers." *Foreign Affairs* 89(6):44.

Pearson, Margaret M. 2006. "China in Geneva: Lessons from China's Early Years in the World Trade Organization." In *New Directions in the Study of China's Foreign Policy*, ed-ited by Alastair Iain Johnston and Robert S. Ross. Stanford: Stanford University Press.

Peck, Jamie, and Adam Tickell. 2002. "Neoliberalizing Space." *Antipode* 34(3):380–404.

Pereira, Carlos, and Joao Augusto de Castro Neves. 2011. "Brazil and China: South-South Partnership or North-South Competition?" Washington, DC: Brookings Institution.

Pieterse, Jan Nederveen. 2011. "Global Rebalancing: Crisis and the East-South Turn." *Development and Change* 42(1):22–48.

Pinto, Sanjay, Kate Macdonald, and Shelley Marshall. 2011. "Rethinking Global Market Governance." *Politics and Society* 39(3):299–314.

Pitts, Jennifer. 2005. *A Turn to Empire: The Rise of Imperial Liberalism in Britain and France.* Princeton: Princeton University Press.

Polanyi, Karl. 1944. *The Great Transformation: The Political and Economic Origins of Our Time.* Boston: Beacon Press.

Polaski, Sandra. 2006. *Winners and Losers: Impact of the Doha Round on Developing Countries.* Washington, DC: Carnegie Endowment for International Peace.

Porter, Tony. 2005. "The United States in International Trade Politics: Liberal Leader or Heavy-Handed Hegemon?" Pp. 204–20 in *The Politics of International Trade in the Twenty-First Century*, edited by Dominic Kelly and Wyn Grant. New York: Palgrave Macmillan.

Prashad, Vijay. 2012. *The Poorer Nations: A Possible History of the Global South.* London: Verso.

Qin, Julia Ya. 2007. "Trade, Investment and Beyond: The Impact of WTO Accession on China's Legal System." *China Quarterly* 191:720–41.

Quark, Amy A. 2013. *Global Rivalries: Standards Wars and the Transnational Cotton Trade.* Chicago: University of Chicago Press.

Raghavan, Chakravathi. 2000. "After Seattle, World Trading System Faces Uncertain Future." *Review of International Political Economy* 7(3):495–504.

Raman, Revti, and Doren Chadee. 2011. "A Comparative Assessment of the Information Technology Services Sector in India and China." *Journal of Contemporary Asia* 41(3):452–69.

Ray, E. J. 1987. "The Impact of Special Interests on Preferential Tariff Concessions by the United States." *Review of Economics and Statistics* 69:187–93.

RBI. 2010. "Remittances from Overseas Indians: Modes of Transfer, Transaction Cost and Time Taken." Reserve Bank of India, Monthly Bulletin, April.

Reardon, Lawrence C. 2002. *The Reluctant Dragon: Cycles in Chinese Foreign Economic Policy.* Seattle: University of Washington Press.

Reisen, Helmut. 2015. "Will the AIIB and the NDB Help Reform Multilateral Development Banking?" *Global Policy* 6(3):297–304.

Reuters. 2009 (February 19). "India to Put Safeguard Duty on China Aluminium."

———. 2014 (September 4). "'Made in China' Clothing Sales May Shrink under Pacific Trade Pact."

Roberts, Cynthia. 2010. "Introduction to Polity Forum: Challengers or Stakeholders? BRICs and the Liberal World Order." *Polity* 42(1):1.

Roberts, J. Timmons. 2011. "Multipolarity and the New World (Dis)order: US Hegemonic Decline and the Fragmentation of the Global Climate Regime." *Global Environmental Change* 21(3):776–84.

Rodrigues, Tiago E. G. 2009. "Agricultural Explosion in Brazil: Exploring the Impacts of the

Brazilian Agricultural Development over the Amazon." *International Journal of Sociology of Agriculture and Food* 16(1):1–12.

Roemer-Mahler, Anne. 2012. "Business Conflict and Global Politics: The Pharmaceutical Industry and the Global Protection of Intellectual Property Rights." *Review of International Political Economy* 20(1):121–52.

Ruggie, John Gerard. 1982. "International Regimes, Transactions, and Change: Embedded Liberalism in the Postwar Economic Order." *International Organization* 36(2):379–415.

———. 1993. *Multilateralism Matters: The Theory and Praxis of an Institutional Form.* New York: Columbia University Press.

———. 1996. *Constructing the World Polity: Essays on International Institutionalization.* London: Routledge.

———. 2005. "American Exceptionalism, Exemptionalism, and Global Governance." Pp. 304-38 in *American Exceptionalism and Human Rights*, edited by Michael Ignatieff. Princeton, NJ: Princeton University Press.

Ruiz-Diaz, Hugo. 2005. "G20: The South Fights for the South." *Le Monde diplomatique*, September, P. 10.

Saad-Filho, Alfredo. 2013. "The 'Rise of the South': Global Convergence at Last?" *New Political Economy* 19(4):1–23.

Sauvé, Pierre, and Robert Mitchell Stern. 2010. *GATS 2000: New Directions in Services Trade Liberalization.* Washington, DC: Brookings Institution Press.

Sauvé, Pierre, and Arvind Subramanian. 2004. "Dark Clouds over Geneva? The Troubled Prospects of the Multilateral Trading System." In *Efficiency, Equity, and Legitimacy: The Multilateral Trading System at the Millennium*, edited by Roger B. Porter, Pierre Sauvé, Arvind Subramanian, and Americo Beviglia Zampetti. Washington, DC: Brookings Institution Press.

Schirm, Stefan A. 2010. "Leaders in need of followers: Emerging powers in global governance." *European Journal of International Relations* 16(2):197–221.

Schnepf, Randy. 2014. "Agriculture in the WTO: Limits on Domestic Support." Congressional Research Service, Washington, DC, January 27.

Schwab, Susan. 2009. "The Future of the US Trade Agenda." In *Opportunities and Obligations: New Perspectives on Global and US Trade Policy*, edited by Terence P. Stewart. Frederick, MD: Kluwer Law International.

———. 2011. "After Doha: Why the Negotiations Are Doomed and What We Should Do About It." *Foreign Affairs* 90(3):104–17.

Scott, James. 2015. "The Role of Southern Intellectuals in Contemporary Trade Governance." *New Political Economy* 20(5):633–52.

Scott, James, and Rorden Wilkinson. 2013. "China Threat? Evidence from the WTO." *Journal of World Trade* 47(4):761–82.

Sell, Susan. 2002. *Private Power, Public Law.* Cambridge: Cambridge University Press.

———. 2006. "Big Business, the WTO, and Development: Uruguay and Beyond." Pp. 183–96 in *Political Economy and the Changing Global Order*, edited by Richard Stubbs and Geoffrey Underhill. Don Mills: Oxford University Press.

Shadlen, Kennneth C. 2005. "Exchanging Development for Market Access: Deep Integration and Industrial Policy under Multilateral and Regional-bilateral Trade Agreements." *Review of International Political Economy* 12(5):750–75.

Shaffer, Gregory, and R. Meléndez-Ortiz. 2010. *Dispute Settlement at the WTO: The Developing Country Experience.* Cambridge: Cambridge University Press.

Shaffer, Gregory, Michelle Ratton Sanchez, and Barbara Rosenberg. 2008. "The Trials of Winning at the WTO: What Lies behind Brazil's Success." *Cornell International Law Journal* 41(2):383–501.

Shahi, Deepshikha. 2014. "India in the Emerging World Order: A Status Quo Power or a Revisionist Force?" Transnational Insititute Working Paper, Shifting Power: Critical Perspectives on Emerging Powers Series. Available at www.tni.org/category/series/shifting-power-critical-perspectives-emerging-economies.

Shen, Guobing, and Xiaolan Fu. 2014. "The Trade Effects of US Anti-dumping Actions against China Post-WTO Entry." *World Economy* 37(1):86–105.

Siles-Brügge, Gabriel. 2013. "Explaining the Resilience of Free Trade: The Smoot-Hawley Myth and the Crisis." *Review of International Political Economy* 21(3):1–40.

Silver, Beverly J., and Giovanni Arrighi. 2003. "Polanyi's 'Double Movement': The Belle Epoques of British and U.S. Hegemony Compared." *Politics and Society* 31(2):325–55.

Sinha, Aseema. 2007. "Global Linkages and Domestic Politics: Trade Reform and Institution Building in India in Comparative Perspective." *Comparative Political Studies* 40(10):1183–210.

Snidal, Duncan. 1985. "The Limits of Hegemonic Stability Theory." *International Organization* 38(4):579–614.

Snyder, Quddus Z. 2011. "Integrating Rising Powers: Liberal Systemic Theory and the Mechanism of Competition." *Review of International Studies* 39(1):209–31.

Srivastava, Sadhana. 2006. "The Role of Foreign Direct Investment in India's Services Exports: An Empirical Investigation." *Singapore Economic Review* 51(2):175–94.

Stanway, David. 2014. "China, U.S. Agree Limits on Emissions, but Experts See Little New." *Reuters,* November 12.

Stedman Jones, Gareth. 1972. "The History of US Imperialism." Pp. 207–37 in *Ideology in Social Science,* edited by R. Blackburn. New York: Vintage.

Steger, D. P. 2010. *Redesigning the World Trade Organization for the Twenty-first Century.* Ottawa: International Development Research Centre (IDRC) and Centre for International Governance Innovation (CIGI).

Steinberg, Richard. 2002. "In the Shadow of Law or Power? Consensus-based Bargaining in the GATT/WTO." *International Organization* 56(2):339–74.

Steinmetz, George. 2005. "Return to Empire: The New U.S. Imperialism in Comparative Historical Perspective." *Sociological Theory* 23(4):339–67.

Stephen, Matthew D. 2012. "Rising Regional Powers and International Institutions: The Foreign Policy Orientations of India, Brazil and South Africa." *Global Society* 26(3):289–309.

Stiglitz, Joseph E. 2004. *The Roaring Nineties: Why We're Paying the Price for the Greediest Decade in HIstory*. London: Penguin Books.

Strange, Susan. 1985. "Protectionism and World Politics." *International Organization* 39(2):233–59.

Subacchi, Paola. 2008. "New Power Centres and New Power Brokers: Are They Shaping a New Economic Order?" *International Affairs* 84(3):485–98.

Subramanian, Arvind. 2011. "The Inevitable Superpower: Why China's Dominance Is a Sure Thing." *Foreign Affairs* 90(5):66.

———. 2014. "India's WTO Problem—A Proposal." RealTime Economic Issues Watch. Washington, DC: Peterson Institute for International Economics.

Subramanian, Arvind, and Martin Kessler. 2013. "The Hyperglobalization of Trade and Its Future." Working Paper 13–6. Washington, DC: Peterson Institute for International Economics.

Swinnen, Johan, Alessandro Olper, and Thijs Vandemoortele. 2012. "Impact of the WTO on Agricultural and Food Policies." *World Economy* 35(9):1089–101.

Taylor, Ian. 2007. "The Periphery Strikes Back? The G20 at Cancun." Pp. 155–68 in *The WTO after Hong Kong: Progress in, and Prospects for, the Doha Development Agenda*, edited by Donna Lee and Rorden Wilkinson. New York: Routledge.

Textile Outlook. 2014 (May 27). Issue No. 168. Available at www.textilesintelligence.com/til/press.cfm?prid=488.

Thakur, Ramesh. 2014. "How Representative Are BRICS?" *Third World Quarterly* 35(10):1791–808.

UN. 2006. "Loss of Textile Market Costs African Jobs." United Nations, AfricaRenewal Online, April, P. 18. Available at www.un.org/africarenewal/magazine/april-2006/loss-textile-market-costs-african-jobs.

UNCTAD. 1997. *Trade and Development Report*. New York: United Nations.

———. 1999. "Quantifying the Benefits Obtained by Developing Countries from the Generalized System of Preferences." UNCTAD/ITCD/TSB/Misc.52. Geneva: United Nations.

———. 2012. *Trade and Development Report*. New York: United Nations.

———. 2013. *World Investment Report*. New York: United Nations.

UNDP. 1997. *Human Development Report*. New York: United Nations Development Program.

US. 2000. "China's WTO Accession: Trade Interests, Values and Strategy." Speech by US Trade Representative Charlene Barshefsky, National Conference of State Legislators, Washington, DC, February 4.

———. 2011. "The President's 2011 Trade Agenda." Ambassador Ron Kirk, US Trade Representative, March 1.

———. 2013. "Foreign Direct Investment in the United States." Department of Commerce and President's Council of Economic Advisors.

US Congress. 2008. "The United States Senate Committee on Finance Press Release: Finance, Ways and Means Leaders Urge President to Stand Firm on Doha Round." December 2.

US Government Accountability Office (GAO). 2006. "US–China Trade: Eliminating Non-Market Economy Methodology would Lower Antidumping Duties for Some Chinese Companies." Available at: http://www.gao.gov/new.items/d06231.pdf.

USDA. 2009. "USDA Economic Research Service, Brazil Briefing Room."

Utar, Hale, and Luis B. Torres Ruiz. 2013. "International Competition and Industrial Evolution: Evidence from the Impact of Chinese Competition on Mexican Maquiladoras." *Journal of Development Economics* 105:267–87.

Valdes, Alberto, and Alex McCalla. 1999. "Issues, Interests and Options of Developing Countries." Paper presented at the *World Bank Conference on Agriculture and the New Trade Agenda in the WTO 2000 Negotiations*. Geneva, October 1–2.

Valdes, Constanza. 2006. "Brazil's Booming Agriculture Faces Obstacles." USDA Economic Research Service. Washington, DC.

Veiga, Pedro da Motta. 2007. "Trade Policy-making in Brazil: Changing Patterns in State-civil Society Relationship." Pp. 143–82 in *Process Matters: Sustainable Development and Domestic Trade Transparency*, edited by Mark Halle and Robert Wolfe. Winnipeg, MB: International Institute for Sustainable Development (IISD).

Veltmeyer, Henry. 2012. "The Natural Resource Dynamics of Postneoliberalism in Latin America: New Developmentalism or Extractive Imperialism?" *Studies in Political Economy* (90).

Vestergaard, Jakob, and Robert Wade. 2012. "The Governance Response to the Great Recession: The 'Success' of the G20." *Journal of Economic Issues* 46(2):481–90.

———. 2015. "Still in the Woods: Gridlock in the IMF and the World Bank Puts Multilateralism at Risk." *Global Policy* 6(1):1–12.

Vogel, S. K. 1996. *Freer Markets, More Rules: Regulatory Reform in Advanced Industrial Countries*. Ithaca, NY: Cornell University Press.

Wade, Robert H. 2003. "What Strategies Are Viable for Developing Countries Today? The World Trade Organization and the Shrinking of 'Development Space.'" *Review of International Political Economy* 10(4):621–44.

———. 2011. "Emerging World Order? From Multipolarity to Multilateralism in the G20, the World Bank, and the IMF." *Politics and Society* 39(3):347–78.

Wall Street Journal. 2013 (December 22). "Spotted Again in America: Textile Jobs."

———. 2014 (July 27). "India Blocks WTO Agreement to Ease Trade Rules."

Wallerstein, Immanuel M. 1995. *After Liberalism*. New York: Norton.

———. 2006. *World-Systems Analysis: An Introduction*. Durham, NC: Duke University Press.

Wallis, William, and Frances Williams. 2002. "West Africa Unites for Attack on Subsidies." *Financial Times*, September 28, P. 3.

Walt, Stephen M. 2011. "The End of the American Era." *National Interest* (116):6–16.

Warwick Commission. 2008. *The Multilateral Trade Regime: Which Way Forward?* Coventry, UK: University of Warwick.

Washington Post. 2010 (August 10). "Indian Government Calls HIB Visa Fee Hike 'Discriminatory.'"

Weaver, Catherine. 2010. *Hypocrisy Trap: The World Bank and the Poverty of Reform.* Princeton: Princeton University Press.

Weiss, Linda. 2005. "Global Governance, National Strategies: How Industrial States Make Room to Move under the WTO." *Review of International Political Economy* 12(5):723–49.

Weiss, Linda, and Elizabeth Thurbon. 2006. "The Business of Buying American: Public Procurement as Trade Strategy in the USA." *Review of International Political Economy* 13(5):701–24.

Whalley, John. 2006. "Recent Regional Agreements: Why So Many, So Fast, So Different and Where Are They Headed?" CIGI Working Paper No. 9, September.

Whyte, Martin King. 2009. "Paradoxes of China's Economic Boom." *Annual Review of Sociology* 35(1):371–92.

Wilkinson, John. 2009a. "The Globalization of Agribusiness and Developing World Food Systems." *Monthly Review* 61(1).

Wilkinson, Rorden. 2006. *The WTO: Crisis and the Governance of Global Trade.* New York: Routledge.

———. 2007. "Building Asymmetry: Concluding the Doha Development Agenda." Pp. 248–61 in *The WTO after Hong Kong: Progress in, and Prospects for, the Doha Development Agenda*, edited by Donna Lee and Rorden Wilkinson. New York: Routledge.

———. 2009b. "Language, Power and Multilateral Trade Negotiations." *Review of International Political Economy* 16(4):597–619.

———. 2011. "Measuring the WTO's Performance: An Alternative Account." *Global Policy* 2(1):43–52.

Wilkinson, Rorden, Erin Hannah, and James Scott. 2014. "The WTO in Bali: What Mc 9 Means for the Doha Development Agenda and Why It Matters." *Third World Quarterly* 35(6):1032–50.

Wilkinson, Rorden, and James Scott. 2008. "Developing Country Participation in the GATT: A Reassessment." *World Trade Review* 7(3):473–510.

———. 2013. *Trade, Poverty, Development: Getting beyond the WTO's Doha Deadlock.* New York: Routledge.

Williams, Marc. 2005. "Civil Society and the World Trading System." Pp. 30–46 in *The Politics of International Trade in the Twenty-first Century*, edited by Dominic Kelly and Wyn Grant. New York: Palgrave Macmillan.

Winters, L. Alan, Terrie L. Walmsley, Zhen Kun Wang, and Roman Grynberg. 2003. "Liberalising Temporary Movement of Natural Persons: An Agenda for the Development Round." *World Economy* 26(8):1137–61.

Wolf, Martin. 2004. *Why Globalization Works.* New Haven: Yale University Press.

Wolfe, Robert. 1998. *Farm Wars: The Political Economy of Agriculture and the International Trade Regime.* Cambridge: Cambridge University Press.

———. 2004. "Crossing the River by Feeling the Stones: Where the WTO Is Going after Seattle, Doha and Cancun." *Review of International Political Economy* 11(3):574–96.

Wood, Ellen Meiksins. 2005. *Empire of Capital*. New York: Verso.

Woods, Ngaire. 2006. *The Globalizers: The IMF, the World Bank, and Their Borrowers*. Ithaca, NY: Cornell University Press.

———. 2010. "Global Governance after the Financial Crisis: A New Multilateralism or the Last Gasp of the Great Powers?" *Global Policy* 1(1):51–63.

World Bank. 1998. "The Present Outlook for Trade Negotiations in the World Trade Organization." Policy Research Working Paper No. 1992, Washington, DC: World Bank.

———. 2001. *Global Economic Prospects and the Developing Countries*. Washington, DC: World Bank.

———. 2004. *Sustaining India's Services Revolution*. Washington, DC: World Bank.

———. 2008. *World Development Report: Agriculture for Development*. Washington, DC: World Bank.

———. 2009. "From Poor Areas to Poor People: China's Evolving Poverty Reduction Agenda." Poverty Reduction and Economic Management Department Report No. 47349-CN. Washington, DC: World Bank.

———. 2012. "Developing Countries to Receive over $400 Billion in Remittances in 2012, Says World Bank Report." Press Release, November 20. Washington, DC: World Bank.

———. 2013. "The State of the Poor: Where Are the Poor and Where Are the Poorest." Washington, DC: World Bank.

———. 2014. "World Development Indicator Tables." Washington, DC: World Bank.

World Trade Organization (WTO). 1998. "The Multilateral System: 50 Years of Achievement." Geneva: WTO.

———. 2000. "Implementation of Special and Differential Treatment Provisions in WTO Agreements and Decisions." Note by Secretariat.WT/COMTD/W/77. Geneva: WTO.

———. 2001a. Speech by Mike Moore. WTO Symposium. July 6. Geneva: WTO

———. 2001b. "Agriculture's Stake in WTO Trade Negotiations." Speech by WTO Director General Mike Moore. Washington, DC, February 22.

———. 2003a. "10 Common Misunderstandings about the WTO." Geneva: WTO

———. 2003b. "Brazil: Statement by H.E. Mr. Celso Amorim, Minister of External Relations, at Cancun Ministerial Conference." Geneva: WTO.

———. 2005a. "EC—Export Subsidies on Sugar—Complaint by Brazil—Report of the Appellate Body." Geneva: WTO.

———. 2005b. "United States—Subsidies on Upland Cotton—Report of the Appellate Body." Geneva: WTO.

———. 2006. *Statement by Pascal Lamy, Director-General to National Press Club*. Tokyo, July 6.

———. 2008a. "Fourth Revision of Draft Modalities for Non-Agricultural Market Access." TN/MA/W/103/Rev.3, December 6. Geneva: WTO

———. 2008b. "Revised Draft Modalities for Agriculture." TN/AG/W/4/Rev.4, December 6. Geneva: WTO

———. 2009. "World Trade Report." Geneva: WTO.

———. 2010. "World Trade Report." Geneva: WTO.

————. 2011. "Chair's Concluding Statment, Eighth Ministerial Conference." WT/MIN(11)/11. December 17. Geneva: WTO.

————. 2012. "International Trade Statistics." Geneva: WTO.

————. 2013. "Trade Profiles." Geneva: WTO.

Wright, Tom, and Harsh Gupta. 2011. "India's Boom Bypasses Rural Poor." *Wall Street Journal*, April 29.

Xiao, Ren. 2013. "Debating China's Rise in China." In *After Liberalism?: The Future of Liberalism in International Relations*, edited by R. Friedman, K. Oskanian, and R. P. Pardo. New York: Palgrave Macmillan.

Young, Alasdair R. 2007. "Negotiating with Diminished Expectations: The EU and the Doha Development Round." In *The WTO After Hong Kong: Progress in, and Prospects for, the Doha Development Agenda*, edited by Donna Lee and Rorden Wilkinson. New York: Routledge.

Zakaria, Fareed. 2008. *The Post-American World*. New York: Norton.

Zeng, Ka, and Wei Liang. 2010. "US Antidumping Actions against China: The Impact of China's Entry into the World Trade Organization." *Review of International Political Economy* 17(3):562–88.

Zoellick, Robert. 2003. "America Will Not Wait for the Won't-do Countries." *Financial Times,* September 9, P. 23.

————. 2010. "The End of the Third World? Modernizing Multilateralism for a Multipolar World." President of the World Bank, Speech at the Woodrow Wilson Centre for International Scholars, April 14.

Index